American Commonwealths.

VOLUME 5

MICHIGAN

AMS PRESS

NEW YORK

American Commonwealths

MICHIGAN

A HISTORY OF GOVERNMENTS

BY

THOMAS McINTYRE COOLEY

WITH A SUPPLEMENTARY CHAPTER BY CHARLES MOORE

BOSTON AND NEW YORK
HOUGHTON MIFFLIN COMPANY
The Riverside Press Cambridge

Library of Congress Cataloging in Publication Data

Cooley, Thomas McIntyre, 1824-1898.
  Michigan: a history of governments.

  Original ed. issued as v. 5 of American commonwealths.
  1. Michigan--History. 2. Michigan--Politics and government. I. Moore, Charles, 1855-1942. II. Title. III. Series: American commonwealths, v. 5.
F566.C77   1973   977.4   72-3764
ISBN 0-404-57205-7

Reprinted from the edition of 1905, Boston and New York
First AMS edition published, 1973
Manufactured in the United States of America

International Standard Book Number:
Complete Series: 0-404-57200-6
Volume 5: 0-404-57205-7

AMS PRESS, INC.
New York, N.Y.   10003

PREFACE TO THE REVISED EDITION.

During the quarter of a century since Judge Cooley completed this history of Michigan, students have given much attention to the early history of the Northwest. Although a large mass of details has been gathered to enrich the story, little has been discovered to change the general outlines as herein sketched. We now know that to Jean Nicolet's adventurous voyage in 1634 is due the discovery of the Straits of Mackinaw and Lake Michigan; and that Grosseilliers and Radisson dispute with Father Mesnard the title of discoverers of Lake Superior; but beyond the mention of these names there is nothing which demands the attention of the reviser.

Advantage has been taken of the opportunity now presented to extend the record of the State, by means of a supplementary chapter covering the most important events in the history of Michigan during the last part of the nineteenth century, and setting forth the conditions that prevail at the opening of the twentieth century.

CHARLES MOORE.

DETROIT, *January*, 1905.

PREFACE.

THE changes of sovereign as well as of subordinate jurisdiction have been greater in Michigan than in any other part of the American Union. France, Great Britain, and the United States have successively had dominion over it, and under the United States it was part of the Northwest Territory and of the Territory of Indiana before it became the Territory of Michigan. As Michigan Territory it passed through all the grades of subordinate jurisdiction, and the circumstances attending its admission to the Union made its history at that period quite unique. Altogether it seemed appropriate that in the series of American Commonwealths the history of Michigan should be sketched as a history of governments; but this would be incomplete without a summary view of the relations of States to the Union at the time Michigan was received into it, or without some notice of the remarkable changes which have been going on since that time, and which have so greatly affected constitutional questions and the political habits of mind and tendencies of the American people. It was also thought proper to present the financial history of the State with some fullness, because it was believed to inculcate a lesson of more than local importance. But no attempt has been made to give the annals of the State as a substitute for other histories, nor, with the field so well occupied as it now is with Judge Campbell's Political History, was any such attempt thought desirable.

CONTENTS.

CHAPTER I.
MICHIGAN IS EXPLORED, AND MISSIONS AND TRADING-POSTS ESTABLISHED 1

CHAPTER II.
DETROIT IS FOUNDED, AND AT LENGTH SURRENDERED TO ENGLAND 16

CHAPTER III.
PONTIAC'S VAIN STRUGGLE FOR THE HOMES OF HIS PEOPLE 40

CHAPTER IV.
A DECADE OF MILITARY ABSOLUTISM 66

CHAPTER V.
THE NORTHWEST CONQUERED FOR THE AMERICAN UNION 79

CHAPTER VI.
GREAT BRITAIN RELUCTANTLY SURRENDERS THE NORTHWEST 105

CHAPTER VII.
THE FOUNDATIONS OF A FREE STATE ARE LAID IN THE NORTHWEST 120

CHAPTER VIII.
MICHIGAN BECOMES A TERRITORY AND IS GIVEN RULERS 140

CONTENTS.

CHAPTER IX.
War, and the Conquest and Reconquest of Michigan 163

CHAPTER X.
The Beginnings of Active American Settlement . 189

CHAPTER XI.
The Territory advances to the Dignity of a State 205

CHAPTER XII.
The State and its Elements 232

CHAPTER XIII.
Money is made abundant in the New State . . . 254

CHAPTER XIV.
The State enters upon Internal Improvements. . 279

CHAPTER XV.
Economy, Recuperation, and Progress 294

CHAPTER XVI.
The State provides for Universal Education . . 306

CHAPTER XVII.
The War in Defense of the Union 330

CHAPTER XVIII
The New State and the Union 344

CHAPTER XIX.
Michigan in the Twentieth Century 372

MICHIGAN:

A HISTORY OF GOVERNMENTS.

CHAPTER I.

MICHIGAN IS EXPLORED, AND MISSIONS AND TRADING POSTS ESTABLISHED.

It was between the great lakes that the western currents of French and English colonization, starting from distant points upon the St. Lawrence and along the Atlantic, after a century and a half of unfriendly rivalry, with occasional bloody and devastating wars, met at last and blended in a peaceful and prosperous commonwealth.

Europe was dazzled by the discovery of a new world, and every maritime nation hastened to share with Spain the fame to be won in adventurous exploration. But in colonization Spain was long without a rival. Attracted by the amazing wealth of tropical production, but far more by the inexhaustible mines of precious metals of which fame brought such wondrous reports from the interior, that country was not long in seizing and occupying the Antilles and the mainland from Mexico to Peru, and the Spanish crown could boast possessions in America of which Rome would have been proud in the height of her supremacy. Portugal, a little later, had obtained a foothold in Brazil; but it was some time before any people or any ruler in Northern Europe appeared to take in the full significance of American discovery, or seemed to appreciate the great fact that a vast and fertile continent, whose possibilities for humanity were beyond calculation, was now offered for the acceptance of European civilization. For more than a century after the discovery by Columbus, the attention of the people of England was so far absorbed by the polemical controversies and the bitter political contests attendant upon a change in the state religion, that the mysterious continent across the ocean excited only occasional and transitory interest. And France, which then, in rivalry with England, was preparing to contest the claim of Spain to the leadership of the world, contented herself for a long time with a lion's share in the harvests which hardy fishermen were gathering on the banks of Newfoundland, and with voyages of adventure and exploration upon the bay and the river St. Lawrence, through which it was hoped there might be found an avenue for trade with the Indies. Roberval and Jacques Cartier attempted a colony at Cape Roque in 1542, but it failed to take root; La Roche with forty transported convicts made a like attempt on Sable Island in 1598, but took off five years later all whom death had not already removed; and De Monts, in 1604, made a settlement on an island near the mouth of the St. Croix, which the next year he abandoned for Port Royal, and Port Royal in its turn was abandoned in 1607 when the fur monopoly, which had been granted to De Monts, was taken away. It was Samuel de Champlain who was the father of New France; and by him, at Quebec, the first permanent settlement was made the year following the planting of the English colony at Jamestown. Other points were soon occupied, of which Montreal was the most important.

The primary objects of French adventure in Canada were profitable trade with the savages and their conversion to the true faith of Christ. Every company of adventurers had its priests, and the eagerness of the trader for gain was more than equaled by the self-sacrificing zeal of the missionary of the cross. Champlain himself was a sincere and devoted son of the Church; and while he endeavored to foster and advance the fur trade, he gave his best energies to establishing and maintaining missions among the Indians, and to protecting against their enemies the tribes which submitted to his guidance, and tacitly acknowledged the French supremacy. In 1615 he visited the shore of Lake Huron, where for the powerful tribe of that name he established a mission of the Récollets, intended by him for a centre of French influence, and of hostility to the Iroquois Confederacy, which he had early encountered in battle near the lake afterwards named for him.

The history of New France from this time to the end of the seventeenth century is a history of one long struggle with the Dutch and English at Albany and New York for the good will and trade of the Indians, in which the Iroquois in general antagonized the French, and the Hurons, with the Algonquin tribes, were their firm friends and supporters. But the French were unable to protect their allies against the proud and fierce confederacy, and the Hurons were driven from their ancient home and took up their abode at Michilimackinac, where they were joined by the Ottawas. But at Michilimackinac they were again assailed by their old enemies, and fled in terror before them to the country beyond Lake Superior, only to come there into conflict with the Illinois, who drove them on to the Mississippi. But there they encountered the Sioux, an enemy not less fierce or formidable than the Iroquois, and finding neither peace nor safety elsewhere, they returned to the Straits of Michilimackinac, and there, in 1671, Father Jacques Marquette founded a mission for them.

The Jesuits took early possession of the mis-

THE POLICY OF THE JESUITS.

sions in New France, and members of that order devoted themselves to the conversion of the Indians with a zeal that spared no endeavor and no artifice, shrank from no privation, quailed before no danger, and was fully in accord with the religious spirit of the day, which could persecute to the death, or submit to martyrdom at the hands of others, with undoubting confidence in either case that Heaven approved the cruelty or the sacrifice. But nothing in the policy of the order favored colonization from Europe; the fathers had come into the wilderness as apostles to the Indians, and it was no part of their mission to people America from France. On the contrary, their mission was to bring the religion of the cross to the people by whom America was already possessed. New colonies must bring with them the vices of civilized life; and the savage nature would be quite certain to add these to such as already belonged to it. A French settlement must, therefore, to some extent be inimical to the success of a mission; and in so far as the colonists failed to observe the sacred precepts of the religion they professed, their proximity would tend to bring religion into contempt in savage eyes, and greatly to increase the labors and perplexities of religious teachers.

But the policy of the fur traders was scarcely less unfriendly to colonization than was that of the Jesuits. Monopolies in the fur trade were granted from the very first, and though conditions were attached to the grants which required the settlement of colonists within territory indicated, it was not to be expected that attention would be given to the conditions any farther than it should be compelled. The grants were made and received for the profit of the grantees, and as their gains were to be gathered in the wilderness, their interest was to preserve the forests, not to destroy them. The conditions for colonization never had more than nominal fulfillment until settlement began in earnest upon the rock of Quebec. Even then the earnestness was but partial, for most of those who were brought over came for hire, and not in pursuance of any deliberate choice to exchange their native country for a home in the new world. Finding everything in New France given over to monopoly, these men either became irregular traders, or took up a roving and lawless life among the Indians, constituting that peculiar class of men known as *coureurs de bois*, whose ambition was fully satisfied if by gun and trap they were able to provide for the limited wants of a life of careless indolence. In 1637, when Richelieu was at the head of affairs, an effort was made in the direction of colonization which seemed to promise great results. Previous grants of monopoly were annulled, and a company of a hundred associates was formed, with Richelieu at its head, to which was granted a permanent monopoly of the trade in furs, skins, and leather, and a monopoly for fifteen years of the whole colonial trade, by land and sea, with the exception of the cod and whale fisheries, which were left free. The scope of the grant embraced the whole of New France, from Florida to the Arctic circle, and on its part the company undertook to convey to New France within the next year two or three hundred men of various trades, and before the year 1643 to increase the number to four thousand, lodging and supporting them for three years, and then giving them for their maintenance lands ready for cultivation. In another age and under other circumstances this undertaking might have borne fruit; but bigotry was then dominant and unrelenting in France, and it would neither tolerate a heretic at home, nor permit him to become the means of extending the glory and power of his native land in the distant wilderness. Every settler was, therefore, required to be a Catholic, and for every settlement at least three ecclesiastics must be provided. The scheme was doomed by its very conditions, for the French nature is little disposed to expatriation, and the class of the people to whom persecution had made emigration a temptation was vigorously excluded from the offer the associates were permitted to make. The company was not prosperous, and in 1663 it was dissolved.

But the dissolution of this company did not

result in freedom to trade. The next year the French West India Company was formed, to which a monopoly still more extensive was granted; but this also was not prosperous, and in 1674 its privileges, with some reservations, were surrendered. Other grants of monopoly followed in succession, the last expiring in 1731; and while they had the effect to prevent immigration and settlement, they also tended to paralyze trade of every sort, to check enterprise, and to incline the lower classes to prefer a life of slothful ease and independence in the woods to one of unprofitable service for the monopolists.

Had trade been free there would still have been serious impediments to settlement in New France. Among the chief of these was the complicated despotism of the government. No English colony had anything similar, and none would have tolerated it. First of its officers was the governor-general, usually a man of noble birth, and nominally the king's immediate representative. Then there was the intendant, who was the king's spy upon the governor-general, possessed of large independent judicial powers, and expected to report fully and frequently, as well as secretly, to the minister. He judged all the king's causes, and might create inferior courts. Commonly, the governor-general and the intendant were at loggerheads, and their correspondence with the minister was burdened with mutual complaints.

There was also a Superior Council, composed of the governor-general, the intendant, and the bishop, which constituted the legislative authority. The Council had an attorney-general, a secretary, and attendant officers, but many times the disputes of the governor and the intendant in regard to their respective powers and privileges made the meetings a scene of disorder, or prevented their being held. The Jesuits were also a power in the colony, which, in the pursuit of its policy, bent its will to no other except when compelled by a necessity which was known to be irresistible. And the king of France wanted no self-government in America. When Frontenac in 1672 assembled the people of Quebec, administered the oath of allegiance, prescribed for them a form of municipal government, and reported the facts to the king, the minister, Colbert, responded: "Your assembling the inhabitants to take the oath of fidelity, and your division of them into three estates, may have had a good effect for the moment; but it is well for you to observe that you are always to follow, in the government of Canada, the forms in use here; and since our kings have long regarded it as good for their service not to convoke the states of the kingdom, in order, perhaps, to abolish insensibly this ancient usage, you on your part should very rarely, or, to speak more correctly, never give a corporate form to the inhabitants of Canada. You should even, as the colony strengthens, suppress gradually the office of the syndic who presents petitions in the name of the inhabitants; for it is well that each should speak for himself and none for all."[1] It was not by such a policy that a power was to be created in New France which could compete successfully in the long race for wealth and power with the English colonies. The matchless skill and prowess of Frontenac for a time made New France preëminent in Indian councils, and humbled and half annihilated the Iroquois Confederacy; but Frontenac in 1698 rested from his long struggles with Iroquois and with Jesuit, and he had no successor who was equal to his responsibilities, or worthy to wear his honors.

Before the opening of the eighteenth century the shores of the great lakes had been well explored by the fur traders and the priests, and important stations had been established, which were at once missions and trading posts. So early as 1641 the Jesuit fathers Raymbault and Jogues had visited the Sault Ste. Marie and had established a mission there for the Chippewas, but the sickness and death of Raymbault caused its early abandonment. The position was too important to permit of its being permanently given up, and Father Marquette was sent there in the spring of 1668, and renewing the mission, he founded there the first permanent settlement in Michigan. This

[1] Parkman's *Frontenac,* p. 20.

illustrious man had come to Canada in 1666, in the twenty-ninth year of his age, to devote his life to mission work, and had received with enthusiasm the order to repair to the upper lakes. In the following year he was joined at the Sault by Father Dablon, to whom he left the work at that place, while he repaired to a new field of labor with the Hurons, then west of Lake Superior. When in 1670 the Hurons fled before their new enemies the Sioux, Father Marquette cast his lot with them, and in the following year gathered them about him at the Straits of Michilimackinac. Michilimackinac, he says, "is the key, and, as it were, the gate, for all the tribes from the south, as the Sault is for those of the north, there being in this section of the country only these two passages by water; for a great number of nations have to go by one or other of these channels in order to reach the French settlements. This presents a peculiarly favorable opportunity, both for instructing those who pass here, and also for obtaining easy access and conveyance to their places of abode." He adds further that the place is "'the home of the fishes.' Elsewhere, although they exist in large numbers, it is not properly their 'home,' which is in the neighborhood of Michilimackinac. It is this attraction which has heretofore drawn to a point so advantageous the greater part of the savages in this country, driven away by fear of the Iroquois."

The mission now established by Father Marquette was located on the north side of the Straits, and was named by him for St. Ignatius. The Hurons and Ottawas, as well as fragments of other tribes, had villages in the vicinity; and in administering to their wants and baptizing their children Father Marquette and his associate, Nouvel, found, as he informs us, "consolation which God sends us, which makes us esteem our life more happy as it is more wretched."

But attractive as were to him the place and the duty, Father Marquette was fired with zeal for more dangerous and venturesome missions, and was ready, as he writes Father Dablon, to leave his charge in the hands of another missionary, in order to seek new nations towards the South Sea, and to become their teacher. Accordingly, when Joliet was sent out to explore the Mississippi, Marquette had orders to accompany him, and he expresses himself as "enraptured at this good news," which put him under the "happy necessity" of exposing his life for the salvation of the nations on the Mississippi, and particularly for the Illinois, who had entreated him when on Lake Superior "to carry the word of God to their country."

The parties started on their mission of exploration May 17, 1673, and proceeding by way of Green Bay, and the Fox and Wisconsin rivers, in a month had reached the Mississippi, which they followed as far down as the Arkansas. Returning they ascended the Illinois, crossed to Lake Michigan at the site of what is now Chicago, and then coasted the western shore of that lake to Green Bay, which they reached in September. Here they separated, and Joliet returned to Quebec. In the fall of the following year Marquette started to fulfill his desire to establish a mission among the Illinois, but his health failed him, and he spent the winter upon the Chicago River. In the spring he proceeded to his destination and began his labors, but continuing to grow feeble in health, and fearing that his end was approaching, he sorrowfully turned his face again to the north, in the hope that his strength might be sufficient to enable him once more to reach the mission he had founded at Michilimackinac, and to worship in the midst of his converts in the chapel of St. Ignatius. But the will of Providence was otherwise. Coasting along the eastern shore of Lake Michigan, he landed for brief rest and for worship near the mouth of the river which has since been named for him, and there, after a few hours' delay and almost without warning, he passed peacefully and quietly to his eternal rest. He was buried on the spot by his sorrowful companions, but two years later a party of his Indian converts removed the body to the place of repose he would have chosen for himself, beneath the chapel which overlooked the Straits of Michilimackinac.

From the time of the founding of the mission on the Straits, that place became a point of resort for the fur traders of Quebec and Montreal, and a point of competition with the English located on the shores of Hudson Bay, and the merchants at Albany. It is not known when Michilimackinac became a military post; we have incidental mention of it by travelers from time to time; La Salle, in the Griffon, the first vessel to plough the waters above Niagara, passed it in 1679, and in 1688 Baron La Hontan visited and described it. La Motte Cadillac was here in command of the post in 1695, and he says of it that "this village is one of the largest in all Canada." The garrison consisted of about two hundred men, and savages to the number of six or seven thousand souls lived in the vicinity, by whom sufficient corn was produced for both the French and themselves. But the capture of the Hudson Bay stations by the French in 1697, and the founding of Detroit in 1701, deprived Michilimackinac of much of its importance, and in 1705 the Jesuits who were stationed there, discouraged by the opposition at Detroit, burned down their chapel and their school building, and took up their departure for Quebec. A few traders and many Indians continued to reside there, and Father Marest soon came to care for their spiritual needs, and remained there until the post was reëstablished, but on the south side of the Straits, in 1714.

EARLY SETTLEMENTS. 15

The importance of the Sault Ste. Marie was greatly diminished by the mission of Michilimackinac, but the Chippewas, a fierce and warlike people, had a village there, and the French government deemed it the suitable point for convening a Congress of Nations in the summer of 1671. Great numbers of Indians came, from the St. Lawrence on the one side to the Mississippi on the other, and even, it is said, from so far down as the Red River, to form or to strengthen a friendship with the French. A post was planted marked with the lilies of France, and the assembled nations were assured that they were now under French protection.

These were the settlements which preceded Detroit. A fort was also built by La Salle at the mouth of the St. Joseph, on Lake Michigan, in 1679, but there was no European settlement about it, and its importance as compared with Michilimackinac was small. A fort at the outlet of Lake Huron was built by Du Lhut in 1686, and named by him St. Joseph. It was constructed to command the passage from Lake Erie to the upper lakes, and its value for this purpose was evident, but with no settlement about it its maintenance would have been troublesome and expensive, and it was abandoned two years after its construction. The founding of Detroit soon rendered any other post on the passage of little or no importance.

CHAPTER II.

DETROIT IS FOUNDED, AND AT LENGTH SURRENDERED TO ENGLAND.

The pathway for Indian traffic and missionary enterprise from Quebec and Montreal was by way of the Ottawa and French rivers to the Georgian Bay, and thence to Michilimackinac, St. Marie, and other stations. The existence of the connecting strait between lakes Huron and Erie must have been known to the French at an early day, but it is not certain that any one of that nation passed through it prior to the expedition made by Joliet, under the command of the intendant Talon, to discover and explore the copper mines of Lake Superior, of which rumors were prevalent. Indeed, that Joliet passed through this strait is only matter of plausible conjecture, for he left no record of this part of his journey; but on his return from his unsuccessful search for mineral wealth in 1669, he encountered, near the head of Lake Ontario, La Salle and the Sulpitian fathers Dollier and Galinée, who had started on their journey of exploration for a passage to the South Sea, and the information he imparted to

LA SALLE'S PARTY DIVIDES. 17

them respecting the upper lake country and the spiritual wants of the Indians of that region so fired the zeal of the worthy fathers that, in spite of the remonstrances of La Salle, they determined to part with him and take their course to the upper lakes by way of Lake Erie. The separation took place at the end of September, 1669, but they did not cross Lake Ontario until the following spring, and they arrived at the Sault Ste. Marie on May 25, 1670, having landed on or near the site of Detroit on the way up, and seized and destroyed with iconoclastic fury and indignation a stone idol which they found there, and whose remains they threw into the middle of the river, that it "might never be heard of again." At the Sault they were received with frigid reserve by the Jesuits, who plainly gave them to understand they were not wanted there, and they returned in discouragement by way of the Ottawa. A crude map made by Galinée and a minute journal of their travels were the valuable results of the expedition, and the importance of Detroit was from this time known to the colonial authorities. It seems probable, also, that at times it was temporarily occupied as a military post. But it was soon to receive more attention, and become a post of first importance, for Antoine de la Motte Cadillac, a man of mark and ability, now appears upon the scene.

We first hear of Cadillac in America in the

year 1687, when he was married at Quebec, being then in the thirtieth year of his age. Two years afterwards he went to France, and returned with a large grant of lands, with manorial rights, on the shores of Maine. He was subsequently employed in positions of importance in the naval and military service of the king, and was so highly esteemed for his judgment and his knowledge of colonial affairs that, in 1692, at the request of Count Pontchartrain, he was sent to France by the governor-general, to give advice respecting the military affairs of the province in its dealings with New York and New England. In the fall of 1694 he was appointed to the command of Michilimackinac, where he remained for five years. Surveying the field of French trade and influence from that remote post, Cadillac had become convinced that Detroit, rather than any of the upper stations, was the point from which the fur trade could best be controlled, and where the friendly Indians could most conveniently be concentrated for the mutual protection of themselves and their French allies. Impressed with this view, he again went to France in 1700, determined, if possible, to obtain the necessary authority as well as the necessary assistance for the establishment of a settlement at Detroit. In a long interview with Count Pontchartrain he presented very fully the advantages of Detroit, its supreme importance as a military and trading post, the excellence of the soil about it, and the desirability of planting in that country an agricultural colony. The sagacious minister was so impressed with his earnestness, and with the reasons assigned, that the desired permission was cordially given, and Cadillac returned to Canada early in 1701, bearing a grant from the king of a tract of land fifteen arpents square, "wherever on the Detroit the new fort should be established," and with assurance of military and other assistance. Making brief pause at Quebec he pushed on to Montreal, where he completed his arrangements for the new undertaking. Fifty soldiers and fifty Canadian traders and artisans were secured by him, and with these in canoes, well supplied with the essentials to a new settlement in the woods, he started from La Chine at the beginning of June. The younger Tonty was commander of the military force, a Récollet priest accompanied the party as chaplain, and a Jesuit as missionary to the Indians. The old route by the Ottawa and Lake Huron was followed, and the boats were drawn up on the shore at the point of destination, on July 24th. A stockade fort was immediately constructed which, in honor of the minister, was named Fort Pontchartrain, and log houses thatched with grass soon went up, in which the settlers found shelter and a home.

At this time the solitude of the vast forests of Michigan was unbroken by the sound of the woodman's axe. The great oaks, hickories, walnuts, and maples towered secure in majestic grandeur, and in all the region of the pine there was audible as yet neither promise nor prophecy of the rich harvest which the lumberman of another day was to reap. In the openings of Southern Michigan, which Nature had decked with more than royal adornments, the elk and the deer found abundant pasturage, and the bear fed on mast and tracked the honey bee to his secret store. The beaver was still building dams in the forest watercourses, and the buffalo fed on the prairies and frequented the abundant salt licks. Choice fish were abundant, but undisturbed, in the lakes and streams of the interior. The iron of Lake Superior was still unknown, and the wealth of its copper was but a rumor, of which the copper ornaments sometimes displayed by the Indian women furnished the only confirmation. The Indian population of the southern peninsula of Michigan was not great; the terror of the Iroquois had made their enemies seek safety in the distance. Around the trading posts and missions, or within easy reach, they had gathered, and many of them under Jesuit teaching had become nominally Christian. But their conversion had scarcely made them less savage and brutal than before; it had not changed their nature, and they could torture the prisoners taken in battle or by treachery, and on great occasions devour their flesh as a stimulant to courage, with the same delight as ever. The Ottawas, said Cadillac a little later, " would be baptized a hundred times a day for a hundred drinks of brandy." " The only good that the missionaries do consists in the baptism of children, who die after having received it, and perchance administering the same rite to some old man at the hour of death." But Cadillac did not like the Jesuits, and he underrated the value of their services. It was a great and lasting benefit to the Indians, that under the influence of the priests they were taught foresight, and in the enlarged cultivation of the soil were induced to provide against the contingencies of bad seasons and occasional failures of the chase, and thus to forestall and prevent the famines that sometimes had visited them with destructive severity. Their agriculture at the best was crude and limited, but it became at length adequate to their wants, and they were the farmers and the gardeners for the soldiers and traders.

Of the traders with the Indians at this early period some were regular, and traded under the existing grant of monopoly, or by special permits. More, however, were irregular. In the woods about every station were many *coureurs de bois*, or bushrangers, who carried on a lawless traffic in furs and peltry with the Indians, and lived with them much of the time in their wigwams. Their trade, though illegal, was generally connived at by all but the regular traders, whose profits it would diminish, and even these sometimes found the bushrangers valuable agents in bringing to their places of business the traffic that otherwise might have been secured by the English. To the colony at large these people were an undoubted advantage, for they gave valuable assistance in maintaining friendly relations with the Indians, and if danger threatened they had early knowledge of it and could give warning in season. But they lived like savages and loved the savage life. At the same time they were never weaned from their native attachments, but were Frenchmen in spirit even when they had abandoned the manners and methods of civilization.

Dominion over the territory lying between the great lakes was claimed by both Canada and New York, on similar grounds of prior discovery and possession. But most of the claims on both sides, so far as can now be ascertained, had little foundation in fact. A sharp correspondence had taken place on the subject between Governor Dongan on the one side and De la Barre on the other, and this was renewed when De la Barre had been succeeded by Denonville. But the correspondence had no result; each party continued its efforts to obtain the trade of the Lake region, while jealously watching the other, and stirring up strife against their rivals as opportunity offered. In all intercourse with the Indians the French had one very great advantage over their rivals: they affiliated with them more readily; they met them more freely and easily on terms of fellowship; their manners were less austere and abrupt; and they took more pains by friendly attentions and courtesies to conciliate favor. In many cases, too, their young men formed lasting attachments and family relations with the forest maidens, and a thousand ties were woven between the Indians and the French, which in the intercourse of the former with the English were comparatively unknown. On the other hand, the English goods were always cheaper, and the Indians had shrewdness enough to discover the fact, and to avail themselves of it whenever they were permitted and found it practicable and safe to do so. But after the founding of Detroit the French generally monopolized their trade. Cadillac assigned to the minister many reasons for this. "One is that each savage, one with another, kills per year only fifty or sixty beavers, and as he is neighbor to the Frenchman, frequently borrows of him, paying in proportion to his returns by the chase; with the little that remains to him he is compelled to make purchases for his family. Thus he finds himself unable to go to the English, because his remaining goods are not worth the trouble of carrying so far; not being sufficient to pay him for the expense of his journey. Another reason is that in frequenting the French he receives many caresses; they are too cunning to allow his furs to escape, especially when they succeed in making him eat and drink with them. The will to go to the English still exists among the savages, but they are skillfully reduced to the impossibility of its execution."[1] Thus early in America do we encounter the slavery of a mortgaged future. But the French had not relied exclusively on their influence with the Indians for the protection of their trade, but had on some occasions made use of force. Robert Livingston thought Detroit should be occupied by the English, and in 1699, after the treaty of Ryswick, a plan was submitted by him to Lord Bellamont for establishing a military post at that point, and settling there both whites and Iroquois Indians; but the plan was not promptly acted upon, and two years thereafter Cadillac was in possession. More fortunate than Livingston, he had succeeded in convincing his government that Detroit "is a door by which one can go in and out to trade with all our allies;"[2] and the king had made him the doorkeeper.

Cadillac was not less impressed with the beauty of Detroit and its desirability as a home than with its commercial and strategic importance, and he grows eloquent as he describes the passage through which flows with moderate current "the living and crystal waters" of the upper lakes,

[1] Sheldon's *Early Hist. of Michigan*, 87, 88.
[2] *Ibid.* 116.

"which are so many seas of sweet water" rolling on to mingle with the distant ocean. The borders of the strait, he says, are vast prairies, and "the freshness of the beautiful waters keeps the banks always green." Natural orchards "soften and bend their branches under the weight and quantity of their fruit towards the mother earth which has produced them," and "the ambitious vine, which has never wept under the pruning-knife, builds a thick roof with its large leaves and heavy clusters, weighing down the top of the tree which receives it, and often stifling it with its embrace." The woods are full of game; the forest trees are straight as arrows, and of prodigious size; above them the courageous eagle soars looking fixedly at the sun; the swans in the river are so numerous that one might take for lilies the reeds in which they crowd together, and the fish are none the less delicious for their great abundance. And he adds, with covert allusion to his enemies, the Jesuits, that "none but the enemies of truth could be enemies to this establishment, so necessary to the increase of the glory of the king, to the spread of religion, and to the destruction of the throne of Satan."

The glowing description of the adventurous founder of Detroit was written with the pen of truth, and expressed but inadequately the sentiments of the writer respecting the beauty and desirableness of his new location. And here he proposed to found the mart of commerce for all the northwest: a town which should be the nucleus of an agricultural colony. But Detroit was born in chains, and weighed down with manacles in all its struggling infancy. The old system of repression under which Canada existed and languished from the first was vigorously applied to it. Commerce must not for a moment be free; individual energy and enterprise must be kept in strict restraint, or if it escaped restraint it must be left to act in defiance of law, or in evasion of it. On October 31, 1701, a contract was entered into by the governor-general and intendant with "The Company of the Colony of Canada," whereby the posts of Detroit and of Frontenac on Lake Ontario were ceded to the company for traffic in furs, to the exclusion of all others, the company assuming various obligations, the chief of which were to put and keep the forts in repair, and to maintain at Detroit the commandant and one other officer. The contract provided under severe penalties that the commandant and soldiers at Detroit should make no trade in furs with the savages or French, directly or indirectly, and the colonial authorities thus evinced their willingness that the new settlement should neither be "nourished by their indulgence," nor "grow by their neglect."

Cadillac, having established his post, proceeded to gather the Indians about it, and for this purpose he looked as far as those at Michilimackinac, and urged them to join him. He was a zealous son of the Church, but affiliated with the order of St. Francis, and his cordial dislike of the Jesuits may have quickened his zeal in the endeavor to break up the mission at Michilimackinac, where the Jesuits were supreme. The obnoxious order reciprocated his dislike most fully, and his stay at Detroit was one long struggle with them, the varying phases of which are all brought out in the correspondence of the parties with the authorities of Canada, and that of Cadillac with Count Pontchartrain. Meantime the wishes of the minister concerning the permanent settlement at Detroit seem not to have been expressed with the precision and certainty which were important to the purposes of Cadillac, who in 1703 anxiously addresses him on the subject, with full statement of his own views. To make success sure, he says, there must be liberty of settlement. He wishes to know whether the soldiers should not have grants of land and be permitted to marry when able to support families; he gives his own opinion decidedly in the affirmative, and he would have dwelling-places granted to the Canadians, who are persecuting him continually for them. He urges the minister to speak decidedly on this point, for he cannot conceal the fact that the company which controls the trade does not wish to do anything about it. Nothing, he affirms, is to be accomplished at Detroit without more inhabitants.

But Cadillac was soon in a quarrel with the company, growing out, as he informed the minister, of his endeavors to protect its interests against thieving officers. This might seem a strange reason elsewhere, but it was not strange in Canada, where official peculation and knavery, in public as well as in corporate service, was the rule, and continued to be so until the French power was overthrown. Montcalm, half a century later, declared that Canada was a land where the knaves grew rich, and the honest men were ruined. Being at Montreal in the autumn of 1704, Cadillac was arrested and charged before the intendant with tyrannical conduct, and though acquitted of the charge he was not given leave to return to his post until September of the following year. When he received permission he did not avail himself of it until he had met Count Pontchartrain, who came to Quebec to satisfy himself, by personal investigation, of the true nature of the difficulties which appeared to hinder the prosperity of the new post. The full and minute explanations which were given him by Cadillac proved satisfactory,[1] and it was when, with his approval, the commandant returned to his post in 1706, that the Jesuit fathers at Michilimackinac gave up the

[1] The examination and defense are given at length in Sheldon's *Early Hist. of Michigan*, 142 *et seq.*

struggle with him and abandoned their station. But when Father Marest succeeded them at that place the old strife was renewed, and continued thereafter as active as ever.

The chief anxiety of Cadillac was now the behavior of the Indians about his fort. They were of various tribes, and not harmonious; and the longing among them for the cheap goods of the English caused some discontent. A fire at the fort was with much reason believed to have been the work of dissatisfied Indians. A number of the Ottawas, by invitation, went down to Albany in 1703, and while there were cunningly made to believe that the building of Fort Pontchartrain was for the purpose of holding them in subjection to the French. They returned discontented, and there were continuous difficulties thereafter. For five years or more the settlement was in a state of disquietude, and Vaudreuil, the governor-general, in 1707 summoned the principal chiefs to a council at Montreal, where he received them with displeasure and rebuke, and after some delay sent them back submissive, but with jealousies and bitterness towards each other. Meantime Cadillac was urging the entire abandonment of Michilimackinac, but Aigrement, who was sent to inspect Detroit and remained at the post nineteen days, reported strongly against the plan of the commander.[1] How far his report was

[1] See report, Sheldon's *Early Hist. of Michigan*, 280.

meant to be truthful may be a question, but the unfriendly animus is apparent. The ground about Detroit, he says, is full of water, and the grasshoppers eat up all the garden plants, so that it is necessary to plant and sow the same things even to the fourth time. But even if the land were ever so productive there would be no market for the surplus, and the trade of the post would never be useful to France; the result of which would be that the establishment would always be a burden. Michilimackinac, on the other hand, is the advanced post of all Canada; the most important as well for its advantageous position as for the commerce that might be made there. But as matters now are, brandy and ammunition are all the goods sold to the Indians by the French: all else are furnished by the English. Cadillac, he takes pains to add, is generally disliked for his tyranny.

Such, in brief, was the report; but it was more damaging in intent than in effect. The minister, though sometimes hesitating, did not fail in any case, after full explanation had been called for and received, to come to the support of Cadillac, and of his favorite post. The faithful and persistent commandant remained at Detroit, and continued to be the life of the settlement and the chief figure in the public affairs of this peninsula until 1710, when private affairs took him away from the colony. We hear of him afterwards as governor of Louisiana for a brief period, and still later in unconspicuous public employments in France, where he died in 1730. His life was one of varied usefulness, but his chief claim upon the regard of posterity rests upon his having had the sagacity to perceive that the site of Detroit commanded a great highway of nations, and the courage and persistence essential to the planting, under many difficulties and against powerful opposition, of the foundations of the City of the Straits.

Among the complaints made of Cadillac was one of the manner in which he dealt with the traffic in intoxicating drinks. How to deal with the traffic was a problem that perplexed him, as it has many a statesman before and since; and if his wisdom was inadequate to its mastery, he was but one in a long line of American rulers who have been equally at fault, and equally unsuccessful. Brandy in Canada, as elsewhere, had been found the readiest and most effective means of making friends with the savages. The Indian tasted it with delight, and he loved it not for its taste merely, but for the demon that was in it. The drunken stage which the white man would gladly avoid, the Indian craved; and the Jesuit soon found that strong drink would prove a chief obstacle to the success of his labors, and that for the Indian, if not for the white man, brandy and Christianity were irreconcilable. The Jesuits, therefore, launched anathemas against the trade, and when these proved idle they obtained prohibitions; but when the sale could no longer be made at the posts, it was made in the woods. Severe punishments were no restraint; at one time the penalty was death, and several executions actually took place;[1] but so desperate a remedy excited other passions among the people, without cooling the passion for drink. Repeatedly we find it declared in official reports and papers that the traffic in brandy is essential to trade and to friendship with the Indians: they must have it from the French, or they will obtain it from Albany, and even religion is concerned in their not going to Albany, where they may be taught heresy to the peril of their souls. Cadillac himself, when at Michilimackinac, had strongly attested the necessity of the trade, but he seems at Detroit to have become firmly convinced of the need of restraints, and to have labored faithfully to establish them. Among the complaints which Aigrement makes of him is one upon this subject: —

"In order to prevent the disturbances which would arise from the excessive use of brandy, M. La Motte causes it all to be put into the storehouse, and to be sold to each in his turn, at the rate of twenty francs a quart. Those who will have it, French as well as Indians, are

[1] Journal des Jesuits, Oct., 1661. See Parkman's *Old Régime in Canada,* 121, 324.

obliged to go to the storehouse to drink, and each can obtain at one time only the twenty-fourth part of a quart. It is certain that the savages cannot become intoxicated on that quantity. The price is high, and as they can only get the brandy each in his turn, it sometimes happens that the savages are obliged to return home without a taste of this beverage, and they seem ready to kill themselves in their disappointment." [1]

But Cadillac's method of limiting the sale was probably wise for the day, and the occasional fury of disappointment was less to be feared than the voluntary madness of drunken savages. A subsequent attempt of one of the successors of Cadillac to induce the Indians voluntarily to abandon the use of brandy had much the same basis in reason as an attempt to teach the wolf voluntarily to abstain from the taste of blood. In a council held on the subject in 1721, when it was intimated that the French would refuse to sell brandy longer, Sastaretsi, the Huron orator, admitted their right to do so, and did not deny that it would have been much better if his people had never been taught to use it; but now, he declared, they had become so much accustomed to the use that they could not do without it. The inference was that whether openly or secretly, from French or from English, the brandy they must and would have, and it was useless to think of preventing it.

[1] Summary of inspection of Detroit and Michilimackinac, given at length in Sheldon's *Early Hist. of Michigan*, 280 *et seq.*

And that Sastaretsi was right in this is proved by all subsequent Indian history. The restraints which the law has cast over the traffic have always been mere gossamer threads, seldom felt, and noticed only as suggesting prudence in methods of dealing and skill in evasion.

Detroit was maintained as a military and trading post under Cadillac, but it did not grow. The opposition to him and to his settlement was so vigorous and persistent that he was barely able to prevent its being uprooted and removed. The force which, in 1710, was transferred to Dubuisson as temporary commandant was smaller than that with which possession of the strait was first taken and the stockade fort erected. The weakness of the post invited attack, and in May, 1712, the Outagamies and Mascoutins, who had settlements near it, undertook to capture and destroy the fort, but Dubuisson had discovered their purpose and was on his guard. The Ottawas and the Hurons were not then returned from their winter's hunt, but they came in time to save the fort. The besiegers were assailed with overwhelming force, and after flying for a distance of twelve miles were captured and slaughtered to the number of a thousand. But the Outagamies, though fearfully weakened by this destruction, were not annihilated, and they remained unfriendly and a source of danger and difficulty afterwards.

And now for forty-eight years, until the final

surrender of New France to the English, the history of Detroit is a monotonous record of the bare existence of a post, the maintenance of which depended upon a trade which was uncertain and subject to many contingencies, upon the friendship of savages who were proverbially treacherous and were given abundant occasions for unfriendliness, and upon the favor of the government, to which it proved an almost constant expense. Incessantly, the question was coming up in public councils, whether Detroit should not be abandoned. La Foret, who had commanded there in 1714, felt under the need of writing a memorial insisting upon its importance as a military post, but he thought settlement about it should be stopped, and the settlers excluded from the fort, since the danger from the savages rendered improvement impossible. Charlevoix, on the other hand, who visited the post in 1721, when Tonty was commandant, speaks in glowing terms of the agriculture about it, and of the Hurons as sharp traders, who raise much for sale. Beauharnais, who was governor-general in 1732, wrote to the minister: "It is impossible for that establishment to become considerable so long as a sufficient number of troops are not sent thither, to whom lands would be granted for the purpose of improvement, by which course farmers would eventually be introduced." With a farming population about it "this post would become considerable in a short time, and by its strength keep all the nations of the upper country in check." In 1745 Beauharnais complained that licenses to trade at Detroit and the upper straits, for which before that time large sums had been paid, could scarcely be given away; provisions were threatening to give out, and the Indians were mutinous. The year 1747 was one of constant alarms of Indian hostility, and some warlike movements were observed among the Hurons, which it became necessary to suppress. And not long after, news began to come from the valley of the Ohio which plainly foreshadowed a struggle for that region of marvelous wealth and beauty, which would be certain to draw within its desolating vortex the people of Detroit and the Indian tribes that lived near or traded with them.

The teeming valley was fit prize for the contention of mighty nations, and each party could advance claims to it which, according to the ideas then prevalent, had plausibility: the French by right of discovery and actual occupation; the English by the occupation and settlement of the seaboard in the same latitude, but especially in the right of the Iroquois Confederacy, which in 1684, when they dominated all this region, had in solemn council at Albany placed themselves and their country under English "protection." In 1748 the Ohio Company was formed, with the avowed purpose to establish settlements in the Ohio valley, and five years later the youthful George Washington led into the valley a small military force, and the war began which was to convulse Europe, and to end only with the entire overthrow of French power in America. Fortunately for Detroit the Indians about it sympathized in this war with the French, and so far as they took part in it did so as the allies of France. Detroit, therefore, heard the thunder of war only in its distant reverberations, and felt the shock but faintly. But though undisturbed it was not prosperous. In 1750 Gallissonière, who had been succeeded as governor-general by Jonquiere, in a paper addressed to the minister, pointed out in strong and clear terms the necessity for an agricultural population at the military and trading posts. Of Detroit he said, " Did it once contain a farming population of a thousand, it would feed and defend all the rest. Throughout the whole interior of Canada it is the best adapted for a town, where all the trade of the lakes would concentrate; were it provided with a good garrison and surrounded by a goodly number of settlements, it would be enabled to overawe almost all the Indians of the continent." Through persistent effort he succeeded in having a few settlers sent out, who for a time received assistance from the government, but the gain to the population was not great. Vaudreuil, the governor-general, writing in 1755 to the minister, could say of Detroit, " That post is considerable; well peopled; but three times more people than it possesses could be easily located there. The misfortune is that we have not enough of people in the colony."

This continued to be the misfortune until Canada became a British province. Colonies had grown to greatness under English neglect, and in the shadow of governmental disfavor; but under the fostering care of French supervision and nursing, they could only languish in the weakness of absolute dependence. When Canada became British there was within the limits of Michigan no settlement which, under existing conditions, gave promise of substantial growth and expansion. At Sault Ste. Marie the Chevalier de Repentigny, under a large grant made to him with manorial rights, had made some effort to plant a settlement, but it took no root and was soon forgotten. At Michilimackinac a trading post and a mission were still maintained, and Indians had their villages about it, and practiced such imperfect agriculture as sufficed for the limited needs of their indolent and unthrifty mode of living. Detroit alone had pretensions to be called a settlement; but when its age and its magnificent natural advantages are considered, the pretensions must be called but slight. For sixty years the Indians had gathered in considerable numbers about it, and raised their scanty crops in its vicinity, and been given such Christian instruction as they would consent to receive, and far more than they were capable of understanding; but they still remained savages, and were watched more than they were trusted. The few French agricultural settlers kept within easy reach of the shelter and protection of the fort. Sixty years of the French system of governmental absolutism, official venality, trade monopoly, and individual dependence had maintained for the king a nominal sovereignty over the Lake country, but it had established no colony worthy the name. On all the upper lakes not a vessel unfurled sails to the breeze; the canoe and other row-boats met the wants of such transportation as the existing traffic called for. There was no printing-press in Michigan, for there was none in all New France. The time was to come when at many a waterfall and crossing of trails in the peninsula, some small company, less numerous than that with which La Motte Cadillac founded Detroit, coming with their axes and other agricultural implements, but above all with their families for permanent homes, would within a single year have more of permanent worth to show for their labors.

CHAPTER III.

PONTIAC'S VAIN STRUGGLE FOR THE HOMES OF HIS PEOPLE.

ON the memorable eighteenth of September, 1759, the garrison of Quebec sorrowfully opened its gates, and the investing British army marched in and took possession. It was the stronghold of all Canada; and from New Hampshire to Georgia Americans welcomed the news with exuberant rejoicings as the prelude to the inevitable submission of all New France, and the termination of the savage warfare that under French inspiration had so long disquieted and at times devastated their northern and western borders. Canada also was alive to the significance of the great event; for it was plain to all men that the permanent occupation of Quebec by British forces involved the overthow of French power in America. Accordingly a vigorous effort was made to recover the place the following year, but it proved abortive, and on September 8, 1760, M. de Vaudreuil, the governor-general, surrendered Montreal, and with it all Canada, to General Amherst, the British commander. By the articles of capitulation the undisturbed enjoyment of their property and the free exercise of their religion were guarantied to the people, but an article stipulating for the preservation of existing laws was refused, and the people were given to understand that they had become subjects of the British crown, and would be treated as such.

Four days later General Amherst issued an order to Major Robert Rogers, directing him to proceed with a military force to Detroit and Michilimackinac and take possession of those posts and administer oaths of allegiance to the inhabitants. Rogers was the most noted partisan leader of the day: he had been active and conspicuous in the war from the first; no Indian had surpassed him in woodcraft or in cunning, and few either white or red had equaled him in daring or in prowess. He had suffered hardships of every nature incident to war: sickness, and wounds, and captivity, and starvation; but his endurance was equal to every emergency, and he had come out of every trial with no abatement of courage or determination. From Lake Champlain to Quebec forest glens had echoed the deadly reports of his rifle, and were red with the bloody footsteps of his men. He received with pleasure the order which was to complete on the upper lakes the victory at Quebec, and started the next day, taking the route by Lake Ontario, the Niagara River, and Lake Erie to Presque Isle, from which he diverged for the delivery of dispatches to General Monckton at Pittsburgh. Returning to Presque Isle he resumed his journey along the south shore of Lake Erie until November 7th, when he encamped at the mouth of a river which he called the Chogage, and which has been variously conjectured to have been the Chagrin, the Cuyahoga, and the Grand. Here he was met by a party of Indians who announced themselves messengers of Pontiac, the ruler and king of all that country, and who admonished the British commander in the name of their master, that no further advance should be made until Pontiac, who was near at hand, should arrive and give permission. The chief soon followed the embassy, and in haughty tones demanded of Rogers how he dared to enter his country without permission. Rogers replied that he had come with no hostile purpose against the Indians, and that his sole business was to remove from the country the French, who had been an obstacle to peace and trade between the Indians and the English. In token of friendship, strings of wampum were then delivered to Pontiac, who received them graciously, but signified his will that the party should proceed no farther until the morning; and after exchange of friendly courtesies he took his departure. The next morning he again appeared, smoked the pipe of peace with Major Rogers, gave consent to his proceeding on his journey, and offered to accompany him to Detroit and give him any necessary protection against unfriendly or excited Indians. The offer was accepted by Major Rogers, and the party proceeded, sending forward in advance a notification of the coming and of its purpose. M. Bellestre, then in command at Detroit, was still vainly hoping that Canada, by a supreme effort, might be recovered by the French, and he seems to have made some effort to arouse the animosity of the Indians in the neighborhood against the English, and to induce them to aid him in resistance; but Rogers gathered them in council near the mouth of the Detroit River, and having assured them of his fixed purpose to send the French away, promised to leave the Indians in possession of their own country, and to settle with them amicably all matters which might be the subject of controversy. The Indians received his assurances as satisfactory, and when on November 29th Rogers reached Detroit, the French commandant, perceiving that resistance would be futile, surrendered the post. From Detroit was sent out a detachment which took possession of Fort Miami on the Maumee and Fort Ouatanon on the Wabash, and Rogers himself started with a force to occupy Michilimackinac, but found the season too far advanced, and was obliged to abandon the undertaking. It was not until the fall of the next year that small forces, sent out from Detroit by command of Sir William Johnson, took possession of the forts at Michilimackinac and St. Joseph, and placed garrisons in them for the British crown.

Thus ninety years after the establishment of the mission on the Straits of Michilimackinac, and more than a century and a half after the founding of Quebec, the French were compelled to yield to their persistent rival the vast country for which they had sacrificed so much, and whose possession, in the eyes of the world, added so considerably to the glory and grandeur of the crown and promised such great things for the future. The national pride was humbled, and the national heart was touched also by the necessary abandonment of the French colonists. Vaudreuil, the governor-general, truthfully said in taking his departure: "With these beautiful and vast countries France loses seventy thousand inhabitants of a rare quality; a race of people unequaled for their docility, bravery, and loyalty. The vexations they have suffered for many years, more especially during the five years preceding the reduction of Quebec, — all without a murmur, or importuning their king for relief, — sufficiently manifest their perfect submissiveness."[1] The treaty of peace was not made between the two countries until February 10, 1763, but when it came it made final concession of Canada to the British crown.

With the triumph of Wolfe on the heights of

[1] Garneau's *Hist. of Canada*, by Bell, vol. ii. p. 71.

Abraham, it has been said, began the history of the United States. Voltaire, in his retirement at Ferney, rejoiced at the fall of Quebec, and the inevitable surrender of Canada, and celebrated it by a banquet as the precursor of American enfranchisement. But this great event meant more than American enfranchisement: it meant the overthrow of the despotic principle in America, and the surrender of the continent, with all its immense possibilities, to the growing and expanding ideas of English liberty. American enfranchisement from the British rule was an event of first importance, but its value to the world would have been infinitely lessened had it not been grounded on the assertion and maintenance of rights assured to the subject by English law. For many centuries now the germs of free institutions had been planted in England, nurtured by the robust thought and defended by the vigorous arms of its people; and when from time to time despotism trampled in the dust the incipient attempts of other nations to win recognition of rights or to gain relief from intolerable burdens, the seagirt island, in maintaining her independence, preserved her liberties also, and the slow but certain development of free institutions went on unchecked. The two opposing principles in government had now grappled in a final struggle for mastery in America, and when despotism fell, a Britain, no longer needing the protection of the four seas, but stepping boldly out to occupy a continent as master, began immediately to give prophecy of that vast confederacy of commonwealths which was successively to become the rebellious child, the hated rival, and at last the chief glory of the island parent, and the precursor of other confederacies of commonwealths which should speedily give to the English tongue and to English liberty an undisputed leadership on both continents.

But the immediate result of the conquest to the conquered people was far from being either beneficial or agreeable. The French rule had been arbitrary and irresponsible, but the English rule did not promise to be immediately any less so. It was, besides, the rule of the stranger over a people compelled to submit by force of arms, and every oppressive act would seem doubly oppressive from that fact. The British commander at once assumed supreme authority, and for the purposes of the administration of justice created a series of military courts to which was given jurisdiction of all controversies, with no appeal in case of dissatisfaction except to other military authorities, or to the commander himself. A military judiciary, always arbitrary and always obnoxious, was made preëminently obnoxious in this case by its being required to govern its decisions by the English law, of which the people knew nothing, instead of the preëxisting laws and usages of the country to which they were accustomed, and which were dear to them as the laws and customs of their native land. If by English law had been understood the common law of England, whose rules for the protection of rights were definite and just, there would have been less reason to complain; but military judges are to be expected to have some degree of contempt for common law methods, and are likely in rejecting the methods to put substance aside also, and make their will the test of right. With the intelligent among the people the sense of oppression was increased by the knowledge that this uprooting of the existing law by the conquering power was not according to the customary practice of civilized nations, and might for that reason be justly suspected as promising a rule exceptionally despotic even for the military; and many of the most enterprising and thrifty abandoned the country, leaving the population sensibly diminished. Some of these returned to France; many accepted the invitation of the people of Louisiana to remove to that district; and when St. Louis was founded in 1764 some became residents of that town. Those who remained under British rule submitted with outward cheerfulness, but without the loyalty of feeling and spirit so essential in times of public danger.

If the establishment of unrestricted military tribunals was not likely to please the French, still less would the management of public affairs tend to conciliate the Indians, or to establish relations of trustworthy amity with them. Most of the savages living in the upper lake region, having taken the part of the French in the wars which preceded the conquest, still looked upon the French as their friends, and would gladly have seen the country restored to their dominion. A strong hope prevailed among them, which might easily become a belief, that a reconquest would yet take place, and the advances they made towards cordial relations with the English were half-hearted and such only as temporary interest seemed to prompt. On the other hand the English authorities, with strange disregard of the demands of the situation, not only neglected to take proper steps to wean the Indians from their French attachments, and to convert them from enmity to friendship, but by a cold, haughty, and reserved demeanor they repelled advances, and thereby gave serious offense even in the case of influential personages, whose favor and friendship were necessary to amicable relations. Where the French officer was easy and complaisant, and by his courteous bearing avoided wounding the self-respect of the Indian, the English officer, conscious of his superiority over the brutal and disgusting savage, and impatient of any assumption of equality, took little pains to conceal his contempt and repugnance, and was perpetually allowing himself to be guilty of slights and affronts to which only the most abject could be expected to submit without resentment. The customary presents which the Indians expected, and which the French had made on a scale of liberality, the English either discontinued entirely or measured by a standard of economy which showed them to be given not in friendship, but grudgingly, and deprived them of all efficacy as a means of preserving amicable relations. Lieutenant Gorrell, when he was sent to receive the surrender of the more western posts, was instructed to give the Indians no more presents than was absolutely necessary to keep them in temper,[1] — instructions which he might well say made him uneasy, so different were they in spirit from the policy which had prevailed with the French. And what was nominally given was often dishonestly appropriated by agents, or only delivered to the Indians to whom it was sent when they had paid for it such sum as the agent saw fit to exact.[2] In Western Pennsylvania and Virginia the settlers were continually encroaching upon the lands of the Indians, and though the tribes west of the lakes were as yet unmolested, they saw in the case of their brothers what they might soon expect from the restless and greedy English, and they perceived very clearly that in this particular, at

[1] *Wis. Hist. Col.* vol. i. p. 32
[2] Stone's *Life of Sir Wm. Johnson*, vol. ii. p. 137.

least, the cause of one tribe was the cause of all. Jefferson did not exaggerate when he said that the settlers in many cases regarded neither the laws, treaties, nor proclamations of their own government, nor the remonstrances of the Indians, and that the lives of men, women, and children were ruthlessly taken by them.

More than ever before trade with the Indians was now the occasion of injustice and outrage, and exasperations arising from it were frequent. Under French sway some degree of fair dealing was secured to the savage; the trader became his friend and boon companion, and made his coming to dispose of his peltry an occasion for festivity and roisterous goodfellowship, when all would partake of the same fare, drink of the same beverages, and indulge in the same sports. At Detroit and elsewhere some of these traders remained, and of the new-comers some were Scotch, with many characteristics resembling those of their predecessors, who sought, while making great profits out of the Indians, to win and preserve their favor. But there were many of a different sort, whose greed knew no bounds, and in whose service, as Parkman has forcibly said, " were ruffians of the coarsest stamp, who vied with each other in rapacity, violence, and profligacy. They cheated, plundered, and cursed the Indians and outraged their families, offering, when compared with the French traders who were under better regulation, a most unfavorable example of the character of their nation."[1] Liquor was the ever ready means by the use of which the Indian was defrauded. Returning from the chase after long abstinence, his eagerness for intoxicating drinks was passionate, and when once indulged, his reason and his self-restraint were overcome, and he was powerless for any purpose of self-protection. We get a vivid picture of what must have been a frequent occurrence at Detroit from the narrative of a white person who was taken prisoner in Western Pennsylvania and adopted into one of the Indian tribes.

"A trader [he says] came to town with French brandy; we purchased a keg of it, and held a council about who was to get drunk and who was to keep sober. I was invited to get drunk, but I refused the proposal; then they told me I must be one of those who were to take care of the drunken people. I did not like this, but of two evils I chose that which I thought was the least, and fell in with those who were to conceal the arms and keep every dangerous weapon we could out of their way, and endeavor, if possible, to keep the drinking club from killing each other, which was a very hard task. Several times we hazarded our own lives, and got ourselves hurt in preventing them from slaying each other."[2]

[1] *Conspiracy of Pontiac*, 155.
[2] *Account of Remarkable Occurrences, etc.*, by Col. James Smith, 76.

The debauch went on while a beaver skin remained, and when it was over the Indian found he had exchanged for it the results of his labors for weeks or months. If he ventured to make complaint he was answered with curses and blows, and was driven off as a creature whose presence, now that his immediate usefulness to the unscrupulous trader was exhausted, had become repulsive. Nor was the trader any more regardful of the rights or of the safety of the white settlers than of the Indians; for in the time immediately preceding Pontiac's war, when the government of Pennsylvania had forbidden trade with the Indians from regard to the public safety, traders did not scruple openly to disobey the law, and supplied the Indians freely with the maddening liquors and with the very guns and ammunition by the use of which they were subsequently enabled to plunder and ravage the frontier. So bold and reckless was the defiance of law by the dealers that in some cases the indignant people retaliated with violence, and seized and destroyed their stores. When, however, the Indian alone was the sufferer from fraud and lawless rapacity, his complaints received little attention from either the authorities or the people, and any resentment on his part that went to the extreme of violence was certain to be regarded as the outrage of a savage, which must be visited with swift and condign retribution. But there was very general recognition of the fact that difficulties began with the traders, and so loud and so general had become the complaints of misconduct and outrage on their part, that in the summer of 1761 Sir William Johnson was sent to Detroit with full authority to correct such evils as he might find to exist, and to take into his own hands complete supervision and control of Indian trade in the Northwest. He reached Detroit in the beginning of September, where he held council with a number of Indian tribes, and no doubt did whatever seemed to him possible in the correction of abuses. But the correction, when the restraining power was to be at a distance, could at best be only temporary and partial; greed was more powerful than the sense of justice or the feeling of humanity, and the story of one year was repeated in the next with variation only of actors and minor circumstances.

Meantime nothing was being done in the Northwest to strengthen the exposed settlements by bringing about them what they needed most of all, a class of agricultural laborers, who would live on the results of their own industry. The French were not brought into sentiments of attachment to their new government by a conciliatory deportment towards them, and with both French and Indians the hope was indulged that the overthrow of French power would prove but temporary, and that before long that great nation might be expected to put forth its mighty energies for the recovery of its lost prestige and dominion.

The fires of discontent were smouldering everywhere, and nothing was needed but the breath of a bold and daring spirit to blow them into flame. And such a spirit promptly appeared on the stage. Pontiac, who with such haughtiness had interposed to stay the advance of Major Rogers, was one of those rare characters among the Indians whose merits are so transcendent that, without the aid of adventitious circumstances, they take by common consent the headship in peace and the leadership in war. In battle he had shown his courage, in council his eloquence and his wisdom; he was wary in planning and indefatigable in execution; his patriotism was ardent and his ambition boundless, and he was at this time in all the region between the head-waters of the Ohio and the distant Mississippi, the most conspicuous figure among the savage tribes, and the predestined leader in any undertaking which should enlist the general interest. Of the Ottawas he was the principal chief, and he made his home at their village opposite and a little above Detroit, with a summer residence on Peche Island in Lake St. Clair. But he was also chief of a loose Confederacy of the Ottawas, Ojibwas, and Pottawatamies, and his influence extended far beyond those tribes, and placed him above rivalry in all the lake region and the valley of the Ohio. The change in territorial sovereignty had not been agreeable to him; he perceived very clearly that with the accession of the English to undisputed sway in the interior, the greatness and even the security of his people were threatened, and that unless bounds could be set to English encroachments the Indians must inevitably be debased by their enticements, robbed by their unscrupulous arts, and at last driven from their homes and their hunting grounds by a rapacity that seemed insatiable. While the French held Canada the Indians had been courted by both sides as holding a certain effective power which made their friendship of high value; but now that France had apparently abandoned the long struggle for a share in the new world, the Indian was made to feel that he no longer had an importance entitling him to respect, but was an inferior being whose rights were subordinate to the interests of the superior race, and who in all controversies would be held presumptively in the wrong, and compelled to submit to such justice as his adversaries should see fit to concede to him. To a bold and haughty spirit like that of Pontiac, this condition of things was intolerable, and he resolved to strike a blow that should at once break the yoke of servitude, and be ample warning against further encroachments upon Indian rights and territorial and personal independence. In the preparation for this blow he had the important, if not indispensable, assistance of a prophet, who sprang up among the Delawares at the need of the hour, and who promised his people restoration to their former importance and power, on condition, however, that they should abandon the arts and the habits of civilized life, throw away the implements which they had received from the white people, and return once more to their primitive simplicity.

The British advanced posts at this time comprehended Niagara, Pitt, formerly Du Quesne, Ligonier, southeast of Pitt, Le Bœuf and Venango on the Alleghany, Presque Isle, Sandusky, Miami, where Fort Wayne was afterwards built, Detroit, Michilimackinac, Le Baye at the head of Green Bay, St. Joseph near the mouth of the river of that name, and Ouatanon on the Wabash. The plan devised by Pontiac for their reduction, while thoroughly characteristic of his race, was worthy of his masterly mind. He proposed by preconcerted action on the part of the Indians in the neighborhood of all these posts to surprise and capture them simultaneously, and thus at one blow to annihilate British power in the West. To make his scheme successful he needed to enlist not only all Indians under his immediate control, but the Senecas of New York also; and this he found means to accomplish.

Detroit being the most important and commanding of all the posts, Pontiac in person took charge of the movement against it. The fort had

FAILURE OF THE INDIAN STRATAGEM. 57

a garrison of a hundred and twenty-eight men, under command of Major Gladwin; a number of fur-traders with their servants were living within the stockade, which also inclosed the town proper, and the dwellings outside along the shore were almost exclusively of French farmers and gardeners. Below the town on the western side was a village of the Pottawatamies; opposite was one of the Wyandots, and farther up was that of the Ottawas, as before stated. The stratagem which Pontiac devised was to have his warriors shorten their rifles to a length which would admit of their being concealed under their blankets, and then, under pretense of a council, obtain admission to the fort, and at a given signal fall upon and slaughter the unsuspecting and unprepared garrison.

The plan came so near success that its failure seems almost providential. The process of shortening their guns by files and saws was observed by some of the French settlers, one of whom communicated the fact to Major Gladwin, and warned him that danger was brewing. But Gladwin paid no heed to the warning, and seems to have had a strange and unaccountable confidence in his savage neighbors. On the following day, however, which was May 6, 1763, an Indian maid who had become possessed of the plan, and who cherished kindly feelings for the commandant, managed to obtain a private interview with him, and revealed the full extent of the conspiracy and of his danger. Pontiac, she informed him, with sixty other chiefs was to come the next day to the fort, with their shortened guns under their blankets, and demand a council. This being granted he would deliver his speech, and then offer a belt of wampum, but holding it in reversed position, which would be the signal for attack. The chiefs were instantly to spring to their feet and shoot down the officers, and the other Indians were immediately to rush in and massacre the soldiers and the traders. Not an Englishman was to be left alive, but all Frenchmen were to be spared as not being their enemies.

Gladwin immediately prepared for the emergency, and when Pontiac with his subordinate chiefs entered the gateway of the fortress the next morning, he was startled at perceiving the garrison under arms, and the fur-traders posted with their rifles at commanding positions, as if awaiting attack. It was evident his treachery was discovered; but he preserved his composure and proceeded to the council-house, where Gladwin and the other officers were awaiting him as if anticipating only a friendly interview. The wily chieftain demanded to be informed why the men were in hostile array, and was told they had been ordered under arms for discipline and exercise. With hesitation and evident distrust he rose at length to make his speech, which in terms was friendly, and expressive of attachment to the

GLADWIN BAFFLES PONTIAC.

English. Gladwin answered calmly, without intimating any suspicions of their intentions, and after receiving some trifling presents, the Indians retired to their camp. The next morning Pontiac came with three of his chiefs and renewed the friendly professions, and again on the morning of May 9th he made his appearance, but this time accompanied by a great crowd of Indians. The gate was shut against them, and Pontiac demanded to be informed why he was refused admittance to the fort. The commandant replied that the chief should be free to enter, but that the crowd which accompanied him must remain outside. To this the savage rejoined that he desired his warriors to enjoy with him the fragrance of the pipe of peace. But Gladwin was immovable, and Pontiac, baffled and enraged, turned away, and entering a boat, proceeded to the Ottawa village on the opposite shore. His followers were now fully aware that further attempts at deception would be useless; the war-whoop was immediately raised, and while some rushed to a house on the common occupied by an English woman with her family, whom they immediately slaughtered and scalped, others pulled off in a boat to Isle au Cochon, where an Englishman had his home, and subjected him to the same fate.

That night the Ottawa population was transferred to the western shore, and at daybreak a desperate attempt was made upon the fort, and for six hours was kept up continuously, but without avail. Two armed vessels anchored in front of the fort rendered valuable assistance to the garrison, and the efforts of the besiegers soon began to show indications of discouragement. Gladwin now hoping that the whole affair was but a temporary ebullition of anger on the part of the Indians, attempted to open negotiations with their commander, but this only resulted in Major Campbell and Lieutenant McDougall being inveigled into the hands of Pontiac, where they were treacherously detained. McDougall in a short time succeeded in escaping, but Campbell met a tragic fate, being seized, bound to a tree, and shot to death with arrows in revenge for the death of an Ojibwa chief whose scalp had been foolishly exhibited in derision at the fort. That no circumstance of horror might be wanting, his heart was torn out and devoured.

From this time savage ingenuity was exhausted in vain endeavor to capture Detroit. The assaults upon other posts were attended with more success. Sandusky, St. Joseph, Miami, Ouatanon, Presque Isle, Le Bœuf, and Venango were all captured in the months of May and June, and in order of time as here enumerated. The fate of Michilimackinac was highly dramatic and tragical, and the story as told by Alexander Henry,[1] the trader who

[1] *Travels and Adventures in Canada and Indian Territories,* 1760–1766.

chanced to be present and was fortunate enough to escape, is one of the most exciting, as well as most familiar, in the literature of savage warfare. The succession of dramatic incident could not be given in brief without marring its intensity of interest; but in the narrative of Henry and in a subsequent letter from the commandant to Gladwin,[1] we are presented the picture of the Indians gathering about the fort as for a day's sport, the unsuspicious commandant opening his gates to their squaws, who strolled in one by one with arms concealed under their blankets, the Indians engaging in their favorite game of baggatiway, and throwing the ball back and forth, nearer and nearer the stockade, until at last it lands in the fort, when they rush in as if to recover it, and once in, raise the war-cry, and seizing the concealed weapons, fall to the work of scalping and slaughter. All the English not slain were made prisoners, but no violence was offered to any Frenchman.

Detroit so far had escaped, but its fate for a long time seemed uncertain. One detachment sent from Niagara for its relief was intercepted and driven back; another, under Captain Dalzell, was more successful. Desirous of signalizing his coming by some marked achievement, the captain planned and executed a night attack on the Indian camp, but was ambushed at a stream two miles

[1] June 12, 1763: *Conspiracy of Pontiac*, 596.

above the fort and slain with many of his men. This fight occurred on July 30th, and thereafter for a time the siege was pushed with vigor. But the reinforcement had put the garrison in better condition for resistance than before, and though the siege went on, the prospects of success continually diminished. Early in October the Ojibwas made some advances towards peace. At the end of that month, Pontiac, who up to that time had cherished hopes of French intervention and assistance, was advised by letter from M. Neyon, commandant at Fort Chartres, that hopes of assistance from that quarter were idle, and that it would be wise for him to abandon hostilities. From that time the siege was substantially raised for the winter, and the Indians went off on their annual hunt. In the spring hostilities were renewed about the fort, but to little effect. Meantime Sir William Johnson, who best of all the English officials understood the Indian character, and was fitted by temperament and sympathy to deal with the savages, was arranging for a grand council at Niagara in the summer, with a view to bringing about a general peace. The meeting which he succeeded in procuring was attended by a great number of Indians, including not only many from the several tribes of the Iroquois Confederacy, but Caughnawagas from Canada, Ottawas, Ojibwas, Wyandots, Winnebagoes, Menominies, Sacs, and Foxes, and even the Osages from

END OF PONTIAC'S SCHEME. 63

beyond the Mississippi, and many others. The conciliatory deportment of Sir William Johnson and a liberal distribution of presents had the desired effect upon the Indians, and they returned to their homes in a peaceful frame of mind. General Bradstreet, with a considerable army, was then on his way to Detroit, where he arrived at the end of August, relieving the garrison from its long beleaguerment. A detachment was immediately sent up to take possesssion of Michilimackinac and to reoccupy the abandoned posts of Sault Ste. Marie and Green Bay, all of which was accomplished without noteworthy incident.

Pontiac haughtily held aloof from all negotiations, and repelled all advances. In the summer of 1764 he was in the West endeavoring to stimulate the Western tribes to vigorous measures. He was also soliciting aid from the French; but all his efforts were without avail. He even sent an embassy to New Orleans, where the French, though the territory had been ceded to Spain, were still in possession; but he received no encouragement from that quarter. This was the end of his hopes. On August 27, 1765, he met George Croghan, the emissary of Sir William Johnson, in a conference at Detroit, and smoked with him the pipe of peace. "It is your children's pipe," he said, " and as the war is all over, and the Great Spirit and Giver of Light, who has made the earth and everything therein, has brought us all together this day for our mutual good, I declare to all nations that I have settled my peace with you before I came here, and now deliver my pipe to be sent to Sir William Johnson, that he may know I have made peace and taken the King of England for my father." But he was then settled on the Maumee, and declined the invitation to return to his old home, assigning for his refusal a reason that, to one who loved his race and desired its preservation, should have been conclusive. "If we dwelt near you at our old village of Detroit our warriors would always be drunk, and quarrels would arise between us and you." "Where we live is so nigh to you that when we want to drink we can easily come for it."[1] Pontiac plainly saw that the struggle for the independence of his people was ended, and that nothing remained for them now but present subjection and, if they remained in the vicinity of white settlements, degrading dissipation with ultimate extinction. In July of the next year he met Sir William Johnson himself at Oswego, and renewed in the most formal manner his assurances of friendship. He assumed to speak the voice of all the Western nations, and Sir William was assured by him that what he agreed to do would be a law to them. With vague reference to what had gone before, he submissively said that " He who made the Universe would have it so."

[1] *Conspiracy of Pontiac,* 556; Hildreth's *Pioneer History,* 76.

DEATH OF PONTIAC. 65

The masterly but unavailing effort of Pontiac for the independence and preservation of his race is often spoken of as a conspiracy; but making due allowance for the barbarous methods of Indian warfare, the fair mind must admit that it was as patriotic and as deserving of generous commemoration as the struggle of Cromwell for the liberties of Englishmen, or of Kosciusko for the independence of Poland. A year later the great chieftain was assassinated at Cahokia, Illinois, by a Kaskaskia Indian instigated to the crime by an English trader, and by the gift of a barrel of liquor and the promise of further reward. The dastardly murder brought speedy vengeance upon the assassin, his tribe, and all their allies. But the chief criminal was unmolested, and as only Indians were the victims, the constituted authorities abstained from all interference.

NOTE. — The story that Gladwin was warned by an Indian girl appears in Carver's *Travels through North America*. Carver visited Detroit five years after the siege. The tale is inherently improbable, is not borne out by subsequent events, and is strongly contradicted by The Pontiac Diary, a daily record of events, which gives the details of an interview between an Indian named Mahigan and Major Gladwin and Captain Campbell. The Indian revealed the plot under promise of secrecy, which promise Gladwin faithfully observed. The Indian maiden story belongs to a class of imaginative frontier tales familiar to the student of Western history.

CHAPTER IV.

A DECADE OF MILITARY ABSOLUTISM.

PONTIAC'S war had desolated many settlements, and left behind only the ashes of burned habitations and the bleaching bones of the people. But in the vicinity of Detroit its desolating tracks were few and soon effaced. The French people then resident in Michigan had not been looked upon by the Indians as enemies, and the war had been waged not against them, but against the English, who held them in subjection by force of arms. "It is not to avenge myself alone," said Pontiac to the French of Detroit, "that I make war on the English. It is to avenge you, my brothers. When the English insulted us they insulted you also. I know that they have taken away your arms and made you sign a paper, which they have sent away to their country. Therefore you are left defenseless, and I mean now to avenge your cause and my own together." So their possessions were spared, and they were treated as friends whom the fortune of war had subjected to a hated foreign yoke, which they would willingly embrace the first favoring opportunity to cast off. A people so regarded by the enemy must necessarily be distrusted by their own government, and when the war was over the condition of the people of Detroit, under the government of suspicious rulers, was very far from being enviable. The king's proclamation on the ratification of the treaty of cession, in 1763, had established military control, and not until the dawn of the American Revolution, when conciliation of Canada seemed to promise the opportunity for a revival of the former antagonisms between that colony and those which were now becoming rebellious, were any steps taken to give this vast country civil government.

Nominally Detroit was within the jurisdiction of the governor-general of Canada, but its great distance from the capital, and its complete isolation from other settlements, enabled the officer in command to wield at pleasure an authority which was almost autocratic. Complaints of oppression do not appear to have been numerous, but in this there is nothing surprising. The only authority competent to give relief was the military commander of the province. To reach him would be difficult, and if reached, it might be expected he would listen with little favor to complaints of abuses which must naturally attend the administration of a system of which he was himself the head. And moreover, the natural inclinations of the French settlers, who were docile and submissive, would lead them to submit silently to such wrongs as were found endurable, rather than to make complaint of the officials whose authority over them was in no manner restricted by law, and might in many ways be abused with impunity.

While Bradstreet remained in command at Detroit he held court for the trial of offenders, and banished some persons on the charge of having given assistance to Pontiac. But this officer had the good sense to perceive that regular courts and a steady administration of the law were essential, and he urged the need of them upon the attention of government. He also believed that encouragement should be given to settlers, though it does not appear that he suggested any particular measures to that end. But at home his views elicited no favorable response. The government showed little inclination to limit the absolutism of military rule, and its regulations in respect to land, while in the main just in so far as they were intended for the protection of the Indians, were well calculated to prevent any extension of the settlements.

By royal proclamation of October 7, 1763, warrants of survey and patents of any lands beyond the heads or sources of any of the rivers falling into the Atlantic from the west or northwest, or of any lands not ceded by the Indians, were strictly forbidden. Private persons were also for-

DEALINGS IN LAND.

bidden to purchase from the Indians, and grants were only to be solicited from them by the governor or commander-in-chief of the proper colony at public meeting or assembly of the Indians held for the purpose, under proper regulations. The proclamation had some effect in restraining the acquisition of land for settlement and cultivation, but did not prevent speculative dealings with the Indians, and Governor-General Gage, fifteen years later, in a letter to Captain Stevenson, then in command at Detroit, found it necessary to deal very summarily with the local land transactions. Calling attention to the fact that none but the governors of provinces had had authority to make grants, and that no purchases from the Indians, without the king's permission, could be of any validity, he proceeds to say: —

"I am now to require of you as soon as this is received to annul and make void by public act every concession made by Monsr Bellestre in the year 1760; every grant made by any British commander without exception, and all Indian purchases whatever, or Indian deeds not obtained by the king's permission and authority; and that you do not suffer any settlements to be made with the above titles, or any new settlements to be begun on any pretense whatever, and that you pull down as fast as any persons shall presume to build up, and that you do seize and send down the country all persons who shall be endeavoring to settle among the savages."

And he adds with good reason: —

"I imagine the Indians will be set up to talk to you on these subjects; you will answer them that the king is tender of their property, and has made regulations to prevent their being cheated and defrauded; that his majesty has been induced to make these rules upon the frequent complaint of the Indians against the white people, who have defrauded them of their lands by making a few of them drunk, and getting them in that condition to give away their country, to the great disgust of the rest of the nations; and that by such means the Indians have represented the white people have taken great part of their hunting grounds. This has happened to many Indian nations, and unless you stop it at the beginning at the Detroit, the same thing will happen there."

If the government orders for the protection of the Indians had been accompanied by regulations for the gift or sale to actual settlers of the lands to which the Indian title had been extinguished, they would have indicated a wisdom on the part of those in authority of which there had as yet been little evidence in the management of colonial affairs. But up to this time America had been to British statesmen simply a vast domain existing and to be managed for the benefit of Britain herself, and the question of its management presented only the problem in what manner it could best be made to contribute to the wealth and glory of the imperial island which owned it.

What would be best for America itself; what would best promote the welfare and prosperity of the people who had found homes in that distant country, might abstractly be a question of some interest, but it was not a question which British statesmanship of the day deemed it necessary to take into consideration. It was not entirely certain that it was for the interest of Great Britain that there should be a further extension of settlements in America, especially in that part of America which was drained by the St. Lawrence. The trade in furs and peltry which, even when shared with France had been largely profitable, was now wholly in English hands, and if nothing were done to check its natural supplies, there was reason to expect it would now be more remunerative than ever. But to open the country for settlement was to destroy or drive out the animals upon whose abundance the trade depended, and must immediately diminish and in the end destroy this profitable industry. It might be thought, perhaps, that there was something unnatural and inhuman in preserving for wild animals the territory by the settlement of which the poorer classes of Britain might greatly better their own condition; but the preservation of forests for game was in the line of British traditions and practice, and so long as the nation permitted a considerable portion of the home country to be kept from cultivation, to gratify a passion for the chase, it was not likely to let sentimental considerations interfere with the preservation for profitable hunting of this distant wilderness.[1]

Another reason also had its influence in restraining any active encouragement of settlements in the interior. As matters now were, the colonies were dependent upon the mother country for all the more important manufactures, and they furnished a large and profitable market for which public opinion would expect from the government a fostering and protecting care. But as the colonies increased in population and wealth, and pushed farther and farther into the wilderness, this dependence must diminish. Manufactures would spring up to supply the local wants, and the people would be taught an undesirable reliance upon themselves and their own resources. The period was one when narrow and selfish ideas controlled the policy of governments; Detroit, like other frontier settlements, suffered from them, and it was kept in the condition of a mere trading post, stationary in population and importance, until America, in the struggle for political liberty, had burst the chains which fettered industry and enterprise.

In the treaty with Pontiac, that "King and Lord of all the Country" had ceded to the crown

[1] For a full illustration of this policy, as exhibited by the action of the Hudson Bay Company, in relation to the Oregon question, see Barrows's *Oregon*, American Commonwealths Series. — ED.

the land between Detroit and Lake St. Clair. As sovereign he doubtless had authority to make this cession; but he made grants at the same time to individuals, the competency of which would seem more questionable. The chieftain of an Indian tribe was not proprietor of the soil, and there was no known custom which authorized him to convey away the lands of the tribe to persons not members of or adopted into it. Moreover, the proclamation of the British king had forbidden the acquisition of the Indian title by private persons, and the grants of Pontiac were therefore doubly invalid. But nobody cared at the time to offend the great chief by questioning his conveyances, and as the new inhabitants who now came to Detroit came for temporary purposes only, — mostly as traders, — ownership of land for those purposes might well pass unnoticed, or be regarded with indifference.

No monopoly of the fur trade existed at this time, and any one might take out a license to engage in it. But with an autocratic and irresponsible government entire freedom of trade was not to be expected; something of arbitrary intermeddling was to be looked for, and no doubt the love of power, or the passion of avarice, or the desire to enrich favorites, often found methods of gratification at the expense of regular trade and industry.

The absolute and irresponsible character of the

government at Detroit is made specially conspicuous in the manner in which the military commander made use of the judicial power with which he had been clothed. Some delegation of that power was perhaps a necessity, and those which were earliest made were moderate and judicious. At the beginning of 1767 Captain Turnbull, who was then in command, issued to Philip Dejean a commission as justice, but with such specification of powers as seemed designed to make his court one of arbitration and conciliation only. But this authority was soon enlarged by another commission, in which Dejean was designated "second judge," and given cognizance of small civil causes. As magistrate, however, his legitimate business was small; the population was devoted to the church, and the spiritual adviser was oftener than the civil judge the arbiter of controversies. But Dejean, who appears to have been a favorite of successive commanders, and was the incumbent of other important offices, did not limit his authority to the terms of his commissions, but unhesitatingly magnified his office to meet the requirements of the situation and the wishes of his superiors. In three instances, at least, persons were tried before him on capital charges and sentenced to execution, and one of the trials was attended by such circumstances as excited great indignation, and led to a presentment by the grand jury of Montreal district. One

Contencinau, a Frenchman, and Nancy, a female slave, were accused of larceny and attempted arson, and convicted; the woman, it was said, was promised pardon on condition that she would act as executioner of the man, which she did, and was then hanged also. These facts were affirmed by the grand jury, who called for the punishment of the judge; but Hamilton, who was then in command at Detroit, and was not likely to be disturbed by a stretch of power that only took the life of a friendless negro, interfered for the protection of the judge, and appealed to the governor-general on his behalf, with the ever-ready plea for detected official rogues, that he was "a man who has made enemies by doing his duty." But Hamilton went farther, and took upon his own shoulders all the responsibility. He was busy just then in directing Indian hostilities against the western settlements, and was too useful a man to be parted with or to be put on defense for a comparatively petty atrocity, and the crime of the judge, who now came to be known as "Grand Judge of Detroit," was suffered to pass unpunished.

General Amherst was succeeded as governor-general of Canada by General Murray, and he in turn by Sir Guy Carleton, who was in office at the opening of the American Revolution. The commandant at Detroit was lieutenant-governor under him, with jurisdiction over all the northwestern posts. Carleton was a man of more just and humane sentiments than commonly prevailed in his day, but he seems to have had very little knowledge respecting the western portion of his province, and there is abundant evidence that it could never have received much of his attention. When examined as a witness before the House of Commons in 1774, he was asked whether Detroit and Michigan were under his government, and he replied, "Detroit is not under the government, but Michigan is." To the further question, whether he looked upon Illinois as a part of old Canada, he replied, "I believe so. New Orleans was under the government of Quebec, but where the precise district ends I really do not know." It is very plain that the governor-general was having very little supervision of his subordinates, either at Detroit or elsewhere in the Northwest.

For the most part the period from the treaty with Pontiac to the beginning of the Revolutionary War was without noticeable incident. A garrison maintained in idleness; a governor who was at once law-maker, judge, and military commander, but with little to do in either capacity; a people without political and almost without civil rights, an unprogressive town with stationary and limited industries, — these were the prominent features at Detroit, and such they remained while British occupation continued. The assurance in the capitulation of Montreal that the people were to be treated as British subjects never bore satisfactory fruit. If this assurance meant anything, it must have meant that the people should have conceded to them the fundamental rights belonging to native Britons: the right of security against arbitrary arrest and imprisonment; the right of trial by their peers; the right to be judged by settled and definite laws. Against anything less than this Britons would have rebelled; but with the people of Canada "it fell out that when they hoped to enjoy legality under peaceful sway, they saw their tribunals abolished, their judges repelled, and the whole social organization upset, to make room for the most insupportable of all tyranny, that of courts-martial." But despotic sentiments ruled in England, and even the liberals of the day were little inclined to concede to Frenchmen, who were also Catholics, equality of rights with Protestant Englishmen. So the state of military despotism continued until the mutterings of discontent in the English colonies, and the occasional instances of determined resistance to royal authority, warned the government that danger was impending. Then the Quebec Act was adopted, as a measure at once firm and conciliatory, and which was thought calculated, while attaching the people of Canada to the crown by removing the causes of just complaint, to give warning to the other colonies that resistance to authority would meet with stern repression.

The isolated post of Michilimackinac, now coming to be known as Mackinaw, acquired exceptional temporary importance through suspicions of a treasonable scheme of Major Rogers, who had been sent there as commandant in 1765. He was charged with scheming to seduce the Indians from the English to the Spanish interest, and to hand the post over to the New Orleans authorities. Rogers was arrested and sent to Montreal for trial, but whether he was actually tried is not known. He was soon at liberty, but did not return to Michigan, and his schemes, whatever they were, came to nothing. His subsequent career was not honorable, and was well calculated to lend plausibility to the accusations of treasonable purposes which had been made against him.

An attempt was made about this time, in which Alexander Henry participated, to explore and work the copper mines of Lake Superior, of whose exceeding richness there had been rumors ever since the upper lakes had been first visited. But the time had not yet come for such an undertaking; the copper mines, which ages ago had been worked by the people who ante-dated the Indians in America, and which since then had remained in neglect and forgetfulness, were only to be opened again when improved methods of transportation should make their working profitable. Their day would come when the whistle of the steamboat should wake the echoes along the rock-bound coast of Superior, but not before.

CHAPTER V.

THE NORTHWEST CONQUERED FOR THE AMERICAN UNION.

When France surrendered Canada to Great Britain the population of the English colonies in America exceeded that of several countries in Europe which in former times had won lasting renown in defending their liberties and independence against the assaults of more powerful neighbors. Two millions of people accustomed to a share of liberty which was altogether uncommon at that period, and schooled by hard necessity to independence of action and the use of arms, must at any time and in any part of the world be a formidable power, and entitled, in all matters which concerned their relations to government, to a respectful hearing. This must be especially the case when their numbers are increasing with great rapidity, and when their distance from the seat of authority is so considerable that their government as a discontented people must necessarily be exceedingly difficult and enormously expensive. But these obvious truths were either overlooked or haughtily disregarded, and a course of treatment for the American colonies at once unjust in its essentials and offensive in its methods was deliberately entered upon. The Stamp Act as a measure of internal taxation, the attempt to collect a revenue from importations of tea, the closing of the port of Boston, the abrogation of the charter of Massachusetts Bay, and the proposal to send persons charged with crimes in America to Great Britain for trial in certain cases, and to quarter troops upon the colonists, were each and all indications of settled despotic purpose, and resistance to them went on from step to step, until delegates were chosen to a Continental Congress, which, when other measures failed to secure redress, was to declare the colonies free and independent states.

But while the British colonies were preparing, with an earnestness that admitted of no doubt or question, for an appeal to arms, Canada neither participated in the excitement nor cared for the causes of it. The Canadians shared in common with the people of the other colonies in no traditions of liberty; they knew nothing of Magna Charta or the Bill of Rights, and they had justly been praised by their last French governor-general for their docility and "perfect submissiveness." These were not the men to resist government because denied the right of self-taxation; king and church had their implicit obedience; and having little in common with the sentiments from which sprang the American Revolution, and quite as little with the men who led it, they were not likely to see attractions in martyrdom for political liberty. The *coureurs de bois* and *voyageurs* about Detroit, French in their gayety and buoyancy of spirits, and Indian in their unthrift, their grossness of life, and their alternations of excess and privation; the little farmers in their whitewashed and vineclad cottages, living a life of easy and thoughtless cheerfulness upon what they produced, were none of them likely to concern themselves with theories of political equality, or with questions of popular enfranchisement. A certain lot in the order of Providence had fallen to them, which they found abundant means of making a cheerful if not a happy one. The traders indeed were not now exclusively French, as they had been a few years before; a few Irishmen and Englishmen had come in, and more Scotchmen; but these seem in coming into the wilderness to have found the habits and methods of those who had preceded them congenial, and they soon displayed in their own ways the characteristics of their French neighbors. They had their seasons of devotion to business, and their seasons of social hilarity and profuse expenditure in the enjoyments of the table; their hospitality was unbounded, and they delighted equally in the rough athletic sports of the day and in the dance and other enjoyments of social life. Nothing could be more agreeable than the picture handed down to us of the best society of the day, and nothing as we look back upon it would be impressed more distinctly upon the mind than that these agreeable and social people were not the men to evolve from the intellectual warfare of troublous times the foundation principles upon which may be builded great states.

But the people of Canada had grievances peculiar to themselves, which they felt at all times, and in which people of both sexes and all conditions participated. One of these concerned their church; they had been promised the unrestricted enjoyment of their religion, but the church complained that its property rights had not always been respected, and this, while not a breach of the letter of the promise, was felt to be in disregard of its spirit. But a second and more palpable grievance was that of being deprived of their ancient laws. If the complaints they made of these grievances were more subdued in tone and deferential than the complaints by the English colonies of attempted imperial taxation, they were not the less sincere or persistent, and they were more universally concurred in by the people.

Accordingly, we find measures for the conciliation of Canada proceeding hand in hand with measures for the punishment of the other colonies. The act for the regulation of the affairs of the province of Quebec was a measure of conciliation

OPERATION OF THE QUEBEC ACT.

from which very much was anticipated. The act sanctioned in Canada the free exercise of the religion of Rome, and confirmed to the clergy their accustomed dues and rights, including tithes established by the edict of Louis XIV. In all civil matters it restored to the people the benefit of their ancient laws, it relieved them from the operation of the English test acts, and it gave to the colony a governing council with powers of legislation subject to the king's negative. The selection of the members was to be made by the king, but a part of the number were to be Catholics, and this was a step in the direction of political liberty which was peculiarly agreeable to the people because of its recognition of their church, — a church not tolerated in England, and abhorred in the other colonies. The act extended the boundaries of the province of Quebec so as to include within it all the British possessions from the Ohio to the Hudson Bay Territory.

The Quebec Act had for one purpose to prevent the disloyalty of the other colonies from extending to Canada ; and the bigoted king, who by it made concessions to the Catholics which he would peril his crown rather than make in England and Ireland, declared when he signed it that it was founded on the plainest principles of justice and humanity, and that he anticipated from it the best effects in calming the inquietudes and promoting the well-being of his Canadian subjects.

Mr. Fox would have gone farther, and given the people an elective chamber. "Nobody has said that the Romish belief naturally disqualifies a man from becoming politically enfranchised, and I for one will never listen to such an assertion. No man intimately acquainted with the Catholic mind will say that there is anything in it opposed to the principles of political freedom. Its aspirations, though repressed by rulers in Catholic countries, exist in the breasts of the people, Catholic and Protestant alike." But this just and manly sentiment of the great statesman was in advance of his day. London made an imposing protest against the approval of the act by the king, and the English colonies included it in the list of their grievances against the British crown. Much of their complaint was born of the bigotry of the time, and may be passed now without remark. But some grounds of objection to the bill were substantial and permanent. It gave to the people no security against arbitrary arrests and imprisonments, and the semblance of a share in the enactment of law was without substantial value. Without the habeas corpus and without a responsible participation in legislation, the people must of necessity be under a political despotism, tempered only by such humane characteristics and such sense of justice and right as might be in the nature of their rulers for the time being. But Thurlow said: "The Quebec constitution is the

IMPORTANCE OF DETROIT.

only proper constitution for colonies; it ought to have been given to them all when first planted, and it is what all ought now to be reduced to." Some of the colonies had objections to the Quebec Act which were peculiar to themselves. In the extension of the boundaries of the province to include the territory south of the lakes and north of the Ohio, the claims of Massachusetts, Virginia, New York, and Connecticut, under their charters, were ignored, and ground for controversy and contention was thus laid which might have become serious had not the course of military events soon deprived it of practical importance.

The government at the opening of the Revolutionary War was represented at Detroit by Colonel Henry Hamilton, first appointed by Governor-General Carleton as his lieutenant; a man of capacity and energy, and thoroughly loyal to the service of his king. The post, next to Quebec, was the most important in the newly created province: it commanded all the upper lakes; all the important points in the country from which have since been formed the states of Ohio, Indiana, and Illinois were easily accessible from it by water highways; it was the place of largest habitual concentration of Indians, and presented means for communication and negotiation with the savages not equaled by any point in possession of the Americans. If the British were to employ the savages in the war, Detroit was the natural and most convenient point for enlisting them in the service, distributing presents among them, and furnishing them with supplies; if they were not to be employed, their very neutrality would constitute a protection to the British authority over the Northwest; for the Americans must either respect the neutrality and put a stop to the intrusion of settlers upon Indian lands, or the Indians on their own account might be expected to wage war upon them.

In all the American wars between the French and the English, the Indians had been enlisted on both sides, but much the more largely on the side of France. To Canada the aid of the Indians had always been essential. The population of the colony was insignificant as compared with that of the colonies in arms against her, and if compelled to rely exclusively upon her own resources, Canada might have been overwhelmed by sheer force of numbers. The dependence upon Indian assistance was, therefore, considerable, and it had been effective in enabling the colony to maintain its relative importance until the time of final struggle. On the side of the English the Iroquois Confederacy had generally been found giving valuable assistance, but though, after the habitual barbarity of their race, the Six Nations destroyed, without distinction, men, women, and children, the colonial authorities had never expressly enlisted them for such indiscriminate slaughter, and would willingly, had it been possible, have restrained their belligerent acts within the limits admitted by the rules of civilized warfare. Nor was Sir Guy Carleton any more disposed to make use of Indian allies for barbarous work, and he declined to sanction their being sent beyond the boundaries of his province to wage war without restraint upon the defenseless American settlements.

But the Americans had not waited for the Indians to be let loose upon them by their enemies; bad men among them, by the most wanton and cruel outrages, had brought upon the West a fury of Indian hostility, which was not extinguished until a great number of lives had been taken and many settlements devastated. In the spring of 1774 a party of land-jobbers exploring the upper Ohio made outcry that Indians had stolen from them a number of horses. It was never made certain that the charge was true; many people believed it a mere pretense for the barbarities which followed. War upon the Indians was immediately begun, with determination to slaughter without distinction all who should fall into their hands. Two were met and killed the same day. A larger number who were encamped a few miles away were approached in pretended friendship, and, as treacherously as ever a savage took life, were wantonly put to death. Other like outrages followed in quick succession. Among the murdered Indians were all the members of the family of Logan, son of a Cayuga sachem, who had lived at Canestoga, and had been the friend and patron of Count Zinzendorf, the Moravian missionary. Logan himself had become a chief in the Shawanese country, and wherever he was known his pacific disposition and his friendship for the white people were also known and recognized. But he would have been neither Indian nor human if this wanton destruction of his family had not stirred his passions to their lowest depths, and made him thirst for vengeance. With others who had in like manner been wronged he entered upon a war of extermination, and the border settlements were soon ablaze with their murderous fires. Dunmore, the royal governor of Virginia, led an army against the Indians, and after a campaign, in which little glory was won, a nominal peace was made, but not till Logan could say, "I have fully glutted my vengeance." It was not possible under the circumstances that the temper of the Indians should be pacific, or that the nominal peace should restore friendship. "Good laws vigorously enforced," said Sir William Johnson, "are the best guaranty against Indian resentments;" a sentiment the truth of which is as obvious as its humanity. The border maxim has always been different; it is that when the Indian has been wronged, the proper guaranty against his resentments is the rifle ball.

Neither party is blameless for bringing Indians

into the field in the Revolutionary War. The British were first in enlisting them; but the Continental Congress, by action of nearly the same date, resolved to take into its service two thousand Indians, and to pay them a reward of one hundred dollars for every commissioned officer, and thirty dollars for every private soldier taken prisoner by them. This arrangement was as humane as any that could have been proposed; but General Schuyler, who was desired to carry the resolution into effect, made strong representations against it as both impracticable and useless, and he prophesied that the aid of the Indians, if enlisted, would be uncertain and fitful, and the value bear no proportion to the cost. In this, as the event proved, he was entirely correct. The Indians might, in their savage way, be of service in carrying an aggressive war into an enemy's country and laying waste his settlements; but such was not the character of the war in which the Americans were engaged. They stood upon the defensive, endeavoring to turn back the tide of war from their own borders, and the lawless habits of the Indians and their peculiar methods of warfare would not only make their aid embarrassing and wastefully destructive of resources, but their very presence would be a constant source of alarm and disquietude to the district which should be the scene of operations. While, therefore, the British might profit by their assistance, through such harassing inroads upon the American settlements as would distract the attention and scatter the forces of the military, until the incessant and pervading alarm of the people and destruction of their resources might possibly incline them at last to accept peace at the cost of submission, the Americans, on the other hand, could look for no corresponding advantages. Nothing was to be gained by them through raids upon the French Canadian settlements; and Indian allies who submitted to discipline with reluctance, and were impatient of the necessary restraints of civilized warfare, were not a promising assistance in encountering in the open field the disciplined armies of England. Neither were rewards which were limited to prisoners alone likely to be attractive to them. It was easier to take scalps than prisoners, and it was also more in accord with their usages and savage instincts. On the part of the Americans, therefore, the value of Indian assistance would practically be limited to such service as they might render against those of their own race taking part with the British.

At Detroit Governor Hamilton saw, or thought he saw, how he could make Indian assistance to the royal cause fearfully effective. He was so decided and earnest a partisan that it is not necessary to charge or even to suspect that he favored useless cruelty; but there is abundant evidence that he had no scruples in enlisting Indians to

THE PRICE OF INDIAN ALLIANCE. 91

fight after their own methods, or in paying them for such effective work as they might accomplish. The effective work which was desired from them was such as would restore the British authority over the western portions of Virginia, Pennsylvania, and New York; and this could only be accomplished by the destruction of the western settlements, and especially those in the valley of the Ohio. But scalps were the rewards and the trophies of such destruction; and for these, if their effective aid was to be had, the Indians must be paid. Hamilton therefore offered rewards for scalps, and he was not ashamed to say, in writing on one occasion to his superior, "Last night the savages were assembled, when I sang the war song, and was followed by Captain Lernoult and several officers."

Captain De Peyster was then in command at Mackinaw, M. de Rocheblave at Kaskaskia, and Mr. Abbot at Vincennes. Captain Langdale, at Green Bay, who was extensively known among the Indians, was commissioned early in 1776 to raise among them a force for the British service, and he proceeded promptly in the execution of his commission. A considerable force was raised, which was sent forward to Montreal under orders from De Peyster which charged them with the duty of "annoying the rebels wherever you meet with them." Several persons who had lived among the Indians were also employed by Hamilton to instigate them to hostilities, and among them were the brothers Simon, George, and James Girty, who were regularly paid as British agents at Detroit, and who personally took part in raids upon the settlements. The monstrous barbarities of some of these men almost stagger belief, and force upon us the unwelcome truth that in civilized society, and within the sound of Christian bells, there may be bred and reared savages as fiendish in their cruelty as any the world has ever known. Hamilton, in his dispatches to his superiors, gave them to understand that he should send out parties of Indians "to fall on the scattered settlers on the Ohio and its branches," and he selected to lead these raids fit instruments who would be troubled by no compunctions and no emotions of pity in making the work of destruction complete.

The year 1777 was distinguished by much military activity, of which Governor Hamilton was the instigation and the head. In the spring several Kentucky settlements were attacked in succession by the Indians, but in each case effective resistance was made, and few scalps were brought back for the governor's bounty. In July Hamilton reported that he had sent out fifteen parties to raid upon the border settlements, but they achieved no considerable success, and only intensified among the settlers a hatred of the government which made use for its purposes of this species of warfare. In September Fort Henry, at Wheeling, was besieged by a considerable force of the governor's Indians, but the defense was skillful, heroic, and successful. In the succeeding year raids were again made upon the Kentucky settlements, and Boonesborough was for a time besieged, but again the besieging party was foiled. So far the bounty money of the government had produced no important results. The settlers retaliated as they found opportunity, and in the destruction of Indian villages and means of subsistence the savages had measure for measure meted out to them for their own barbarities.

But this indecisive warfare, the horrors of which were experienced by only one of the principal belligerents, had results which its instigators little anticipated, and was the inspiring cause and the prelude to movements which were pregnant with mighty consequences. The actors were few, and the scene of conflict so far in the interior that what was done passed at the time almost without observation; but the future of a vast and fertile country from which great states were to be carved depended upon what these few actors, in heroic but unpretending way, were to accomplish.

George Rogers Clark was at this time the most conspicuous figure in the Kentucky settlements. He was a Virginian from the mountain region; like Washington he was a land surveyor; and in 1775 and again in 1776 he had visited the

Kentucky settlements, and made himself thoroughly familiar with their condition. He found them without civil government, the jurisdiction claimed by both Virginia and North Carolina; but neither State was doing anything to justify the claim by giving to the people the benefits of protection and government. The settlers themselves claimed to be Virginians, and in mass meeting in June, 1776, they chose Clark and Gabriel Jones to represent them in the Virginia Assembly. But this was without authority of law, and Clark disclaimed the election, though he consented to go as agent, and did his best to enlist the interest and aid of the State in the defense of his constituents. He had the mortification of finding that his solicitations bore no fruit, and turning his back upon the authorities with the pregnant remark that "a country not worth defending was not worth claiming," he determined to return to Kentucky and initiate a movement for the formation of an independent state. The council of state were made uneasy by this declaration; they knew the hardy mountain surveyor meant what he said and could accomplish what he determined; and yielding to his resolute manner what they had denied to his solicitations, they reversed their decision, and forwarded to the order of Clark a considerable supply of gunpowder for Kentucky use.

But Clark saw very clearly that all warfare in

the West must be desultory and inconsequential unless the British themselves could be made to feel the consequences, and that this could only be done by the reduction of the British posts. Accordingly, in 1777, he sent spies to reconnoitre and report upon their condition, and on their return he submitted to Patrick Henry, then governor of Virginia, a plan for the capture of Kaskaskia and Vincennes. The plan was approved, the necessary legislation was obtained for the attempt, and on January 18, 1778, the resolute leader left Williamsburgh to put it in execution. "Elevated," he says, "with thoughts of the great service we should do our country, . . . the more I reflected on my weakness the more I was pleased with the enterprise." His modesty was great, but, with courage inspired by the occasion, he perceived clearly that the opportunity was offered for an achievement at once glorious for himself and of lasting benefit to his country. With vast difficulty and under numerous discouragements he collected a force at the Falls of the Ohio with which on the 30th of June he started across the country for Kaskaskia. The intervening ground was low and flat, and covered by luxuriant vegetation; the guide was unfamiliar with the way, and at one time lost it; and two days before the point of destination was reached the provisions were exhausted. Nevertheless the intrepid leader of determined men pushed on, and on the evening of

July 4th, a day famous in American annals for many great events, he surrounded and occupied the town, and broke into the fort with such celerity that the astonished commander had no time for any resistance. Assuring the inhabitants of the town of the friendship and protection of the Americans, he quieted their fears, which at first had been greatly excited, and they promptly and cheerfully tendered their allegiance to the American cause. The French settlers of Cahokia, on learning of the capture, made haste to follow the example of their brethren at Kaskaskia, and an Indian force which had been collected in the vicinity dispersed in fear of an attack. Vincennes followed suit, and Clark, with a success beyond expectation or reasonable hope, was put in possession of these several settlements without the loss of a man.

The whole force with which this remarkable achievement had been accomplished consisted of but a hundred and eighty men; and it was so insignificant in numbers and so far from support that Clark deemed it necessary to magnify his strength by circulating a report that a large force at the Falls was at his service. This deception was the more imperative since a portion of his men, thinking their task now fully accomplished, insisted upon returning to their homes. Only about a hundred remained with him, but the French settlers proved true friends, and with their

CAPTURE OF VINCENNES.

assistance he set about establishing friendly relations with the Indians.

It was startling news which was brought to Detroit, that the settlers of Kentucky, instead of being driven back beyond the mountains, as was expected, had taken the aggressive, and captured and were then holding the posts in the Illinois. It was not pleasant intelligence for Governor Hamilton to communicate to his superiors; and he took prompt steps to retrieve the disaster. On December 17th, with a considerable force of British and Indians, he presented himself before Vincennes and demanded its surrender. Captain Helm was in charge with but a single man; for Clark had not been able to spare men for a garrison. Helm made a show of resistance, and Hamilton, who was ignorant of the condition of affairs, and desired to avoid bloodshed, offered him the honors of war. The terms of surrender were accepted, and the valorous captain, with colors flying, marched his one man out, not less to the surprise than to the mortification of his captor.

The vigor displayed in capturing Vincennes bore no further fruit. The Indians soon dispersed, or were sent off by Hamilton on marauding expeditions, and Clark, who was soon apprised of the condition of affairs, determined to make an attempt for the immediate recovery of the post. Volunteers swelled his force to a hundred and seventy-six, and with these, early in February, he began his march. On February 23d he was before the town, having, during the preceding five days, waded several miles in water on the "drowned lands," often with the water up to the breast. A sharp attack upon the fort was at once made, which met with vigorous resistance; but from the first the resistance was hopeless, and at noon of the following day the post was surrendered with all its stores. The men captured were nearly equal in number to the force of Clark, but what was more important was the capture of Hamilton himself. Supplies on their way from Detroit were also captured a few days later, and with these was taken "Dejean, Grand Judge of Detroit."

Thus by the invincible bravery of a single man, with a force so insignificant and under difficulties so formidable that to cool heads the attempt might well have seemed foolhardy, the Northwest was conquered and held for Virginia. The title of the State was doubtful before, but now with "nine points of the law" in her favor, she made practical assertion of her right, and proceeded to organize the county of Illinois. The possession had national consequences of the highest value. To the commissioners who negotiated the treaty of peace which secured American independence, it indicated with unerring certainty that the true northern boundary of the states was not the Ohio, but the line of the great lakes. One

Virginia surveyor, by his valor and wisdom, had secured independence to America, and another had given to the Union this vast Northwest, with its boundless resources and its brilliant future.

Hamilton and Dejean, with one Lamothe, were sent prisoners to Virginia, where they were put in irons for their cruelties, and detained with refusal of exchange. The council of state held inquisition upon their case, and found "that Governor Hamilton has executed the task of inciting the Indians to perpetrate their accustomed cruelties on the citizens of the United States, without distinction of age, sex, or condition, with an eagerness and avidity which evince that the general nature of his charge harmonized with his particular disposition. . . . That Governor Hamilton gave standing rewards for scalps, but offered none for prisoners, which induced the Indians, after making their captives carry their baggage into the neighborhood of the fort, there to put them to death and carry in their scalps to the governor, who welcomed their return and success by a discharge of cannon. . . . That the prisoner Dejean was on all occasions the willing and cordial instrument of Governor Hamilton, acting both as judge and keeper of the jails, and instigating and urging him, by malicious insinuations and untruths, to increase rather than relax his severities, heightening the cruelty of his orders by his manner of executing them. . . . That the prisoner Lamothe was a captain of the volunteer scalping parties of Indians and whites, who went from time to time under general orders to spare neither men, women, nor children."[1] Dejean and Lamothe were suffered to go on parole the following December, but Hamilton was detained until October, 1780. His connection with the Indian cruelties may have justified the hardship of his treatment,[2] but Jefferson in his communications with Washington assigned other reasons also. "You are not unapprised," he said, "of the influence of this officer with the Indians, his activity and embittered zeal against us. You also, perhaps, know how precarious is our tenure of the Illinois country, and how critical is the situation of the new counties on the Ohio. These circumstances determined us to detain Governor Hamilton and Major Hay within our power when we delivered up the other prisoners."[3] He added that on representations of the people of Kentucky of what they had reason to apprehend from these two prisoners in the event of their liberation, assurances had been given that they would not be parted with. If, therefore, they were not detained exclusively for their cruelty, it was their cruelty which excused the policy of their detention.

---

[1] Jefferson's *Works*, vol. i. p. 226, note.

[2] See the narrative of his captivity, *Mag. of Am. History*, vol. i. p. 176.

[3] Jefferson's *Works*, vol. i. p. 258.

But, justly as Hamilton deserved condemnation for his cruelties, it is not probable that he was conscious of deserving the censure he received, or that he was exceptionally cruel when judged by the standard of the times. There are proofs that he sometimes ransomed prisoners who might otherwise have been slaughtered, and showed kindnesses where the interest of his cause did not seem to forbid. The brutality was in the system, rather than in the men who administered it; a system which, in the indignant words of Lord Chatham, was "to turn forth into our settlements, among our ancient friends, connections, and relations, the merciless cannibal, thirsting for the blood of man, woman, and child; against our Protestant brethren, to lay waste their country, to desolate their dwellings, and extirpate their race and name with those horrible hell-hounds of savage war;" and for this the administration was responsible, and not the agencies employed to execute its will. Even De Peyster, who succeeded Hamilton in command at Detroit, and whose reputation has escaped the charge of barbarity, is said on one occasion to have reproached a trader, who rescued from the Indians two female prisoners who were being made to run the gauntlet preliminary to further tortures. If savages were to be employed, they must be left to their savage ways.

The posts in the Illinois being thus captured and occupied, the whole West, if Detroit could be seized by the Americans, would be secure from further forays under British direction. Mackinaw and Montreal were too far away to constitute bases of operations against the settlements in the Ohio valley, and Mackinaw itself was too exposed to be either a gathering place for attack or a secure retreat. The important thing to be now accomplished was, if possible, to seize and occupy Detroit. With three hundred men Clark at the time estimated that he could effect the capture, but three hundred men he had no means of raising, and the State could not spare them for his service. The impatient soldier declared that Detroit was lost for the want of a few men.

De Peyster was transferred from Mackinaw to the command of Detroit, and the post continued to be headquarters of plots against the western settlements until the war was over. A formidable force of British and Indians, under the command of Captain Bird, was sent out in the spring of 1780 upon a mission of devastation, and a couple of settlements were captured and a few non-combatants slaughtered in the Licking River valley; but the force accomplished nothing of which its commander was likely to boast. With Hamilton gone, Detroit proved more disquieting than dangerous. Washington, Jefferson, and Clark are found repeatedly planning to equip an expedition for its capture, but the time seemed never to come when the men or the means could be spared from larger operations on the seaboard. But the American occupation of the Illinois country had put the hostile Indians on the defensive, and the new settlements had such comparative peace that they continued to grow and extend.

When peace came to be negotiated between Great Britain and the United States, the British commissioner was inclined to claim for Canada the boundaries named in the Quebec Act. Mr. Secretary Livingston, writing to Franklin, very pertinently remarked that as that act was one of the laws which occasioned the war, to build anything upon it would be to urge one wrong in support of another. The boundary between us and Canada, he said, had been very well ascertained by grants, charters, proclamations, and other acts of government, "and more particularly by the settlements of people who are engaged in the same cause with us, and who have the same rights with the other subjects of the United States. . . . Our claims are such at least as the events of the war give us a right to insist upon." [1] Nothing was more certain than this. The British, by the fortune of war, had succeeded in holding nothing but a couple of posts on the connecting waters of the upper lakes; all else had been wrested from them, and many little communities had made their homes in the disputed territory. These were Americans, and the United States could not in

[1] *Works of Franklin*, by Sparks, vol. ix. p. 129.

honor abandon them. The proper boundary between the two countries in this part of the world was obviously the line of the lakes, and the British commissioner did not strenuously dispute it. Great Britain was perhaps the more ready to concede the American claims from the fact that Spain also was claiming the Ohio valley, and likely to make trouble for the nation which possessed it.[1]

Thus was the Northwest conquered and secured for the American Union. A different result would have changed the whole current of subsequent American history; how much no one can calculate, or has basis for any reasonable conjecture. The achievement was of incalculable value to America, and it was won with a handful of men by the patriotism, unflinching courage, and energy of George Rogers Clark.

[1] *Secret Journals of Congress*, vol. ii. p. 225; *Works of John Adams*, vol. viii. p. 18; *Works of Franklin*, by Sparks, vol. ix. 128 *et seq.*; Pitkin's *Hist. of U. S.* ch. 15.

CHAPTER VI.

GREAT BRITAIN RELUCTANTLY SURRENDERS THE NORTHWEST.

The valor and endurance of America had won from the mother country an acknowledgment of independence, but had not produced a clear conviction that it was secure and permanent. A loose Confederacy of thirteen states, without army or navy, or treasury, or stable executive, or power of any sort to compel obedience by a single person to its proper requirements or commands, was not a spectacle calculated to excite admiration or to inspire confidence. To the thoughtful and disinterested observer it must have seemed probable that for want of cohesive force it would shortly fall to pieces. The interests of the several states were greatly variant, and for that reason amicable relations with other countries on some subjects might become impossible. The Confederacy owed a large debt which the states were expected to pay, but upon what basis or in what proportions it was not possible to secure consent of opinion or harmony of action. In the treaty of peace stipulations had been inserted in the interest of British creditors and American loyalists, which must depend for their enforcement on the voluntary action of individual states, and the popular opposition to these stipulations was in some quarters so positive and aggressive that enforcement seemed quite out of the question. But these were not all the discouraging circumstances which the patriot was forced to contemplate, and in which the enemies of the country rejoiced. The poverty of the people, and their manifest inability to pay their debts, was in some parts of the country so great that rebellion was threatened if the courts were allowed to perform their regular functions. The Indians also gave occasion for alarm. In the negotiations for a treaty of peace they had not been included, but had been left to be dealt with separately. From central New York to the Mississippi they had in general sympathized with Great Britain in the late war; large numbers had taken arms in its cause, and Joseph Brant, the head chief of the Six Nations, a man of education, of great intelligence and ability, known and respected by all the tribes, had held a commission in the British army. After the war he had removed with his own tribe, the Mohawks, to Canada, that he might be under British, rather than American jurisdiction. Brant had a deep sense of the wrongs his people had suffered and were likely to suffer at the hands of the Americans; reflecting in this particular the general feeling among them. Under all these circumstances a condition of semi-hostility existed on the part of the Indians, which gave no little concern to the state and confederate governments, and kept the new settlements disquieted.

The action of the British authorities tended very greatly to increase this disquiet, and to keep up the belligerent condition among the Indians. When the line of the lakes had been agreed upon as the northern boundary, it had been expected that the British would immediately surrender possession of Oswego, Niagara, Detroit, and the minor posts which fell within the limits of the United States. This expectation was not fulfilled. Baron Steuben was sent by Washington, in July, 1783, to the British General Haldimand to receive possession; but on making known his business he was informed by that officer that he had received no instructions for the surrender of the posts, and did not consider himself at liberty even to discuss the subject. He was so ungracious as even to refuse the baron passports to visit Niagara and Detroit; and the latter was compelled to return with nothing accomplished. For this conduct at the time there could have been no sound or friendly reason. Afterwards, the retention of the posts was excused by the failure on the part of the states to perform some of the stipulations contained in the definitive treaty of peace; and it was continued until the ratification of Jay's treaty, twelve years later. Meantime there was a lingering hope that if the American Confederacy, as was not apparently improbable, should fall to pieces from its own inherent weakness, some of the states at least, to secure to themselves the blessings of permanent government, might be ready to return to their old allegiance, and the possession of the posts by the British would favor that result. What was certain was that the possession contributed largely to keeping up the hopes of the Indians, and to perpetuating the condition of hostility.

In the fall of 1784 the United States had entered into a treaty with the Six Nations at Fort Stanwix, by which that Confederacy was made to consent to relinquish all claims to the country west of a line beginning on Lake Ontario, four miles east of Niagara, thence passing southerly to the mouth of Buffalo Creek, thence to the north boundary of Pennsylvania, and thence west and south along the Pennsylvania line to the Ohio River. This treaty had caused bad feeling: the Six Nations had objected to entering into it without the presence and concurrence of the western tribes; but the government had insisted on negotiating with them alone, and they had very unwillingly assented. It was ominous that Brant was not present: he felt, as did his people generally, that it was unjust to require them thus to make a treaty which affected others as well as themselves, without the presence and counsel of the parties concerned.[1] The terms of the treaty were also greatly disliked; they were vague in their references to territory, and more might be claimed under them than the Indians had intended to concede. They especially objected to any implication that lands west of the Ohio were to be surrendered to the United States; and in December, 1786, a grand confederate council was held at the Huron village, at the mouth of the Detroit, to consider the grievances incident to the excessive claims under this treaty.[2] At this council the attendance was large and imposing: the Six Nations, the Hurons, Ottawas, Miamis, Shawanese, Chippewas, Cherokees, Delawares, and Pottawatamies, and the Wabash Confederacy were represented, and an address to the United States was adopted with general concurrence. The address was pacific in tone, and recommended a further grand council, in which the United States also should be represented, and that in the mean time the United States should prevent surveyors and other people crossing to the Indian side of the Ohio. The address plainly indicated a purpose to insist upon the Ohio boundary as an ultimatum; and there is abundant evidence in the correspondence of Brant with the British authorities that in this purpose the Indians were con-

[1] *Life of Brant*, by Stone, vol. ii ch. 8.
[2] *Ibid* vol. ii. ch. 9.

firmed by the advice of Sir John Johnson and of Major Matthews, who had recently been assigned to the command at Detroit, if not by that of Sir Guy Carleton himself, now become Lord Dorchester. The result of the council was not communicated to the United States until July, 1787, and the proposed grand council was never held. The Indians came together again in 1788, but the result of their deliberations remains matter of conjecture.

Meantime the government was endeavoring to form treaties with the western tribes. General St. Clair was empowered by Washington for the purpose, and in January, 1789, he proceeded to negotiate separate treaties, avoiding all recognition of a confederacy, and all common or concerted action among the tribes. "A jealousy subsisted between them," he said, "which I was not willing to lessen by appearing to consider them as one people." [1] This was statesmanship according to the diplomatic ideas of the day: a broader philanthropy would no doubt have been more expedient, as well as more humane. The object of the government in entering into treaties was to secure peace, but treaties were powerless for this purpose unless they resulted in friendly relations; and it was not possible that friendly relations should be established by encouraging, directly or indirectly, the tribal animosities and jealousies, or

[1] *St. Clair Papers*, vol. ii. p. 113.

by a course of conduct which plainly indicated a purpose to profit by them. The excuse sometimes advanced, that the white people did not create these unfriendly sentiments, was only partly true: from the first they had practiced making use of Indians against each other, and one of the chief purposes which the Indians proposed to accomplish by gathering in grand council was to allay tribal jealousies and put an end to wars among themselves. The western tribes were incensed that the treaty of Fort Stanwix was entered into without their coöperation and advice, and a continuation of the same policy at this time was certain to spread discontent instead of allaying it, and to offend more persons than it would pacify.

Before this a territorial government had been given to the Northwest Territory, with St. Clair for governor, and settlers began to pour into it. Marietta was founded in April, 1788, and Cincinnati in December of the same year. "Arks," bearing one or more families with their household goods, were floating down the Ohio, and it was evident to the most limited comprehension that a tide had set in which, unless promptly checked, must overwhelm or drive out the native tribes. Nor were the new-comers altogether honest emigrants: lawless characters were among them, and instances were not wanting of atrocious outrages upon unoffending Indians.[1] Thus individual in-

[1] The account which Sir William Johnson in his letter to the

jury concurred with national wrong to swell the tide of hostile feeling, and in 1790 statistics were collected from which it appeared that since 1783 no less than fifteen hundred and twenty men, women, and children had, in Kentucky alone, been killed by the Indians or carried away into captivity. It is not likely that the Indians, in the same period, had suffered less than the white people.

This condition of affairs could not be suffered to continue, and in the autumn of 1790 General Harmar, with an army of near fifteen hundred men, was sent into the territory to chastise the Indians. The chastisement inflicted was received by his own army, which was defeated with considerable loss, and the depredations were renewed with greater fury than ever. The Indians also sent an embassy to Lord Dorchester, that they might learn what assistance, if any, could be expected from the British authorities. Lord Dorchester gave them no encouragement whatever; but the tenor of communications made to them by Sir John Johnson and others was such as to confirm them in their belief that they were right in insisting on the Ohio as a boundary; and, as a consequence, all the efforts made by Washington to bring about peace were futile. A year after the defeat of Harmar, St. Clair was given the

Earl of Hillsborough of August 14, 1770, gives of the treatment of the Indians in the West will hold good of a much later period.

command of two thousand men, an army thought to be ample for bringing the Indians to submission; but in one of the bloodiest fights in the history of Indian wars he was defeated and compelled to retire. This disaster was as unexpected as it was alarming: the whole country was made uneasy by it, and the Indians became more bold in their ferocious depredations. It seemed necessary that conciliation should again be attempted, and the President invited Brant to Philadelphia, where he was treated with great respect, and the good offices of the Six Nations were solicited to bring about peace with the western tribes. But the western tribes were not so much bent upon war as they were determined to insist upon what they believed to be their rights; and in a conference at the Au Glaize they would agree upon no peace that did not fix upon the Ohio as a boundary. This was reiterated in a formal conference had with Messrs. Lincoln, Randolph, and Pickering, commissioners on the part of the United States, in the summer of 1793. "We desire you to consider," they said, "that our only demand is the peaceable possession of a small part of our once great country. Look back and view the lands from whence we have been driven to this spot. We can retreat no farther, because the country behind hardly affords food for its present inhabitants; and we have, therefore, resolved to leave our bones in this small space to which we are now consigned. We shall be persuaded that you mean to do us justice if you agree that the Ohio shall remain the boundary between us."[1] But the time when this was possible, if it ever was, had gone by; the commissioners had no power to consent to it, and the Indians were given distinctly to understand that it was out of the question.

Brant was present at this conference, and from a speech subsequently made by him it appears that a treaty was prevented by British interference. "To our surprise," he said, "when on the point of entering upon a treaty with the commissioners, we found that it was opposed by those acting under the British government, and hopes of assistance were given to our western brethren to encourage them to insist upon the Ohio as a boundary between them and the United States."[2] In February, 1794, Lord Dorchester, in a formal talk with the Indians, gave them further encouragement. "From the manner in which the people of the United States rush on and act and talk on this side, and from what I learn of their conduct towards the sea, I shall not be surprised if we are at war with them in the course of the present year, and if so, a line must then be drawn by the warriors." Simcoe, who had become lieutenant-governor of Upper Canada, soon followed

[1] See *Life of Brant*, by Stone, vol. ii. ch. 11.
[2] *Ibid.* vol. ii. p. 358.

this talk with the erection of a new fort at the foot of the rapids of the Maumee, — an act of which the hostile nature was manifest. The Indians were greatly elated, and emboldened to persevere in their hostility, while Washington felt outraged, and wrote to Mr. Jay denouncing it in unmeasured terms. It was, he said, the most daring act yet committed by the British agents in America, though not the most hostile or cruel; " for there does not remain a doubt in the mind of any well-informed person in this country, not shut against conviction, that all the difficulties we encounter with the Indians — their hostilities, the murders of helpless women and innocent children along our frontiers — result from the conduct of the agents of Great Britain in this country."[1] And he added that it was in vain for the administration in Britain to disavow having given orders which will warrant such conduct, while its agents go unpunished.

But remonstrance was idle, and negotiation with the Indians was fruitless, so long as the prestige of success in the field remained with them; and another campaign was necessary to bring hostilities to a conclusion. For its command General Wayne was chosen; and in June, 1794, over the road where St. Clair led his army to disaster, Wayne marched to a bloody but decisive victory. The battle of August 20, 1794, was fought in the

[1] *Writings of Washington*, vol. x. p. 433.

immediate vicinity of the new British fort on the Maumee; and Major Campbell, who was in command of the fort, having witnessed the disaster to his friends, addressed to General Wayne an arrogant and impudent note, expressing surprise at the appearance of an American force almost within reach of his guns, and inquiring in what light he was to view such near approaches to the garrison which he had the honor to command. The American commander replied that were the major entitled to an answer "the most full and satisfactory one was announced the day before from the muzzles of his small arms in an action with a horde of savages in the vicinity of the fort, and which terminated gloriously to the American arms." And he added that "had it continued until the Indians were driven under the influence of the fort and guns mentioned, they would not have much impeded the progress of the victorious army under my command, as no such post was established at the commencement of the present war between the Indians and the United States." Other notes of equal asperity followed,[1] in the last of which Major Campbell warned the American general that he must not approach within reach of the guns of the fort without expecting the consequences that would attend it, and Wayne responded by devastating with fire the land about the fort almost to its very gates.

[1] Dillon's *History of Indiana*, 352–355.

TREATY OF PEACE CONCLUDED.

This was not the last of unfriendly British interference. In October following Governor Simcoe was himself at Fort Miami, and in a conference with chiefs whom he had invited to meet him he endeavored to keep up their faith in British assistance. He was still of the opinion, he said, that the Ohio was their right and title. He had given orders to the commandant of Fort Miami to fire on the Americans if they ventured to make their appearance again. He would go himself to Quebec, and lay their grievances before "the great man." From thence they would be forwarded to the king their father. Next spring they should know the result of everything,—what they should do and what he would do. And he gave them to understand that the next spring the English would be prepared to attack the Americans and drive them across the Ohio.

Although Brant joined his advice to the governor's, the speech made little impression upon the Indians. They had been looking from fall to spring and from spring to fall for twelve long years for British assistance, which had never come, and they had lost faith and courage. Their two great victories had fearfully reduced their numbers, and their defeat by Wayne threatened annihilation. On Wayne's invitation they met him in council at Greenville, where on August 3, 1795, a treaty of peace was concluded. As Brant said, "the Indians, convinced by those in the

Miami fort, and other circumstances, that they were mistaken in their expectations of any assistance from Great Britain, did not longer oppose the Americans with their wonted unanimity. The consequence was that General Wayne, by the peaceable language he held to them, induced them to hold a treaty at his own headquarters, in which he concluded a peace entirely on his own terms." Large grants of lands were made to the United States; among them one six miles in width on the eastern shore of the peninsula of Michigan from the River Raisin to Lake St. Clair, another on the main land north of the island of Mackinaw, six miles in length and three in depth, together with the Island of Bois Blanc, " being an extra and voluntary gift of the Chippewa nation." All claim to the posts of Detroit and Mackinaw and the adjacent lands was also surrendered.

Meantime Jay had negotiated a treaty with Great Britain, by one of the provisions of which it was stipulated that on or before the first day of June, 1796, the British garrisons should be withdrawn from all posts and places within the limits of the United States. The treaty was ratified after a controversy of extraordinary earnestness and acrimony, and the garrisons were withdrawn according to its terms. On July 11, 1796, the American flag was, for the first time, raised above Detroit, and the laws of the United States and of the Northwest Territory were extended over the

Michigan settlements. The occupying detachment was from Wayne's command, but Wayne in person did not reach the town until the following month. He then took command of the post until November, when he started for the East, but at Presque Isle succumbed to a disease which terminated his brilliant and useful career.

CHAPTER VII.

THE FOUNDATIONS OF A FREE STATE ARE LAID IN THE NORTHWEST.

At the opening of their struggle for Independence, the American States had no common bond of union except such as existed in a common cause and common danger. They were not yet a nation; they were only a loose confederacy; and no compact or articles of agreement determined the duties of the several members to each other, or to the Confederacy as an aggregate of all. The attempt to agree upon articles of union, which should determine rights and prescribe duties, encountered difficulties which for a long time rendered it abortive. One of the chief of these concerned the vast territory lying between the Alleghanies and the Mississippi, not yet settled or occupied by people of European race, but which the people of the states were determined not to abandon to the king.

The Confederacy as such could of course make no claim to this territory except as an acquisition resulting from the war; but it was claimed by individual states, and to much of it the claims were conflicting. This was particularly the case with all that part of it lying north of the Ohio and west of the present boundary of Pennsylvania. New York claimed it under the Six Nations, who, by their martial prowess, had established a certain undefined and only partially admitted supremacy over the tribes of the region, and who had themselves acknowledged subordination to the jurisdiction of New York. Virginia, Massachusetts, and Connecticut claimed all or parts of it, under the vague and uncertain terms of their charters, and Virginia claimed also by virtue of the conquest made by Clark under the authority of the State and at its expense; a conquest which the State had made complete and effectual by the organization of counties and the establishment of civil government. The other states did not concede the justice of these claims. Whatever were the rights of the respective colonies before the war, none of them had made its claim effective by taking possession; and if the territory was now wrested from Great Britain, it must be done by common effort and common sacrifices, and if retained after peace, it could only be as the result of a treaty made by the common authority. The obvious use to be made of the territory after acquisition was to put the land upon the market for settlement; and it seemed entirely just and reasonable under the circumstances that instead of being sold for the benefit of one or more of the states, it should be considered a common fund to be managed and disposed of for the advantage of all. Nor did this seem any less politic than it was just. To permit one or a few of the states to appropriate this vast domain to the exclusion of the rest would give to it or them such an advantage over the others in point of territorial extension and of material wealth as would make their preponderance in the Confederacy dangerous to the rights of the others, and might threaten its very existence.

Impressed with these views Delaware, in giving assent on February 1, 1779, to the Articles of Confederation, accompanied the act with the declaration " That this State think it necessary . . . that a moderate extent of limits should be assigned for such of those States as claim to the Mississippi or the South Sea," and further " That this State consider themselves justly entitled to a right in common with the members of the Union to that extensive tract of country which lies to the westward of the frontiers of the United States, the property of which was not vested in or granted to individuals at the commencement of the present war: that the same hath been or may be gained from the king of Great Britain or the native Indians by the blood and treasure of all, and ought therefore to be a common estate to be granted out on terms beneficial to the United States." In this Delaware expressed the common opinion of all the states which made no separate

SURRENDER OF CLAIMS TO THE STATES. 122

claims; but Maryland emphasized the opinion by refusing to ratify the Articles of Confederation until the western lands were ceded to the Union. This refusal made action on the part of the claimant states imperative, and New York in February, 1780, recognized the necessity by giving to its delegates in Congress authority to make on its part the required cession. Connecticut followed in October of the same year by offering to cede its claim to the unsettled territory west of Pennsylvania, but with considerable reservation of lands bounded on the north by Lake Erie and on the east by Pennsylvania; a tract since known as the Connecticut Western Reserve. For this reservation the State could advance a claim of very plausible equity, based upon the fact that a considerable tract, which had been claimed under its charter with much apparent reason within the existing boundaries of Pennsylvania, had been taken away by the decision of a federal tribunal after much of it had been settled by purchasers under Connecticut grants. Virginia, in the December following, offered a cession of its claims to the territory north of the Ohio, but coupled it with a condition that its claims south of that river, which were then the subject of much controversy, should be guarantied. The New York delegates, in March, 1781, exercised the authority which had been vested in them to give a deed of cession, but reserved a right to rescind unless the same guaranty was given to New York as to any other ceding state. Maryland, thereupon assuming that the cessions were so far completed as to render the result certain, gave her adhesion to the Articles of Confederation. But how much the Confederacy had acquired by the public acts so far performed was a question of no small moment. A committee of Congress reporting the next year upon the western claims declared the title of New York to be the valid title. As matters then stood it was for the interest of the Confederacy to take this position, and the report was open to the suspicion that it was made for effect rather than from a belief in the soundness of its conclusions. Thus matters stood until March, 1784, when Virginia again came to the front with a cession qualified only by a reservation for bounty lands for the soldiers who with Clark made the conquest of Kaskaskia and Vincennes, and with stipulations for the reimbursement of the expenses of that conquest, for the security of the French inhabitants, and for the eventual erection of republican states within the ceded territory. Nobody could well complain of these provisions. Massachusetts ceded its claims in April, 1785, and the cession of Connecticut, with the reservation already mentioned, was accepted in the following year. By these several cessions the Union acquired jurisdiction over the territory north and west of the Ohio, and title to its unsold lands except as they had been reserved, but subject to such aboriginal rights as had not already been extinguished by treaties with the Indian tribes.

The Confederacy had thus acquired a vast domain, upon which there were already living many people. These people were without a government; and some provision for this just need of the social state was imperative. Such provision could now be made by no single state; it must be a confederate act; for only the Confederacy had jurisdiction over the territory. Minds inclined to be captious and technical might have interposed the objection that the Confederacy, which derived all its powers from the states, had not been given authority to create subordinate governments. But the case was not one to be disposed of on a technicality; the necessity for action was imperative, and the broad statesmanship of Mr. Jefferson was prompt to recognize and act upon it. Though never at any time inclined to liberal construction of federal powers, he took the lead in the steps to give the people of the territory the benefits and protection of government, and as chairman of a committee of three upon the subject, he matured a plan which, in March, 1784, he reported to Congress. The plan was comprehensive, for it embraced all the territory of the Confederacy, and proposed to divide it into seventeen parts, with provision for temporary governments, contemplating the eventual admission of the several parts as states into the Confederacy, but with certain fundamental principles upon which both the temporary and the permanent governments were to be established. The first of these was, "That they shall forever remain a part of the United States of America;" the last, "That after the year 1800 of the Christian era, there shall be neither slavery nor involuntary servitude in any part of the said States otherwise than in the punishment of crimes, whereof the party shall have been duly convicted to have been personally guilty."

This comprehensive plan, thus embodying the great principles of perpetual union and universal liberty, and proposing to organize all the territory of the United States upon them, was reported to a Congress representing states, every one of which, save Massachusetts, was then slaveholding. If adopted and given full effect, it must inevitably, within a few years, bring into the Union a sufficient number of free states to put the slave-holding states into permanent minority. It would, moreover, so effectually circumscribe the area of slavery and interpose obstacles to its extension, that if permitted to stand, nothing could save the institution from certain and not long-delayed destruction. It seems a bold plan to be proposed to such a Congress; but it expressed the matured convictions of Mr. Jefferson, and it had the support of the leading statesmen of the Virginia of that day.

The states were not fully represented in Congress at the time, and the anti-slavery provision of the proposed ordinance, though the opposition to it was but feeble, failed to receive a sufficient vote. In March of the next year Rufus King proposed in Congress an entire and immediate prohibition of slavery in all the territory belonging to the Confederacy, but the proposition, though exciting little opposition, was not acted upon. Early in 1787, a committee, of which Nathan Dane was a member, reported an ordinance drafted by him, which received the unanimous approval of the eight states then represented in Congress, and was adopted on the thirteenth of July.

This was the immortal Ordinance of 1787 "for the government of the Territory Northwest of the Ohio;" immortal for the grand results which have followed from its adoption, not less than for the wisdom and far-seeing statesmanship that conceived and gave form to its provisions. No charter of government in the history of any people has so completely withstood the tests of time and experience: it had not a temporary adaptation to a particular emergency, but its principles were for all time, and worthy of acceptance under all circumstances. It has been the fitting model for all subsequent territorial government in America, and so far as its provisions have now become customary in organizing territories, they may be passed without particular mention.

The significant provisions were contained in six articles, which it was declared "shall be considered as articles of compact between the original states and the people and states in the said territory, and forever remain unalterable except by common consent." The first of these provided for freedom of religious worship. The second was a comprehensive bill of rights; and in the enumeration was included an unusual and very significant provision making contracts inviolable. The third should be given in the words of the author. "Religion, morality, and knowledge being necessary to good government, and the happiness of mankind, schools and the means of education shall forever be encouraged. The utmost good faith shall always be observed towards the Indians; their lands and property shall never be taken from them without their consent, and in their property, rights, and liberty they shall never be invaded or disturbed unless in just and lawful wars authorized by Congress; but laws founded in justice and humanity shall from time to time be made for preventing wrongs being done to them, and for preserving peace and friendship with them." The fourth declared that the states to be formed from the territory should remain permanently in the Confederacy and share its obligations, and that all navigable waters and the carrying places between them should be free. The fifth provided that not less than three nor more than five states should be formed from the territory, and that these as they attained a population of sixty thousand should be admitted to the Union under republican constitutions. The sixth again should be given exactly as its author framed and the Congress adopted it. "There shall be neither slavery nor involuntary servitude in the said territory, otherwise than in the punishment of crime, whereof the party shall have been duly convicted: Provided always that any person escaping into the same, from whom labor or service is lawfully claimed in any one of the original States, such fugitive may be lawfully reclaimed and conveyed to the persons claiming his or her labor or service as aforesaid."

In all this ordinance, so full and complete in its provisions for government and for the protection of individual rights, framed though it was when popular notions of government were crude and unsettled, not a provision appears — if we except the proviso to the sixth article, which concerned external relations — which after the lapse of a century does not still appear wise and proper; not a line which one could wish had been omitted; not a clause which one could desire modified in any important particular. For its dedication of the territory to freedom credit has been given by partial friends to several different persons; but Jefferson first formulated the purpose, and for him it constitutes a claim to immortality superior to the presidency itself. The one was proof of his greatness and far-seeing statesmanship; the bestowment of the other evidenced only the popular favor. The ordinance was the beginning of the end of American slavery. It checked at the banks of the Ohio the advance of a system fruitful of countless evils, social and political; and the opponents of the system found in its mandate of uncompromising prohibition an inspiration and a prophecy of final triumph in their subsequent warfare.

The convention for framing a constitution for the United States was in session when the ordinance was adopted, and the first Congress of the Union recognized and sanctioned the ordinance, and provided for the appointment by the president, with the advice and consent of the Senate, of the governor, and other territorial officers. But before the federal constitution had been ratified by the states, the Congress of the Confederacy had chosen a governor, judges, and secretary, and on July 15, 1788, Arthur St. Clair, as governor, had in great state made his formal entry into Marietta, and inaugurated civil government amid the plaudits of the people. Shortly afterwards, with the assistance of the judges, he proceeded to give laws to the territory.

But the Ordinance of 1787 did not establish immediately a state of universal freedom. Many slaves were already in the territory; some of them Africans, brought by settlers from New York, Virginia, and elsewhere; but more of them Indians or their descendants. The servants who were generally preferred at that day were Indians who had been held and disposed of as slaves under the French and English governments, and were still detained as such. This species of slavery was founded upon the assumed right, which the Indians had acted upon, of selling their captives as the alternative to putting them to death; and it had existed from the early settlement of the country. The most of these slaves were Pawnees; that tribe was generally considered by the others as degraded, and for that reason the prisoners taken from it were more often sold for degrading service. Traders purchased them to do the drudgery of the fur trade; families procured them as house-servants, and Pawnee, or Pani, came to be the common appellation given to all slaves. But the practice of purchasing them had ceased before the territory came into the possession of the United States; and now the question which concerned them was whether their bonds were sundered by the ordinance.

The slaves in the Northwest Territory, as regards the legal questions affecting their liberty, might be ranged in three classes; the first embracing those who were in servitude to French owners previous to the cession of jurisdiction to England, and who were still claimed as property in which the owners were protected under the treaty of cession; the second, those who were held by British owners at the time of Jay's treaty and claimed afterwards as property under its protection; and the third, those who since the territory had come under American control had been brought into it from the states in which slavery was lawful. In the case of the first two classes the claim of the masters was generally recognized as indisputable, and it was always enforced when contested; the third class, when held at all, as was not unfrequently the case, were quite as generally believed to be held in evasion or defiance of law.

But such slavery as was then in the country existed in very mild form, and no glaring evils or abuses arrested public attention, or excited active hostility to the institution. The anti-slavery provision in the ordinance, therefore, probably for this reason more than for any other, was very generally treated as having only prospective force, and as not designed to disturb existing relations, whether originating under French, English, or American law. And in this treatment of the subject the governor apparently concurred. The anti-slavery sentiment of the day was not aggressive, and it was much less pronounced among the people than it was among the leading statesmen in Congress, who had been active in the Revolution, and for many years had given thoughtful attention to the subject of human rights in all its aspects. By them the elements which go to the making of great states had been carefully considered, and the most of those who were inclined to tolerate slavery at all did so in the expectation that it would prove but a temporary evil. But the people at large had given the subject little attention; they knew the slaves only as servants who seemed to be as well treated as others, and they did not pause to consider their status further, or to speculate upon the effect of degraded labor upon the social or political state.

Subsequent proceedings made it painfully evident that the public sentiment on the subject of slavery was not well advanced. By act of Congress of May 7, 1800, the Northwest Territory was divided and Ohio set off, the remainder receiving a government under the name of Indiana. The boundary line between Ohio and Indiana ran from the mouth of the Kentucky River to Fort Recovery, and thence due north to Canada, thus assigning the eastern portion of Michigan to Ohio. But this arrangement did not long continue; Ohio in 1802 formed and adopted a constitution with more restricted bounds, and by act of Congress the following winter was declared a state in the Union. The territory north of the new boundary of Ohio was annexed to the Territory of Indiana, which was thus made to include all the lower peninsula of Michigan.

William Henry Harrison was the first governor

of Indiana Territory, and among the subjects to which the people invited his early attention was their inability under the ordinance to acquire and hold slaves. Many of them had come from slaveholding states and were accustomed to slave labor; and it seemed to them a hardship that they should be deprived of it. But the inhibition of slavery discouraged immigration, and in many ways, as the people thought, hindered the development of the resources of the country. A popular convention held in 1802, presided over by the governor himself, adopted a petition to Congress which prayed for a temporary suspension of the anti-slavery article. The petition was received with respect, and referred for consideration to a committee of which John Randolph was chairman, but it found no favor with the committee, and received no further attention from Congress. "The rapid population of the State of Ohio," said Mr. Randolph, reporting upon it, "sufficiently evinces, in the opinion of your committee, that the labor of slaves is not necessary to promote the growth and settlement of colonies in that region; that this labor, demonstrably the dearest of any, can only be employed in the cultivation of products more valuable than any known to that quarter of the United States; that the committee deem it highly dangerous and inexpedient to impair a provision wisely calculated to promote the happiness and prosperity of the northwestern country, and to give strength and security to that extensive frontier. In the salutary operation of this sagacious and benevolent restraint, it is believed that the inhabitants of Indiana will, at no very distant day, find ample remuneration for a temporary privation of labor and of emigration." So Virginia stood firm in her purpose to preserve for freedom the domain which had been pledged to it by her early and wise policy.

The petitioners were not discouraged by this first rebuff, but renewed their application; and in two successive Congresses reports of committees were obtained favorable to their views. For unexplained reasons upon neither of these was action taken. A third favorable report was obtained in 1807, which recommended a suspension for ten years from the succeeding January, but this also was ignored by Congress. In the autumn of 1807 Governor Harrison united with the legislature in renewing the request for suspension; but this time a select committee reported against it, and the attempt to secure this change in the organic law, so long and so persistently urged, became evidently hopeless, and was at last abandoned. Albert Gallatin truly said to Badollet, "If you have had a share in preventing the establishment of slavery in Indiana, you will have done more good to that part of the country at least than commonly falls to the share of man."[1]

[1] *Life of Gallatin*, by Adams, 406.

While this last petition was pending in Congress legal proceedings arose in Michigan which called for authoritative examination of the whole subject of slavery in that territory. As there were some slaves on both sides the national boundary, cases of fleeing from servitude sometimes occurred which led to bad blood, and an attempt was made to secure territorial legislation for restoring fugitives from Canada, but the necessary vote in the legislature could not be secured. Several persons held as slaves by masters residing in the territory also demanded their freedom on writs of habeas corpus; and these were made returnable before the chief justice, who gave the subject careful examination. In the case of one held as a slave at the date of Jay's treaty, there was no difficulty in deciding that the relation was still lawful; but as to others the judgment was different. The arguments made on behalf of the masters are not preserved; but it is manifest from the opinion that the discussion took a wide range, and that the competency of the legislation which undertook to prohibit in the territories what was permitted by the states was questioned. But the chief justice met the case squarely, and declared that in cases not covered by treaty slavery could not exist in the territory, either, 1, by the law of nations; or, 2, by the common law; or, 3, by domestic legislation. And he then proceeds to say: —

"In some parts of the United States, and in some

parts also of the British dominions, a judicial character could not lay down these positions; and he must certainly feel a strong sense of shame for his country that she does not permit him; as on the contrary every Englishman feels and must feel a very just pride of country when he reflects on the position laid down by Lord Mansfield.

"But in this part of her dominions my country does enable me to lay down this position, and to act upon it, with a very slight exception, and that entirely in favor of British settlers by virtue of a special treaty. In other respects her will is there shall be 'neither slavery nor involuntary servitude' in this territory. I am, therefore, bound to say and do say, that a right of property in the human species cannot exist in this territory except as to persons in the actual possession of British settlers in this territory on 16th June, 1796, and that every other man coming into this territory is by the law of the land a freeman, unless he be a fugitive from lawful labor and service in some other American state or territory; and then he must be restored." [1]

There was no appeal from this decision, and it settled the controversy finally for this part of the country. It will be remarked that no notice was taken of cases which might have arisen under the French cession; but the great lapse of time had made the question under that treaty of historical importance only.

Illinois, after it had come to be a state, was destined to be the theatre of a pro-slavery agita-

[1] MSS. opinion in possession of Michigan Historical Society.

tion, which was carried on with no little acrimony, and with every appearance for a time of probable success. The question then made was complicated, for it involved both congressional and state action. The State had been admitted to the Union under a constitution adopted by the people, and subject to change only by the people, and which prohibited slavery. The anti-slavery article in the Ordinance of 1787, being one of "compact between the original states and the people and states in the said territory," and "forever unalterable except by common consent," would stand in full force even if the constitution were amended, unless by the consent of Congress it was abrogated or suspended. Thus both the state constitution and the ordinance stood in the way of the agitators for slave labor; the one must be changed by popular voice, the other by the national legislature. In the year 1823 the attempt was made to secure an amendment to the constitution. Had the attempt succeeded, and had that great state as a political force been arrayed for the extension and perpetuity of slavery, the current of subsequent American history and the probable destiny of the Union would have been altogether changed. It was fortunate for the State, for the American Union, and for mankind, that the State had in the person of its governor a statesman at once farseeing and patriotic, fearless and able, persistent in what he knew to be right, and who did not for a moment hesitate when the question was presented to him, whether he would yield to a prevailing sentiment for the sake of personal popularity and a political future, or, on the other hand, would allow himself to be the sacrifice to preserve his commonwealth from the evils of slave labor.

Edward Coles had himself been a slaveholder, and had come to the Northwest that he might emancipate his slaves, and thus sever all connection with a system of labor and dependence which to him was abhorrent. When the pro-slavery agitation began, he took up promptly and fearlessly the gage of battle which was cast at his feet, and in a struggle deserving of perpetual remembrance and praise achieved a victory which was signal and conclusive. To his skill, fidelity to principle, and unflinching courage it is due that the noble commonwealth of which he was executive did not even temporarily lose its place in the category of free states, and that its onward progress in population and wealth, and in all the elements of greatness, was never for a moment delayed or embarrassed by this attempt to turn back the wheels of time and take up again the discarded system of degraded and degrading labor.

CHAPTER VIII.

MICHIGAN BECOMES A TERRITORY AND IS GIVEN RULERS.

The Territory of Michigan was set off from Indiana on June 30, 1805. It was to embrace all that portion of Indiana Territory lying north of a line drawn east from the southerly bend or extreme of Lake Michigan, until it intersected Lake Erie, and lying east of a line drawn from the same southerly bend through the middle of Lake Michigan to its northern extremity, and thence due north to the northern boundary of the United States.

The settled parts of the territory had then for nine years been in possession of the United States, but the increase in population had been insignificant. Some slight addition had been made by French families coming in from Canada, and we have seen that some enterprising persons of other nationalities had come for the purposes of trade. But with the change in jurisdiction there had been some loss of inhabitants also by the removal to Canada of persons who had reasons for preferring to live under British rule.

FATHER GABRIEL RICHARD.

Detroit was still the principal settlement. It had taken on a certain municipal dignity by being incorporated as a "town" by the legislature of the Northwest Territory in 1802, but it was still a small hamlet, and almost without growth. The people, for the most part, professed the Catholic religion; but their piety scarcely went beyond profession; the days of intense zeal had passed away, and general indifference had succeeded. Since the conquest by England the people had been greatly neglected by their spiritual teachers and superiors; and the restraints which had done something to preserve their morals in the half savage life led by so many of them as hunters, trappers, and *voyageurs* had almost entirely been withdrawn. Now, however, they had among them Father Gabriel Richard, a faithful and devoted pastor, who, under many discouragements, was doing what he found it in his power to do to restore or convert the people to Christianity, and to moral and decent lives.

Father Richard would have been a man of mark in almost any community and at any time. He had come to America in 1792 at the age of twenty-eight, and placing himself at the disposal of Bishop Carroll of Baltimore, had been sent by him first to Illinois, where, without evidence of much valuable fruit, he labored until 1798, and was then transferred to Detroit. He was a plain man, simple in all his habits, and abstemious in all his indulgences. In his Christian labors he soon perceived that the intemperance of the people was likely to prove the chief obstacle to success, and to the cure of this he addressed his efforts directly, not limiting them to indulgence in intoxicating drinks, but to the use of tobacco also. But the evil of intoxication was too deep-seated for any one man, however much he might be respected, to make sensible inroads upon it. It pervaded all classes of society, and was not wholly a matter of indulgence of appetite. With well-to-do people it was to some extent a matter of fashion; with other classes a matter of imitation. Burnet has left us a graphic picture of the dinner parties given by the fur traders of Detroit, in which "they competed with each other for the honor of drinking the most, as well as the best, wine without being intoxicated themselves, and of having at their parties the greatest number of intoxicated guests."[1] It was thus that they offset the privation and suffering of their excursions into the wilderness; their lives, as another observer said,[2] consisting in one constant succession of amusements: "dances, rides, dinners, card parties, and all the *et ceteras* of dissipation follow in one long train, treading each on the heels of the other." It was little that the sincere and fatherly advice of any

---

[1] Burnett's *Notes*, 283. As to Indian degradation from intoxication, see Ibid. 389 *et seq*.

[2] Judge Wm. Woodbridge: Memoir by Lanman, p. 14.

priest or pastor could accomplish with the common people when such were the examples set for them by the men of wealth, the leaders in business, and in society.

Father Richard did not confine his labors to Detroit, but in the summer of 1799 he visited Mackinaw, which he found to be a place containing fifty houses, but where a thousand people sometimes congregated. These people also had once been nominally Catholic, but the children among them were mostly illegitimate; and it was "very painful to see so many poor creatures left without instruction, several of them scarcely knowing how to make the sign of the cross." He was informed that the same condition of things prevailed farther on to the northwest "where the great Northwest Company of Montreal employ nearly seventeen hundred men, nearly all Canadians." He visited the settlement of the Ottawas on Lake Michigan, where he was received gladly. He proposed to send a priest among them "for their instruction, or at least for that of their children," but though they seemed thankful for this, and took the offer into consideration, they never made reply to it. "The truth of the matter is," he is mournfully compelled to admit, "they are so much addicted to the use of ardent spirits that they care very little about religion. . . . The trade there is principally in liquors, and as long as this state of things exists there can be no prospect of making them Christians." He repeats the saying of another that the traffic in English rum has destroyed more Indians than the Spanish sword, and wishes it could be abolished, but sees no hope of it. He returned to Mackinaw, where he found ample need for his services, and would gladly have remained for the winter; but duty seemed to demand his presence at Detroit, and he came back to his regular charge.

If Father Richard had tasted the "English rum" of Indian commerce he would have discovered, if he did not already know by common report, that what was sold to the Indians by that name was for the most part neither rum nor any other liquor known to civilized trade. It was a preparation specially made for Indian use. Two gallons of whiskey in a barrel of water, with tobacco sufficient to impart the desired intoxicating quality, made an article as suitable for this trade as any other. The cost to the dealer was trifling, and the profits of the trade enormous.

The condition of the Sault Ste. Marie at this period was quite as repulsive as that of any of the fur-trading stations described by Father Richard. Mackenzie, who visited it in 1793, said of it, "It is dwindled to nothing, and reduced to about thirty families of the Algonquin nation, who are one half the year starving, and the other half intoxicated, and ten or twelve Canadians who have been in the Indian country from an early

CONDITION OF THE WHITE POPULATION. 145

period of life, and intermarried with the natives, who have brought them families." Game was already gone, and the Indians lived mainly on fish; but "whatever quantity they may have taken, it is never known that their economy is such as to make it last through the winter, which renders their situation very distressing."[1] Equally distressing, and for the same reasons, was the condition of the Indians in other parts of the territory. That of the white people was substantially the same at Detroit and elsewhere. The total white population of the territory at this time did not exceed four thousand, and the fur trade was still the leading industry. The number of "settlements" or farms was found on actual count to be four hundred and forty-two, of which more than a fourth were at Frenchtown on the Raisin, where French families had begun to settle in 1784. A few were on Grosse Isle, but the most of them were on the Rouge and other streams flowing eastwardly. Many of them were locations without lawful permission on the public lands, so that in law the settlers were mere trespassers. In all the territory it was believed there were but eight good titles to land. The claims were numerous, and were derived from various sources, but the most of them were either clearly illegal in their origin, or had become invalid by reason of some breach of condition. But nobody was questioning

[1] Mackenzie's *Travels*, xxxviii.

the titles, and the people troubled themselves but little about the defects. They were lively and gay, if not happy; they had no feeling of responsibility in respect to public and governmental concerns, and submitted cheerfully and without question to the authorities placed over them.

The government of the territory was already outlined by the Ordinance of 1787, which was closely followed. The executive was to be a governor appointed by the president, with the advice and consent of the senate, and there was to be a secretary who would perform the duties of governor if the latter officer was absent or the office vacant. The judiciary was to consist of three judges, also of presidential appointment. The legislature was at first to consist of the governor and judges, who were not, however, to originate laws, but were to adopt such as were suitable from the laws of the original states; and the laws so adopted were to be in force unless disapproved by Congress. The whole government thus originated in Washington and centred there, and was neither derived from the people governed nor responsible to them. But as yet the interest of the United States in the territory was greater than that of all the people in it. The nation was proprietor of the soil, and was charged with the duty of protecting a long line of frontier, where the people who were subject to its jurisdiction were in the main aliens in language and feeling, and in sympathy rather with the people across the border than with those with whom by the fortune of war they had come into political association. A temporary government originating at Washington was, therefore, a political necessity; but the organic act provided that so soon as there should be five thousand free male inhabitants of full age in the territory, they should elect delegates to a general assembly, who, with a territorial council of five, to be selected by Congress from ten names nominated to it by the general assembly, should constitute the legislative body. The legislature would, therefore, be representative of the people in both houses, but the veto of the governor was to be absolute.

If the wisdom of the president in his appointments had been equal to that of the legislation, the early history of the territory would have been more orderly, and, perhaps, more prosperous also. But Mr. Jefferson, with singular want of tact and judgment, sent to this distant frontier territory as rulers for its rough and peculiar population a number of persons who were not only ignorant of this part of the country and of its people, but were without practical acquaintance with similar communities elsewhere. It was not to be expected, therefore, that they would readily and easily come into sympathetic and cordial relations with the people they were to govern. Some of them also had personal peculiarities and deficiencies which would render entirely improbable a successful and orderly administration of their offices.

General William Hull of Massachusetts was the selection for governor. He had an excellent and well-deserved reputation, and in point of character and standing the appointment was altogether suitable. He had early entered upon service in the War for Independence, participating in many important battles with credit, and continuing in the service until the surrender of Cornwallis. Steuben had selected him for his assistant in the work of army reorganization, and when the war was over, and Steuben's mission to obtain the surrender of the western posts had failed, he had himself been charged with a similar mission, which also proved unsuccessful, and he then took part in the suppression of Shays's Rebellion. In 1793 he was again sent to Canada; this time to bring to the attention of the authorities the manner in which the hostile Indians were furnished with the supplies that enabled them to continue their destructive depredations. Subsequently he traveled in Europe for observation and mental improvement, and on his return was made judge of the Court of Common Pleas of his native state.

This highly honorable record was without a stain, and that of his whole subsequent life would probably have been equally untarnished and enviable had he declined to accept the appointment of governor of this territory when it was tendered to him. He was at this time fifty-two years of age and inclined to corpulency; he had all his life lived in the smiles of public favor, and his domestic and social relations were agreeable; and had he been made the executive of a staid and orderly commonwealth, with associates in government of similar characteristics, his administration might have been altogether popular and successful. But in Michigan he found uncongenial people all about him, and it soon appeared that he was somewhat lacking in the persistent self-assertion necessary to make the rough characters of a backwoods settlement recognize and accept the fact that within the proper limits of his authority he proposed to be and would be ruler and master. Had the other territorial officers yielded him the deference and respect which was due to his character and station, their example would, in all probability, have been followed by the general public, and his administration might then have had a fair measure of success. But the governor was peculiarly unfortunate in having in one of the judges a person of characteristics much more pronounced than his own, and with not only the power but the will, as subsequently appeared, to embarrass and embitter his whole official life. This was Augustus B. Woodward, who was sent on from Washington as chief justice.

The chief justice was pronounced by one of his subsequent associates to be "a wild theorist, fit only to extract sunbeams from cucumbers;" but this characterization presents only one side of his erratic and peculiar nature. He was a theorist, but not a mere dreamer; his ability was very considerable, and, in some respects, very substantial. In doing what he chose to do he was perfectly fearless, and he succeeded, through the use of his official authority, in dominating public affairs during the whole period of Hull's administration. He was as eccentric as he was able, and his audacity kept him continually in the public eye, and made him, until the war came on, the most conspicuous figure in territorial affairs. Mr. Jefferson had given him for associates Frederick Bates and John Griffin, both Virginians; but Bates had already been in the territory for some little time as an official of the land office, and he alone of all the territorial officers possessed the important qualification for his post, — that he knew the country and knew its people. And it may be added here that he alone of them all had a subsequent career that was satisfactory and altogether honorable. He was not long in discovering that his official relations were to be unpleasant, and he resigned his office and left the territory for conspicuous public service in Missouri. Judge Griffin remained at his post; but his official life was not a happy one, and years afterwards he complained that he was made the mere drudge of the chief justice to do his will.

The journey of Governor Hull to take possession of his government was well calculated to impress him with its exposed condition, and with its vast distance from friendly support in case an emergency should arise which made assistance necessary. From Albany his route was by way of Lake Ontario, which he traversed in boats with his family. Reaching Niagara he proceeded thence to Buffalo, where he found a vessel in which he could take more comfortable passage to Detroit. But before he reached the lakes he had left civilization behind, and whether he turned to the right hand or to the left he beheld a wilderness still inhabited by savages. To the north of the lakes, too, the territory was the property of Great Britain, a country with which the relations of the United States were at the time far from cordial. It was inevitable that the governor should have received, upon his long and tedious journey, impressions of the exposed condition of the territory which abided with him until the great crisis of his life and helped then to unman him.

But the circumstances of the governor's reception at Detroit were not calculated to remove unpleasant impressions or to give augury of official ease and enjoyment. It is not improbable that the veteran soldier who had consented to take up his abode in the far interior as governor of the new-born territory expected to be received with acclamations, and to make triumphal entry, as

St. Clair had done, into his capital; but when on the first day of July, 1805, he came in sight of the town he found nothing but the smoking embers of desolated homes, and tents set up here and there in which a portion of the people had found temporary shelter. The story the people had to tell was a sad one. On the eleventh of the preceding month fire had broken out in the densely compacted settlement, and it had spread right and left, to be stayed only when there was nothing left for it to consume. Public buildings and private alike were gone; only a warehouse and a bakery had escaped destruction. The spectacle was disheartening. Instead of finding his people well housed and comfortably circumstanced, as he expected, the governor found them objects of charity, living in their canvas habitations, or provided for in the outside settlements. A beginning had been made of putting up loghouses, but the gloom of the great desolation was still upon the people, and it could not immediately be driven away.

Obviously the first duty of the new officials was to do what should lie in their power to give relief to the homeless and needy people. The rebuilding of the town must be aided, and the people must have lots upon which to erect their habitations and business houses. Fortunately, in providing for their relief it was possible to convert the present calamity into a permanent blessing. The old town had been constructed with special view to protection against the Indians; it was compact that it might be the more easily fortified; its streets were mere lanes; it was too crowded for comfort, for health, or for business. Some day it would have become necessary to plan the town anew, and to make suitable streets by the destruction of the buildings at great expense to the public. But now accident had removed the buildings as if by providential design; and the bare earth invited the suitable plan, and was incumbered by no obstacles.

In seeking relief for the people, the governor and the chief justice found themselves able to coöperate; and they agreed that the destruction of improvements presented a strong case for the equitable consideration of Congress. Both of them took the long journey to Washington to impress their views upon the national legislature, and their success was reasonably satisfactory. Congress recognized the justice and policy of providing homesteads for the sufferers by the fire; and an act was passed making the governor and judges a land board, with authority to lay out a town, and to convey a lot therein to every person over seventeen years of age who, at the time of the fire, had owned or inhabited a house in the old town. This enabled them all to become freeholders, where before they had had a merely tolerated occupancy.

But the efforts on behalf of the settlers were not restricted to those who had suffered in the destruction of the town. The propriety of recognizing and confirming all actual possessions was strongly urged upon Congress, and with such success that under proper legislation the people of the outside settlements soon became owners of the legal title to the lands they had occupied and brought under cultivation, and were thus encouraged to make lasting and valuable improvements.

Next to looking after the immediate needs of the homeless people, the preparation of a code of laws demanded the attention of the governor and judges. For this purpose they met from day to day, and adopted distinct acts on different subjects as occasion seemed to require. The chief justice was commonly the draftsman; and the several acts were printed together, and in popular speech were collectively known as the Woodward Code.

The plan of the new town was also the production of the chief justice, and he had made one that was his pride and his glory. To some extent it was modeled upon that of the national capital; and though he succeeded in securing its adoption, it was the subject of much contemporaneous ridicule, not only for what seemed to the people its whimsical character, but also for its magnificent distances. It had its Campus Martius and its Grand

Circus, with broad avenues radiating from these into the woods, — avenues which the fertile imagination of its author saw, in the near future, lined with elegant dwellings and stately public and private edifices. But the matter-of-fact people of the day saw only a visionary plan for an immense metropolis on paper, prepared by an eccentric enthusiast for a town which had been more than a hundred years in attaining the proportions of a respectable village; and which, so far as could be seen, had nothing in immediate prospect calculated to give its growth any considerable impetus. The plan, therefore, was ridiculed while it was tolerated, but it was not strictly adhered to, and the departures from it, from time to time, annoyed its author, and were a frequent incitement to ill-temper and controversy.

The chief justice had more occasion for annoyance in the refusal of Congress to sanction his scheme for a great bank. He had planned for a bank with a capital of four hundred thousand dollars, which Boston parties were expected to furnish for nominal use in the fur trade. So confident were he and his associates of entire success in the scheme, that a bank building was erected and all preparations made for beginning business before the charter was granted. But the chief justice was at this time the effective force in the legislature: it was only necessary for him to draft the bill he desired, and to present it to the others for their signature. The bank was soon in operation, with the chief justice for president; and it was charged at the time that the governor was concerned with him in interest; but this was denied, and the probability seems to be that the governor abandoned a purpose which he had once formed to that effect.

A bank in the vastness of its pretensions so out of proportion to the insignificant town where it was to do business, and having the chief legislative and judicial officer of the territory for its manager, was naturally the subject of unfavorable criticism, and the parties concerned were severely attacked in such newspapers as circulated in the territory. Congress refused to sanction the scheme, and the charter became of no force; but the bank, nevertheless, went on as before, until, in September, 1808, in the absence of the chief justice from the territory, the other members of the legislature summoned courage to pass an act denouncing severe penalties upon unauthorized banking. The bank officers petitioned for exemption from these penalties, but were refused.

From this time the governor and the chief justice were in avowed hostility; and as one of the associate judges took sides with the governor and the other against him, the meetings of the four, whether as a land board or as a legislature, were occasions for undignified and angry contests and dissensions which were well calculated to bring public authority into contempt. It does not appear that the governor was wanting in proper observance of the proprieties of his station, or of the rules of law; but his antagonist was less scrupulous, and by his very audacity not only for the most part carried his points, but also carried with him an apparent public sentiment. He was ingenious in finding ways to annoy and mortify the governor, and his own misbehavior furnished opportunities when nothing else did. He did not hesitate, on one occasion, to stretch his prerogative to the extent of fining a citizen as for contempt of court for offensive language to himself in the public street, — an outrage on the law which the governor undertook to redress by the issue of a pardon. But the grand jury of the territory made a presentment denying that the governor possessed the power of pardon, and censuring his usurpation; and the chief justice, thereupon, not only treated the pardon as void, but proceeded to enforce his own illegal judgment. What was more extraordinary still, the grand jury at the instigation of the chief justice presented as unnecessary and a "nuisance" certain legislation which had been adopted when that functionary was absent. Fortified by this presentment the chief justice and his echo in the court treated the offensive legislation as a nullity. Evidently the governor had more than a match in his daring and unscrupulous antagonist.

But other causes were troubling the governor also. He was Indian agent as well as executive; and he had come to the territory with some idea that in his capacity of agent he might be of signal service, both to the territory and to the Indians. For the benefit of the territory he proposed to take steps for the extinguishment of the Indian title as rapidly as it might be accomplished without causing discontent to the tribes. To benefit the Indians he proposed to have them taught agriculture and the mechanic arts. He soon perceived, however, that plans made by a New England fireside for the amelioration of the aboriginal condition lacked fitness of adaptation to circumstances when presented for actual test, and that civilized agriculture and mechanic arts were the last things the savages cared to learn. We hear nothing of his philanthropic purposes after he came to his government; and when he opened negotiations for cessions of territory, he discovered an entire absence of a disposition to respond favorably. On the contrary he found the opposition decided and persistent. The Indians about Mackinaw refused to attend any council, declaring that if their brothers below were fools enough to throw away their lands, they might do so; but for themselves they were determined that the governor must not think of taking away one hair's breadth of their lands, for they had not so much to spare. The governor did succeed, however, in obtaining, in 1807, a cession of all that portion of the territory not before ceded which was bounded on the west by the principal meridian, and extended on the north to the line of White Rock in Lake Huron.

This was a very valuable acquisition; and no complaint has reached us of any overreaching or other unfairness on the part of the governor in obtaining it. But ever since their encounter with Wayne, the Indian tribes of the Northwest had been rapidly sinking into degradation, and the most of them no longer exercised much freedom of will. In their intercourse with white people they were constantly brought in contact with all that was low and base in civilized life, with the inevitable result of adding to their native vices many that were new and in their effects more destructive than those they were born to. When not on the war-path, or on their great hunts, they were easily mastered by their passion for intoxicating drinks; and several classes of white people were ready to cater to this passion for selfish purposes of their own. It was often the case that a treaty of cession by the Indians was an arrangement which scheming persons among them had contrived to bring about for their own interest, and which the Indians were made to conclude with little volition of their own. Reservations in the nature of grants for the benefit of traders and interpreters and their half-breeds came to be a common feature in such treaties; and though these were always nominally made at the desire of the Indians, the management which had created the desire was not often such as would bear the light. What was said of an Indian treaty a little later was already coming to be true. "An Indian treaty now lies chiefly between the various traders, agents, creditors, and half-breeds of the tribes, on whom custom and necessity have made the degraded chiefs dependent, and the government agents. When the former have seen matters so far arranged that their self-interest and various schemes and claims are likely to be fulfilled, and allowed to their hearts' content, the silent acquiescence of the Indians follows of course; and till this is the case the treaty can never be amicably effected."[1]

But the governor, by the time his treaty was concluded, saw plain indications that trouble was brewing. He heard well-authenticated rumors that a prophet was among the Indians throughout all the West, practicing his arts and incantations, and urging in the name of the Great Spirit, — for whom he assumed to speak, — that they should league themselves together for protection against the white men. A great chieftain was also coming upon the stage, who perceived very clearly that the system pursued by the United States was "a mighty water ready to overflow his people;"

[1] Blanchard's *Discoveries and Conquests in the Northwest*, 402.

TECUMSEH'S POLICY.

and he was laboring earnestly among the tribes in the effort to form a confederacy " to prevent any tribe from selling land without the consent of the others." This was " the dam he was erecting to resist this mighty water." The scheme of Tecumseh, even though it had been peacefully intended, must necessarily have excited alarm among the white people; for it sprang from a feeling of antagonism to their encroachments, and must depend for its success upon the prevalence of unfriendly sentiments among the tribes. That such sentiments were already spreading was perceived by those who were brought in contact, officially or otherwise, with the Indians; and the tendency in that direction increased rapidly as the relations between the United States and Great Britain became unsettled and threatening. There had never been any complete sundering of ties between the Indians of the Northwest and their old employers; they were still to some extent pensioners upon Great Britain for services during the Revolutionary War; and as they had nothing to fear from British aggression, there were no suspicions to weaken the former friendship. If war broke out between the United States and Great Britain, the Indians were likely to take the part of their old allies; and if the Indians on their part felt inclined to war, they naturally hoped for the assistance of the nation which they plainly perceived had no friendly feeling for the

Americans. What Governor Hull saw very distinctly was that in the event of war the little settlement on the frontier of civilization, whose destinies were committed to his care, would be encompassed by foes so numerous and so bloodthirsty that they might overwhelm and destroy it before the distant assistance upon which exclusively he must depend could be made effective.

Such was the state of affairs when the "dam" which Tecumseh had arranged broke away under premature pressure with such destructive force in the battle of the Tippecanoe. John Randolph truthfully said: "It was our own thirst for territory, our own want of moderation that had driven these sons of nature to desperation of which we felt the effects."

CHAPTER IX.

WAR, AND THE CONQUEST AND RECONQUEST OF MICHIGAN.

In February, 1812, Governor Hull was in Washington, and reports which gave him great concern were continually coming to him of hostile conduct on the part of the Indians. For a long time the relations between the United States and Great Britain had been growing more and more critical; and if, as there was every reason to fear, war should be declared, no part of the country was so exposed to attack or so difficult of defense as the territory of which he was governor. The people in a petition to Congress the preceding December had justly said that the whole territory was a double frontier, with British on one side and Indians on the other, and they prayed for further protection of military posts and for an additional force at Detroit. There was so little agriculture in the territory that the garrison they already had at Detroit must be dependent for supplies in part at least upon Ohio; and a wilderness of two hundred miles separated that frontier post from the Ohio settlements. Through this wilderness by difficult and exposed roads the supplies must be transported and reinforcements sent forward, unless the Americans should secure command of Lake Erie and establish a base of operations upon it.

At this time the British had complete control of the lake and its connecting waters. Three years before the governor had suggested to the administration the expediency of constructing armed vessels upon Lake Erie as a necessary protection to communication with the territory; and in 1811 he returned to the subject, and gave his views with considerable fullness. After a careful review of the situation, he summed up as follows: —

"This, then, appears to be the plain state of the case. The British have a regular force equal to ours. The province of Upper Canada has on its rolls a militia of twenty to one against us. In addition to this there can be but little doubt but a large proportion of the savages will join them. What then will be the situation of this part of the country? Separated from the states by an extensive wilderness which will be filled with savages to prevent any succor, our water communications entirely obstructed by the British armed vessels on Lake Erie, we shall have no other resource for defense but the small garrisons and feeble population of the territory. Under these circumstances it is easy to foresee what will be the fate of this country. . . . If there is a prospect of war with England, what measures are most expedient? In my opinion there can be no doubt. Prepare a naval force on Lake Erie superior to the British, and sufficient to preserve your communications."

And once more he returned to the subject in the spring of 1812, but every time without avail.

There were not wanting at that day able men in Congress and out of it who ridiculed the suggestion that Canada could possibly be a source of serious danger to the United States. So far from indulging in fears of that sort, they looked upon Canada as a source of weakness to the British government. The people of Canada, as they conceived, were a people held in unwilling subjection by a foreign power; and it was only necessary to raise the flag of liberty and offer them free institutions, and they would be found flocking with alacrity to accept the offer. Mr. Clay, who should have known better, was one of this sanguine class. "We can take Canada without soldiers," he declared. "We have only to send officers into the province, and the people, disaffected towards their own government, will rally round our standard. . . . It is absurd to suppose we shall not succeed in our enterprise against the enemy's provinces. We have the Canadas as much under our command as Great Britain has the ocean, and the way to conquer her on the ocean is to drive her from the land. I am not for stopping at Quebec or anywhere else, but I would take the whole continent from them and ask no favors." Mr. Clay had evidently forgotten the history of Quebec in the war of the Revolution, and the repulse of the brave Montgomery before its frowning citadel. Discontent in Canada there undoubtedly had been under the administration of Governor-General Craig, who was obnoxious to Canadians of French descent; but Craig had been succeeded by Sir George Prevost, an able man who took every pains to make a good impression upon the people, and to remove all ground of just complaint. The French inhabitants, more than willing to be favorably regarded by their rulers, responded readily to the governor's pacific advances, and from all sides there is concurrent testimony that in the preparations for anticipated war the Canadians were more active and also more unanimous than were the Americans. John Randolph was, therefore, abundantly justified by the facts when he ridiculed the anticipated "holiday campaign," in which there was to be "no expense of blood or treasure on our part," but Canada was "to conquer herself," "to be subdued by the principle of fraternity." But Mr. Clay's delusion was the common one, and nothing in his utterances appeared unreasonable to the dominant war party of the day. The journals of public opinion and the speeches of public men in Congress and elsewhere furnish abundant proof of a general expectation that Canada in case of war would be easily conquered with the aid of large numbers of its own people. But Governor Hull, who better knew the condition of things in Canada than did most of his contemporaries, indulged in no such expectation.

THE FATAL BLUNDER. 167

While in Washington the governor was tendered the command of a force, consisting in the main of Ohio militia, which it was proposed to send to Michigan for such service as might be required of it. He declined the appointment, but subsequently, after Colonel Kingsbury, who had been assigned to the command had been disabled by sickness from taking it, he accepted, though with reluctance; and at Dayton, on May 25th, three regiments of militia, commanded respectively by Colonels McArthur, Cass, and Findlay, and numbering twelve hundred men, were placed under his command. Three hundred regulars afterwards joined them, and with the whole body General Hull marched to the Rapids of the Maumee, which he reached at the end of June. From Urbana, then a frontier town, a road had to be cut through the wilderness, and the labor was very great and the progress necessarily slow.

The government made a blunder in tendering the command of this force to Hull, and he on his part made if possible a greater blunder in accepting it. His opinion that the control of the lakes was necessary to the protection of his posts had been fully disclosed; and not having that control he was, according to his own view, if war should break out, at the mercy of the enemy. A courageous and vigorous campaign, and especially an aggressive campaign, it was idle to expect under such leadership: he was conquered by his own misgivings before he moved; and nothing but great and to him unexpected good fortune at the outset could have relieved him of his dismal forebodings and inspired him with the necessary courage for a campaign so far from support. Instead of experiencing any such good fortune he was made the victim of another blunder, the consequences of which were visited upon him with merciless severity when they culminated in the disaster which finally overtook his force.

On July 1st General Hull procured a small vessel, upon which he loaded his baggage, hospital stores, and the invalids of his army, and sent it forward from the Rapids to Detroit. With the baggage he also sent important papers containing full information respecting the force under his command. There would have been nothing unsafe or wanting in prudence in this proceeding under ordinary circumstances, and General Hull might claim with some plausibility that he was aware of no circumstances which could render it improper or imprudent. But as the probability that war might arise was the only reason for placing him at the head of a military force, and as the vessel could not reach Detroit without passing what in the event of war would be a hostile fort, a more cautious man would not have been likely to expose his papers to unnecessary risks under such circumstances. What actually happened, however, he had no reason to anticipate, for the department at

NEGLIGENCE AT WASHINGTON. 169

Washington was guilty of negligence so gross as to be little less than criminal.

On the eighteenth of the preceding month Congress had declared war against Great Britain. As Hull was in command of a military force marching towards an exposed "double frontier," the importance of his receiving the earliest possible information was so obvious and so imperative that it would seem impossible it should be overlooked or neglected by those in authority. But this, through gross and most unaccountable mismanagement in the war department, was precisely what happened. A communication from the secretary of war notifying General Hull that war had been declared, instead of being sent with expedition by special messenger, was intrusted, as far as Cleveland, to the slow-going mail of the day, and only reached the general on the second of July. Another communication from the same office, of comparatively little importance, sent out at an earlier hour of the same day by special messenger, had come to hand eight days earlier. British interests had been looked after with more vigilance, and the authorities in Canada were notified of the state of war with the utmost promptness. The immediate and very natural consequence was that the vessel which Hull had sent forward from the Rapids was seized when passing the British post of Malden, the astonished crew receiving their first notification that hostilities existed from the demand made for their surrender.

But this capture of the general's baggage and papers was not the only injurious consequence of the criminal neglect of the war department. The secretary, in communicating to him so leisurely the fact that war had been declared, had apparently overlooked altogether the exposed post of Mackinaw, which from its situation and surroundings would be liable to immediate and overwhelming assault, unless at once reinforced and strengthened. He assumed that the general might be able at once to take the offensive, and suggested the capture of Malden, and an extension of conquests as circumstances might seem to justify. General Hull on receiving the communication immediately pushed forward to Detroit. But the British authorities had lost no time in communicating the declaration of war to the officer in command on the island of St. Joseph; and that officer, though his own force was insignificant, had experienced no difficulty in collecting, within the short space of eight days, by the aid of British fur companies and the friendly Indians, a force of a thousand men. With this force on July 16th he started to reduce Mackinaw, and landing in the night-time, and taking up a position commanding the fort, he was able in the morning to announce his presence at the cannon's mouth. The garrison consisted of but fifty-seven effective men, and had no alternative but that of surrender.

The possession of Mackinaw as a means of con-

THE BRITISH CONTROL OF LAKE ERIE. 171

trol over the Indians inhabiting that part of the country was at this time of the very highest importance. Nothing but a show of force held those Indians in a neutral position, and not even this remained when Mackinaw was lost. The circumstances of the loss, also, were such as to bring the American authorities into contempt among the savage tribes. The prestige of success was now with the British, and such motives as had tended to restrain the savages from gratifying their inclinations to take arms in the British service were gone. They were emboldened also to expect an easy and speedy success over Hull; and as a consequence the woods about Detroit and other settlements in Michigan were swarming with hostile savages, before there had been opportunity to take precautionary measures for protection.

But by far the most important fact in the existing situation was that which Hull had endeavored to convince the administration must control; namely, that the British had undisputed mastery of Lake Erie. While they held command of that lake, Hull's communications were at their mercy. Such road as then existed between Detroit and the Ohio settlements was poor at the best, and at times almost impassable. It followed along the river and the western end of the lake to the Rapids of the Maumee; and from the post of Malden it was so easy at any time to throw a British force upon it, that a strong military convoy was a necessity whenever supplies were to be sent. For the defense of the communications a considerable force was therefore required beyond what would otherwise be needed for the protection of Detroit; but no force could make them entirely secure against sudden and disastrous assaults. It is not likely that Hull, in this condition of affairs, saw anything to change his previous opinion that control of the lake must be secured, or Detroit sooner or later must fall.

But Hull very well knew it was the expectation of the department and of the country that he would immediately commence operations to reduce a province which was supposed to be ready to fall into his hands. He therefore crossed the river into Canada on the 12th of July, dislodging and scattering a small force which had collected at Sandwich. He also immediately, in pursuance of the policy of "fraternity" which Mr. Randolph had so pointedly ridiculed, issued a proclamation to the Canadians in which he tendered them "the invaluable blessings of civil, political, and religious liberty, and their necessary result, individual and general prosperity." Detachments from his army pushed out into the country and secured some provisions, and one under the command of Colonel Cass took possession of the bridge over Aux Canards in the direction of Malden. The army at the time was eager to attack Malden, but the opinion of General Hull was against it. A council of war, when the river was first crossed, had decided against an immediate attack, and though the army had since received an important supply of field artillery, the commander did not believe an attack would be prudent. Meantime his supply of provisions, which was not very abundant at the outset, was rapidly diminishing, and his alarm was excited on that score. Learning that a company of Ohio troops was at Frenchtown with provisions for his relief, he detached Major Van Horne with two hundred men to escort them to Detroit, but the officer in command at Malden had early information of the movement, and a small force was sent across the river in the night, which fell upon Van Horne and totally routed him. Here was new cause of anxiety to General Hull, and very striking evidence that his previous fears were not groundless.

The calamity to Van Horne was followed by information from Niagara which increased his uneasiness to such an extent as to impress him that his position in Canada was critical. He now learned that the British had sent reinforcements to Malden, and that others were on their way; that their movements indicated an intended attack upon him, and that he could expect no diversion at Niagara in his favor. Impressed by this information with a sense of immediate danger, the general, without counseling with his officers, on the night of August 7th recrossed the river with his whole army to Detroit. The movement had all the appearance of a flight under a panic, and was generally condemned by subordinate officers.

The reason why Hull was to expect no diversion from Niagara in his behalf was that General Dearborn, who was in command of the American forces at that point, had entered into an armistice with Sir George Prevost, the British commander at Queenstown, whereby his hands were tied from rendering General Hull any assistance. Having hurried off to Malden a considerable force under General Brock, Sir George had the address to secure the assent of General Dearborn to an armistice, whereby it was agreed that the forces opposing each other on the Niagara should act on the defensive only; thus protecting his own depleted force by this stratagem, while Hull was left to his own resources and to such aid as an administration of phenomenal inefficiency would be likely to render him. The armistice was subject to disapproval at Washington, but the mischief which the British commander intended was accomplished before the disapproval by the government could be notified.

Immediately on recrossing the river Hull detached Colonel Miller with six hundred men to do what Van Horne had failed to accomplish, namely, to open communications and bring forward supplies from Frenchtown. At Monguagon a force of British and Indians was found intrenched, and this was attacked and routed. A severe rain-storm coming on, and the rations proving to be lost or destroyed, the detachment was ordered back to Detroit, and another sent out under McArthur and Cass, by a route farther back from the river. This was on August 14th. On the next day General Brock appeared at Sandwich with a force which he reports at 1,330, and sent a demand to General Hull for a surrender. This being refused he opened fire, but with little effect. On the morning of the 16th he crossed the river at Springwells, in plain sight of the fort and without opposition, and renewed his demand for surrender. Hull, whose effective force then at the fort was rated by Cass at 1,060, but by himself at much less, immediately entered into negotiations for surrender, stipulating only for the protection of the people and of private property, and for the parole of the state troops which had been sent to his assistance, but were not yet arrived. The forces of McArthur and Cass were included in the stipulation, but the fiery spirit of Cass could not brook the indignity, and he broke his sword rather than surrender it. From all sides the concurring testimony is abundant that the army under Hull, confident in its ability to repel the British assault, was awaiting the attack in good spirits when the order to haul down the American flag was given. They had the mortification to see the flag lowered without a blow in its defense; and with Detroit all Michigan passed under British control.

The indignation of the army at what seemed to them a pusillanimous surrender was intense, and its expression found an answering echo in every part of the country. Great things had been expected of this army, and the ambitious colonels of regiments had anticipated nothing so little as a result inglorious to American arms. The first suggestion to thousands of minds was that Hull, from some corrupt motive, must purposely and treasonably have betrayed his army. He was actually put on trial on a charge of treason, coupled with others of cowardice and criminal neglect of duty, before a court-martial of which General Dearborn was president; and though acquitted of the most serious charge, he was convicted of the others, and sentenced to be shot to death. The president approved the conviction, but in consideration of former meritorious services remitted the penalty.

When time had softened the asperities which the surrender evoked, General Hull appealed from this conviction to the judgment of his contemporaries, basing his defense upon the following propositions. First: That his army was cut off from supplies with no adequate means of opening communications, and that so situated it must inevitably fall. Second: That in his actual situation to fight would have been a useless expenditure of life, and would unnecessarily have exposed the inhabitants of the territory to Indian hostilities. Third: That the situation was not his own fault,

HULL'S FALSE STEP. 177

but was in part the fault of the general government, and of General Dearborn, and in part of circumstances for which perhaps no one was responsible. Fourth: That his force at the time was much inferior to that of General Brock; and Fifth: That his provisions were so nearly exhausted that surrender for that reason would soon have been inevitable even if his force had been adequate. The judgment of the country has not acquitted Hull of fault. That his effective force was smaller than that of General Brock seems probable. The latter in his official report stated the forces captured at 2,500; a gross exaggeration, which must have been intended to magnify his success beyond its true proportions. The same motive might have led him, and possibly did, to understate his own force. And the situation was such that while Brock might expect accessions from Indians and militia, Hull could look for none immediately from any source.

But armies have often, under far more disadvantageous circumstances, won signal victories; and while the men were confident and eager to put courage to the test, the general had no business to be discouraged. The men believed they could repulse the enemy in his attempt to cross; and they should have been given the opportunity for a trial. But when he had crossed they felt safe within the fort; and the scarcity of provisions could have been no ground for surrender until the enemy had demonstrated his ability to keep the garrison behind its defenses.

The ground of defense which has most strongly appealed to the sympathy of the world was that a vigorous resistance would have subjected the inhabitants to the danger of massacre at the hands of the hostile Indians. This the general, who as governor must have been familiar with the face of nearly every man, woman, and child in the little town of Detroit, professed to contemplate with horror. And if the defense of his post had been plainly impossible, he might upon this ground have been excused from making the vain attempt. But as a military commander his first duty was to defend the posts committed to his charge; and he had no right while that was possible to permit his sympathies to overcome his sense of public duty. War is cruel at the best, and the commander of an army expects to inflict cruelties instead of laying down his arms to prevent them. A possible massacre of non-combatants is always incident to a warfare in which savages are employed, and constitutes a reason with civilized nations for refusing to employ them. But General Hull knew very well that for a military commander to suffer the possible barbarities of the opposing force to be accepted as a reason for relaxing the vigor of his efforts, or for surrendering his charge while it was still in his power to make defense, was to give the savage an importance in war beyond his proper military effectiveness, and to make his very cruelty and his disregard of the rules of civilized warfare a reason for employing him. Instead of yielding to such considerations, his duty on the other hand would be to make his defense all the more persistent and vigorous, that his antagonist might be made to see that loss rather than gain was to follow from bringing into the field a force so wicked and so uncontrollable in its barbarity.

But what was put beyond question by Hull's defense was that his fault began when he accepted a task which he believed it was not in his power to accomplish. Without the command of the lake he had declared that Detroit must fall; and yet without command of the lake he had undertaken its defense. When, therefore, the enemy came and demanded a surrender, his judgment, deliberately formed, assented immediately to the demand, because he believed resistance would be hopeless. It was not necessary to suggest physical cowardice: the want of confidence in the ability to make defense of the post had been made known to the government before his appointment. When the government persisted in offering him the command, his duty was either to decline it absolutely, or to let the courage of others supply the deficiency of his own, even though the task might seem to be an attempt to accomplish the impossible.

The judgment of the court-martial upon General Hull has never as a judgment had much weight with the people. It was ordered by an administration whose blunders in management had been at least equally blamable with his own conduct, and it was presided over by an officer whose position in respect to some of the questions involved was such as to suggest a suspicion that he could not be wholly unbiased. The importance to the defense of Detroit of a command of the lake was afterwards so fully demonstrated that the prosecution of the officer who pointed it out in advance, by the government which could not understand or appreciate it, seemed to partake of cruelty.

On taking possession of Detroit, General Brock issued a proclamation announcing that the American laws should continue in force so long as the peace and safety of the territory would admit. Colonel Proctor was made civil governor with full powers, and he immediately issued regulations for the government of the territory, whereby the civil officers remaining in the territory were for the most part continued in the discharge of their respective functions, and the courts were to be open as usual. And what proved to be of more importance to the people than any of the other regulations, Chief Justice Woodward was designated to act as secretary.

This able and fearless official, who in time of

peace had so stretched his prerogative to the annoyance of the governor, had now an opportunity to appear in a character which justly won for him the gratitude of the people whose interests in a measure were committed to his keeping. For a time his influence with Colonel Proctor was considerable, and he was ready on all occasions to employ it in mitigating the evils of war to his countrymen. But Proctor soon gave such unmistakable evidence of a tyrannical nature that no one who sympathized with the people placed by the fortune of war at his mercy could possibly for any considerable time coöperate with him in harmony. It does not appear that any breach took place in their official relations until after the defeat of Winchester at Frenchtown, but the atrocities which attended and followed that disaster to the American arms, and the use which the temporary governor at Detroit would have made of it to bring an unwilling people to abjure allegiance to their own government, not only excited the indignation of the chief justice, but convinced him that he could no longer be useful in the attempt to coöperate with a man so wanting in proper feeling and so unobservant of the common rights of humanity.

The military operations important in their bearing upon the final possession of Michigan, after the capture of Detroit, can be briefly stated. Fort Dearborn at Chicago, which was within the jurisdiction of General Hull, was abandoned on the 15th of August, in pursuance of an order which he had sent, but the garrison in returning was captured by hostile Indians and in part massacred. An army entitled the Army of the West was soon put in process of formation, under the command of General Harrison, who was expected to operate against Upper Canada, and to repossess the country lost by Hull. In January, 1813, General Harrison was at Sandusky, from which place he sent orders to General Winchester at Fort Defiance to move forward and take post at the Rapids of the Maumee, which was promptly accomplished. At the Rapids Winchester received an urgent appeal from Frenchtown for protection against British and Indians who were then threatening to plunder the settlement, and he sent out a detachment of near seven hundred men to their assistance. The enemy were attacked and scattered with considerable loss, and Winchester on receiving information of the affair, went forward himself with a small reinforcement, and assumed the command. The force which had preceded him was quartered behind pickets in the settlement, and the reinforcement encamped in the open field. Here at daybreak of the next morning, January 22d, Winchester was attacked by a British force from Malden under the command of Proctor, and nearly the whole detachment was killed or captured. Winchester himself was among the prisoners, and many of his men in endeavoring to escape were tomahawked by Indians. Meantime an assault upon the pickets had been repulsed with heavy loss; but Proctor having made Winchester believe he could easily destroy the village and drive out the military with his artillery, and that a massacre by the Indians would follow, the latter weakly sent orders for surrender. Major Madison, who was in command, declined to obey until assured of protection against the Indians, and the proper assurances were given. Private property was to be respected, a guard was to be provided for the wounded, and sleighs furnished for their removal to Malden.

If any attempt was made to keep faith with these stipulations, it was so feeble and ill-conducted that it accomplished little or nothing. Proctor did indeed take to Malden under the protection of his own soldiers such of the prisoners as were able to walk, but the wounded were left behind, where they were plundered by straggling savages; and after the main body of the Indians had moved off to Stony Creek, a band, some two hundred in number, unable longer to restrain their savage propensities, hurried back to Frenchtown, and began an indiscriminate slaughter. Well has a historian of Canada said, in alluding to this affair: "It is a subject of eternal regret to every true Briton that those biped bloodhounds should have run under the shadow of our standard so long and so late."[1]

The criminality of Proctor in respect to the massacre of Frenchtown was enhanced, if that be possible, by the fact that citizens, in anticipation of a battle, had specially called his attention to the probability of such an occurrence. Judge Woodward, in a subsequent communication reviewing the facts, reminded him of the previous apprehensions of the people, which had induced them to press the subject upon his attention previous to the battle, and that their fears had been quieted by his assurance that he considered his own honor pledged for their effectual protection. Proctor affected to disbelieve the reports of barbarities, and called upon the judge for proofs. They were furnished in great abundance, and the story, which was cruel enough when told in summary, was only the more sickening and horrible when given in detail. Proctor, also, as if that to any extent could excuse the massacre, intimated, without directly affirming, that the surrender had been made without pledge of protection on his part; but he was very properly reminded that the principles of the law of nations impose an obligation almost equally strong; and the judge might very justly have added that a commander who advances the fact that his prisoners surrendered without first demanding assurances that they shall

[1] Garneau's *History of Canada*, by Bell, vol. ii. p. 293.

be treated according to the rules of civilized war as excuse or palliation for his conduct in suffering them to be massacred, is adding, by the brutality of the excuse, to the original enormity.

For some time after the massacre there might frequently be seen on the streets of Detroit women and children led or driven as the prisoners of savages, and considerable sums were paid by humane people for their ransom. Meantime Proctor, not yet satisfied with the misery inflicted upon the territory, undertook to coerce the citizens of Detroit into taking an oath of allegiance to the king. He seems to have intimated a desire to have the assistance of Judge Woodward in this business; but that officer, with no little indignation, told him that "in a state of open and declared war a subject or citizen of one party cannot transfer his allegiance to the other party without incurring the penalties of treason; and while nothing can excuse *his* guilt, so neither are those innocent who lay temptations before him." Proctor also, without just cause so far as is known, ordered from the town a considerable number of its leading citizens, in palpable violation of the terms of Hull's capitulation, which stipulated for the protection of persons and private property. They made spirited protest, but it had no effect upon the British commander; and Judge Woodward, apparently convinced that he could no longer be of service to his countrymen by remaining in Detroit as the subordinate of so arbitrary a ruler, withdrew from the territory that he might give the facts to the world. He returned when peace was restored, and took up again his judicial functions.

The capture of Winchester was followed by successive attacks under the leadership of Proctor on Forts Meigs and Stephenson, where his repulse was so decided that he deemed it prudent to fall back with precipitation upon Malden. But the career of this obnoxious officer was now rapidly drawing to a close. On the 10th of September, 1813, Commodore Perry won his great victory over Commodore Barclay at Put-in Bay, capturing the entire British squadron. Making use of the captured vessels for convoy, the army of Harrison, now largely reinforced, was transferred to Canada and took up offensive operations. Proctor, in great haste, proceeded to dismantle the fortress at Malden preparatory to flight. To the great Indian chieftain this looked like an act of cowardice, and he made earnest protest against it. In a formal speech Tecumseh said to his superior officer, "You have got the arms and ammunition which our great father sent for his red children. If you have an idea of going away, give them to us, and then for all we care you may go and welcome. Our lives are in the hands of the Great Spirit. We are determined to defend our lands, and if it be his will we wish to leave our bones upon them." But the protest and the plainly implied censure were alike in vain. Malden and Detroit were both evacuated and a hasty retreat made. Detroit on September 29th was reoccupied by an American detachment, and Proctor was pursued and overtaken at the Moravian town, where he sustained a crushing defeat, and only escaped capture by precipitate flight, looking, as some of his own people said, more after his baggage than after his army. Tecumseh, who among Americans had in all respects a better reputation than his superior, and was looked upon as honorable and humane, was killed in the engagement.

This victory effectually broke for the time the British power in Western Canada, and was the end of important military operations in the vicinity of Detroit. Colonel Cass, much to the satisfaction of the people, was stationed with his regiment at that place and given the command. Mackinaw still remained in the hands of the British, and an attempt made by Colonel Croghan to recover it in July, 1814, proved abortive. It was only restored after the conclusion of peace in the spring of the following year.

After the death of Tecumseh a considerable number of Indians abandoned their British allies, and some of them offered their services to Colonel Cass and were accepted and enrolled by him. But it was not easy to subject them to proper discipline, and their thirst for plunder was so uncontrollable that Colonel Cass did not long retain them. Hostile Indians hovered about Detroit and committed occasional depredations until after the peace with Great Britain. A mounted force was sent up from Ohio as a protection against them, and they were soon brought under such fear of punishment as kept them for the most part to a proper observance of the rights of others.

CHAPTER X.

THE BEGINNINGS OF ACTIVE AMERICAN SETTLEMENT.

MICHIGAN had great good fortune in her second territorial governor. Lewis Cass, born in New Hampshire, had settled at Marietta at the age of seventeen, and had had abundant opportunity to become thoroughly acquainted with the Northwest and its people. He was a lawyer of exceptional ability; he had been in the legislature of Ohio when the mysterious conspiracy of Burr excited and alarmed the country, and had drawn and procured the passage of a law to reach and punish such conspiracies. Afterwards he had served as marshal of Ohio, on the appointment of Mr. Jefferson. On the breaking out of war with Great Britain, he had entered into military service, with the ambition and courage to make the aggressive campaign which the country had expected of Hull. His severe condemnation of that officer, in a letter to the war department, had attracted the attention of the country, and been generally accepted as conclusive of Hull's criminality. Afterwards he had taken part in the brilliant campaign of Harrison, which ended in the destruction of the British army in western Canada, the killing of Tecumseh, and the ignominious flight of Proctor. He had then been assigned to the command at Detroit and became military governor of Michigan. The president could have made no appointment of civil governor more likely to be useful or acceptable to the people.

The territory was also fortunate in its secretary. This office was of great importance, as the secretary, in the absence of the governor, would become acting governor *ex officio*. William Woodbridge was selected for this place, like Cass a lawyer of prominence at Marietta. The two men were as different as possible: the governor, a man of the world, of robust health and active temperament, fond of politics and a natural leader; the secretary, more frail and of a retiring disposition, and never so happy as when busy at his quiet home among his books. On political questions the two were commonly found in opposition, but there were no unseemly disagreements during the long time they held offices so mutually related, and their official intercourse was always decorous and agreeable, though they were never specially intimate.

The number of French farms, particularly on the river Detroit, had been slowly increasing. Secretary Woodbridge has left us a picturesque description of their appearance from the river as he came up to take possession of his office: the row of long and narrow farms, with cultivation only in front; the houses of one story, most of them from ten to eighty years old and fashioned a little like the houses of the low Dutch about New York; and the moss-grown crucifixes everywhere on gates, barns, and houses, — this was what appeared on either side the river.

But it was still to be said of Michigan that its few settlements were far on the frontier, and that its leading interest was that which gathered its harvests in the wilderness. John Jacob Astor had appeared in the fur trade a little before the war, and had negotiated with the British fur companies for the purchase of their interests on the American side of the boundary, but the war had broken up the arrangements, and after it was over Congress, in his interest, passed a law prohibiting foreign traders from prosecuting their enterprises within the limits of the United States. This law, as a retaliatory measure, was perfectly just, for the British companies, by their organization and the manner in which they had employed it in the capture of Mackinaw, had given ample demonstration that they were capable of performing the service of a military force, and that they constituted an ever-present danger to the settlements. It was evident, also, that their interests were opposed to the settlement of the country; and if this fact did not prompt them to foster an unfriendly feeling on the part of the Indians towards the Americans, it would without doubt keep alive an influence against further cessions of land by the Indian tribes. The exclusion of British fur dealers from American territory was, therefore, justifiable on sound reasons of public policy; and Mr. Astor as the American Fur Company, with his headquarters on the island of Mackinaw, soon had the woods full of savage and half savage people, working in his interest and gathering for him the forest treasures that soon made him one of the great merchant princes of the world.

The fur trade, however, could neither colonize Michigan nor enrich it. It brought some money and some goods into the territory and assisted in giving a certain activity to business at the centres of trade. But the period immediately following the war was one of great depression and general stagnation in business, and the derangement of the currency was such that losses from that source were constant and unavoidable. Steady progress and prosperity were impossible while this state of things continued.

Michigan also needed to be better known. The country knew almost nothing of it, and the common belief was that there was a fine belt of territory on the eastern border, but that the interior was a vast swamp which might well be abandoned to fur-bearing animals and the trappers and hunters. This belief was countenanced by the geographers of the day; for even Morse, who was considered authority, gave it currency in the books which were made use of in colleges and schools. It was supported also by the reports of surveyors who were sent out by the general government, and who reported without much investigation what they supposed to be the fact. A notable instance is that of the party who were charged with the duty of making surveys for bounty lands for the soldiers who had served in the late war. These surveyors professed to have made an examination of the country, beginning at the northern terminus of the boundary line between Ohio and Indiana and proceeding thence north fifty miles; and they reported finding only tamarack swamps, bogs, and sand barrens, with not one acre in a hundred fit for cultivation; a most astounding report, and quite impossible to have been honestly made, if they had examined the country as they professed to have done. But it was conclusive for the time, and the soldiers were sent farther west for their bounty lands, not probably to their advantage.

Other causes besides ignorance of the country were delaying its settlement. Many Indians were still in the territory, whose presence was disquieting, and the governor deemed it of high importance that, so far as should be found possible consistently with justice, they should be removed to the distant west. They had, now, in two wars been employed by the British against the Americans, and they were regular pensioners on British bounty. They gathered annually in considerable numbers at Malden and at Drummond's Island to receive payments and presents, and while their attachment to the British was thus perpetuated, their animosity to the Americans was to some extent kept alive also. They passed back and forth through the territory in large bands, and were likely to encamp in the vicinity of white settlements, whenever there was opportunity for doing so, and their drunken orgies and savage antics made them a source of constant dread and danger.

Governor Cass, therefore, who was made superintendent of Indian affairs for the Northwest, gave early attention to the extinguishment of the Indian title. One treaty of cession was made as early as 1814; another and very important one was concluded at Fort Meigs, on September 29, 1817, by which the Wyandot, Seneca, Delaware, Shawanese, Pottawatamie, Ottawa, and Chippewa tribes of Indians surrendered nearly all the lands they claimed in Ohio, and large districts in Indiana and Michigan, constituting in all nearly four millions of acres. Sixteen other treaties were negotiated during his administration, mainly through his management, resulting in the transfer of a large part of the Indians to the country west of the Mississippi. In all his dealings with them the governor proceeded in a spirit of perfect fairness, refusing at any time to resort to coercion,

SALES OF PUBLIC LANDS. 195

but waiting for a more propitious day when he found success by fair means impossible. He thus preserved for himself the respect of the Indians, and secured for his people their good will.

It was next important that the lands acquired by the United States should be brought into market. Congress in 1796 had provided for the survey and sale of the public lands in sections of six hundred and forty acres, at a minimum price of two dollars an acre, giving credit for a part of the purchase-price if desired. Changes were afterwards made in the interest of purchasers with small means, and in 1817 sales in eighty-acre lots were authorized. In 1818 the surveys had so far progressed that sales were begun in Michigan. In 1820 the minimum price was reduced to one dollar twenty-five cents an acre. Ten years later preëmption rights began to be given to actual settlers upon the public lands. By this legislation it was made easy for any prudent and industrious person to obtain land sufficient for moderate wants.

Governor Cass meanwhile was active and vigilant in furthering the interests of his government. In 1818, on the admission of Illinois to the Union as a state, the territory of Michigan had been enlarged by the addition to it of all that part of the Northwest Territory lying west of Lake Michigan and north of Illinois; an addition, the value of which was at the time very little known. The governor now determined to visit in person the upper lake region, with a view to inquire into the condition of the Indians, their numbers and sentiments ; to explain to them that their annual visits to the British authorities at Malden were offensive to him and must be discontinued; to obtain further cessions if possible; to investigate the copper region; and to make himself familiar with facts concerning the British and American fur trade. This comprehensive plan was carried out by the governor in 1820, when he traversed the lakes with a party in open boats, holding councils with the Indians by the way, at one of which a cession of land at the Sault St. Marie was secured. But the Indians were generally found to be unfriendly and completely under British control. At the Sault, when the governor signified his purpose to construct a new fort, there were plain intimations that it would not be permitted, and one of the chiefs spurned with a contemptuous kick the presents which had been laid out for him. When the council broke up for the day, the Indians withdrew and raised the British flag before the tent of one of their chiefs; but Governor Cass, on perceiving it, immediately proceeded, without arms and unattended, to take it down and bear it away with him, regardless of the menacing aspect of the savages and of their muttered threats. It was a bold act but as wise as it was bold, and though for a time an armed collision seemed imminent, the undaunted demeanor of the governor had its effect, and the Indians, when they were given distinctly to understand that the fort would be built and American supremacy maintained, returned to the council in a more submissive mood, and consented to enter upon an amicable consideration of the subjects the governor brought before it.

Another matter of immediate and pressing importance was that of roads. Immigrants could not come into the territory in any considerable numbers so long as they must find their way through the woods by trails, or by roads cut out but never worked, and which in a little while by use became nearly impassable. At the conclusion of the war there were no good roads anywhere in the territory. Lake Erie was then open, but there were no regular passenger vessels of any kind upon it. Neither was there any considerable population bordering it from which Michigan might expect accessions. Such immigration as then came to the territory would be likely to take the road around the west end of Lake Erie, a road the national importance of which, not less for military than for civil purposes, had been fully demonstrated in the late war. The governor, therefore, with the efficient aid of the secretary, called the attention of the federal government to it, and the secretary in person pressed it upon the attention of Congress with such effect that an appropriation in aid of it was at length secured. The resources of the territory, so far as with reason they could be applied to this purpose, were appropriated to the construction of a highway from Detroit to Chicago, and other roads of similar importance, and it became possible to penetrate the territory in various directions with the ordinary means of country transportation, as it had never been before. The results were so beneficial that the population of the territory, which for fifty years had been nearly stationary, began steadily, though slowly, to increase, and by 1820 not only had the losses by the war been made good, but the number of the people was found to be twice as great as it was at the preceding census.

Meantime the question of change in the territorial government was being agitated. In 1818, under a belief that the population of the territory now entitled the people to be represented in the legislative department, the question was submitted to a popular vote, whether they desired to be thus represented. The answer by the voters, the most of whom were still French, was a decided negative. The people had found nothing to object to in the existing government and they cared for no change. Moreover, to them the duties and the burdens of government seem to have had no special attractions. They were also still poor from the exhaustion of the war, and the cost of the proposed change in government was used as a powerful argument against it. They were, however, given the privilege of electing a delegate to Congress in 1819, and William Woodbridge was first chosen. After a short incumbency he retired, and was succeeded by Judge Solomon Sibley, and he in turn by Father Richard.

Father Richard was now in his sixtieth year. He had built St. Anne's Church at Detroit under many difficulties of a pecuniary nature, and he now officiated there to a large congregation. He was a favorite with the people at large, and was easily persuaded that, as territorial delegate, he might be exceptionally useful at Washington. But he was not universally liked by his parishioners, with whose faults he was not over-indulgent; and it is a fact not unworthy of mention that when elected delegate he was under arrest on an execution in favor of one of them. One of his people had obtained a divorce from his wife contrary to the laws of the church, and had then married again; and the father arraigned him in church and denounced him, in the presence of the congregation, as an adulterer. For this language he was prosecuted and a judgment of a thousand dollars obtained, which he refused to pay, preferring to suffer imprisonment, rather than recognize the rightfulness of this judicial interference with his clerical functions. His privilege as a member of Congress enabled him to obtain relief for the time being, and eventually the equally plain privilege belonging to his sacred office was very properly recognized by the court, and the judgment arrested. He served one term as delegate to the satisfaction of the people, and was then succeeded by Austin E. Wing, some of the Catholics leading the opposition which defeated him. But he turned patiently and without complaint to his more legitimate work, to which he devoted himself with unwearied assiduity until 1832, when he fell a victim to the cholera, dying full of years, and grateful for the long life of labor and usefulness which had been accorded him.

Long before this time other denominations of Christians had come to be represented in the territory by their teachers and pastors; the Methodists, who in the new West have commonly been the pioneers, were gathering a little congregation at Detroit as early as 1809, and in 1816 the Rev. John Monteith, of whom we shall hear again, was delivering carefully prepared written discourses with decided Calvinistic leaning, to Protestants without distinction. And before long began changes in government. In 1823 the legislative power was finally transferred from the governor and judges to the governor and a council of nine, the members of the council being selected by the president and confirmed by the Senate from eighteen chosen by the people. By this change Michigan was advanced to the second grade in territorial government. Two years later came another change in the increase of the councilmen to thirteen, and in 1827 the exclusive power of choice was left to the people.

This last change, which established the third grade in territorial government, made the people to a large extent self-governing. It may be assumed to have been made on the recommendation of the governor, for it was in entire accord with his well known views. Though in his own office a creature of executive power, he was a thorough believer in self-government of the people, and desired to see the power of appointment which was vested in him transferred to the voters. In one of his messages he urged an application to Congress for a change of the law in this regard, and he sometimes advised the holding of popular elections as a guide to his own action in making appointments. But the democratic tendencies of his mind were perhaps most distinctly manifested in his recommendations on the subject of popular education, of which more will be heard farther on.

Under the organic law the governor had power to organize counties, and this power he exercised freely as occasion required. In 1825 the legislative council was empowered to divide the counties into townships, and the township system was then introduced which in its main features has continued to this day. But other changes were now taking place which were quite as significant in their influence upon the growth and prosperity of the territory as the changes in government. Previous to 1809 there had been no printing press in the territory and Governor Hull was compelled to procure the printing of his orders and proclamations — when they were printed at all — several hundred miles away. Even the laws were not printed as they appeared, and some of them, remaining in manuscript, were mislaid or abstracted and all evidence of them lost. The first printing press was brought to the territory in 1809 by Father Richard, and a little paper called the "Michigan Essay and Impartial Observer" started; but it had brief existence. In 1816 the Cass Code, as it was popularly called, was published. It was, in the main, a mere abstract of the laws in force, the territorial funds not justifying a full publication. In 1817 the day of newspapers for Michigan had come, and the "Detroit Gazette" was begun, followed in 1825 by another paper at Detroit, in 1829 by a third at Ann Arbor, and in 1830 by others at Monroe and Pontiac. These were not merely journals of current news, but at times they discussed public affairs and important political questions with ability and vigor. Now also dawned the day of steamboats. The Walk-in-the-Water made its appearance at Detroit in 1818 and was hailed as the harbinger of a new era. The next year it advanced as far as Mackinaw, to the astonishment of the savages who were mischievously made to believe it was drawn by a team of trained sturgeons. The great event of the period, however, and that which had most to do with giving sudden impetus to the growth of Michigan and bringing to it the population that shortly had planted settlements and reared churches and school-houses all through its central and southern parts, was the opening in 1825 of the Erie Canal. It was not long after this before steamers were abundant on the lakes; no less than seven on Lake Erie in 1826, and four years thereafter a daily line was running between Detroit and Buffalo. The fort at Detroit was abandoned, as having become an anachronism, in 1827, and in the same year flour began on a small scale to be exported. In 1830 the population had risen to 32,538, and the territory was self-supporting. By the time Governor Cass was summoned by President Jackson to a seat in his cabinet in 1831, the little frontier settlements which he had come on to defend in 1812 had extended and spread to the dimensions of a commonwealth under his judicious and statesmanlike care and nurture.

There was some feeling of territorial pride that Jackson had looked to this distant region for a member of his cabinet, but the people of the territory parted with the governor with great reluctance. He had not only managed the public affairs with ability and unquestioned integrity, but his example had been excellent and his influence of the best. Governing frontier settlements where rough characters abounded and roystering habits prevailed, he was always in his own deportment courteous and complaisant, always abstemious, always self-respecting; and as unexceptionable in his private character and in all his domestic and social relations as he was in his public capacity and deportment. Permanent American settlement may be said to have begun with him; and it was a great and lasting boon to Michigan when it was given a governor at once so able, so patriotic, so attentive to his duties, and so worthy in his public and private life of respect and esteem.

CHAPTER XI.

THE TERRITORY ADVANCES TO THE DIGNITY OF A STATE.

WHEN Lewis Cass resigned the office of governor of Michigan, there were living within the territory many men of ability and education, who were thoroughly familiar with its affairs and fully possessed of the public confidence. The appointment of any one of these to the vacant office would have been recognized as that of a competent and suitable person. Some of them — as, for example, William Woodbridge, who had been secretary of the territory, and as such had occasionally acted as governor in the absence of Governor Cass, and who, after resigning the office of secretary, had been successively delegate in Congress and judge, and Austin E. Wing, who had also been delegate in Congress — were already well known at Washington, and others might have been known through Governor Cass had he been consulted. The late governor was a democrat by conviction and not merely in a party sense; it was no new doctrine with him, when, in his famous Nicholson letter, previous to the meeting of the nominating convention of his party in 1848, he laid down the proposition respecting the inherent right of the people of the territories to self-government which, by way of ridicule, was christened by his opponents as the doctrine of squatter sovereignty; he had himself as governor endeavored to devolve upon the people as belonging to them of right such appointing power as the law had confided to him; and it is not probable, had he been consulted by the president respecting officers for the territory he was leaving, that he would have advised looking beyond the territory itself for such officers, or that he would have felt any difficulty in naming perfectly competent men, who had cast their fortunes with the territory, for every important office in it. It is very rare that a new community in a frontier region contains among its members so many men of culture and ability as Michigan had among its citizens while it remained a territory; and there could have been no just excuse for treating it as a community unfit to govern itself, and requiring rulers sent in from abroad to govern it. This had been necessary in the case of the Northwest Territory, for the settlement was in its infancy and everybody was a new-comer when the organization took place; and it was excusable also in the cases of earlier appointments for Michigan, considering its peculiar population and circumstances. The excuse no longer existed in view of the large, intelligent, and self-respecting population which the territory had acquired.

But a period had now arrived constituting a new era in American politics, when for a long time no general maxim of government was to be so powerful at Washington as the maxim that to the victor belong the spoils of office. This maxim of war, when war meant robbery and plunder, was now being adopted in the civil administration of the government, and was to vitalize all political life and be the chief spring of all political action and energy. As the people of the territories had no vote, they constituted no part of the victors who had captured and taken possession of the general government, and were, therefore, entitled to no consideration in the distribution of rewards. These must go to Virginia, Pennsylvania, and other states, where many citizens who had shown their patriotism by their labors in electing the president were now waiting in expectation of receiving their share in the division of what had been won at that election. Personal fitness for office was found in the fact that claims had been established by labors in securing the election of the presidential incumbent, and this, if not sufficient for all cases, would seem to have been thought ample in the case of a merely territorial position. But circumstances of a more personal nature might also have some influence, and it therefore caused no surprise when Mr. John T. Mason of Virginia, brother-in-law to the late Postmaster-general Barry, but wholly ignorant of the territory and its people, was appointed territorial secretary. What fitness he might have developed for the office no one can tell, as he soon elected not to discharge its duties, and went abroad on an enterprise for private parties. The president thereupon transferred the appointment to Stevens T. Mason, his son. The only reason ever advanced for this selection, and the only one that could have existed, was that the father requested it.

The appointment of a successor to Governor Cass had not as yet been made, and by law the new secretary would be acting governor and also acting superintendent of Indian affairs. A rumor soon spread that young Mason was under the age of legal majority; that in fact he was but nineteen years of age; and his personal appearance indicated the truth of the rumor. A committee of citizens was thereupon appointed to inquire into the facts; and on calling upon him was frankly told by the young gentleman that he was indeed under age, but he added that the president very well knew the fact when he made the appointment. Young as the secretary was, he had not failed to imbibe the spirit which was dictating the distribution of political favors; and he justified the appointment to the committee on the ground that the emoluments of the office were needed for the support of his father's family while the father was absent from the country. To a committee, some of whose members had the old-fashioned notion that offices were to be created and filled on public, not on private considerations, the reason assigned seemed only an aggravation of the original wrong. The papers of the day declared that the people of the territory were outraged by this attempt to place a boy in authority over gray heads. Even the Indians, it was said, would know better than this. "They know, if we do not, that age and talents are to be treated with respect, and that boys are not to mingle in the councils of the elders; much less to assume authority over them." But the people wasted breath and the editors their ink. The president was taking care of his friends, and was making precedents to be followed and enjoyed by many successors. If it pleased him to send a boy to sit in the seat of Cass and play governor, complaints of the people concerned would no more move him than the howling of wild beasts in their forests. The official organ at Washington, a large part of whose business it was to defend removals made at the mere will of the president, did indeed take notice of the complaints, but only to advance, with assumed gravity, in reply to their protests, that as young Mason, whether properly appointed or not, was now in office, he could not with propriety be removed so long as he was not guilty of official misconduct; and with this answer the people were forced to content themselves as best they might. But in a new country, with much that is new constantly demanding attention, a good-natured people are not likely to nurture resentments; and when, at a parting banquet to the late governor, after wine had flowed freely and merriment was at its height, the elder Mason appealed to the assembled guests to "give the boy a trial," they responded with hearty good nature, and promised him their support.

The appointment of governor fell to George B. Porter of Pennsylvania, a lawyer in large practice whose engagements kept him away from the territory for nearly a year, and who was frequently absent afterwards. Mason was, therefore, acting governor for nearly the whole remaining period of territorial existence. But the boy-governor was conciliatory in his ways; he was genial according to the customs of the times; there was very little for him to do until the boundary controversy with Ohio broke out, and when it did, he pleased the people by the spirited manner in which he espoused and defended the rights of the territory, and in the end, after by actual occupancy of the office he had acquired some fitness for its duties, his administration became as popular as at first it had been obnoxious.

But Jackson was not satisfied with sending on executive officers from distant states; he removed the judges, who were performing their duties satisfactorily, that he might give their places to gentlemen from New York and Pennsylvania who wanted them. One of the judges removed was William Woodbridge, an able lawyer and an upright man, whose character was above reproach. The feeling against his removal was very strong and the members of the bar gave expression to it in a public testimonial. Seven years later he became governor of the State, and was shortly after elected senator in Congress.

The stream of immigration continued to pour into the territory, and early in 1832 the question of applying for admission to the Union began to be agitated. The major part of the immigration was from New England, New York, and Ohio, and was of people accustomed to self-rule, who valued highly the privilege of choosing their own officers. They were, besides, coming to understand how invaluable were the natural resources of the territory, and were vaguely forming in their minds schemes for development by means of canals and railroads. It was supposed there were, by this time, fifty thousand people in the territory, and in another year there would be more than sixty thousand. It was one of the articles of compact in the Ordinance of 1787 that so soon as any of the three or five states to be formed out of the Northwest Territory "shall have sixty thousand free inhabitants therein, such state shall be admitted by its delegates into the Congress of the United States on an equal footing with the original states in all respects whatever." It seemed proper, therefore, to take the opinion of the people on the question of forming a state government, and an election was held in the fall of 1832 at which a large majority of votes was cast for the proposition. But other matters were this year interesting the people more than matters of government. War with Indians on the Mississippi, known as Black Hawk's War, had broken out and spread a vague terror through the country as far east as Lake Erie. The cholera also made its appearance in Michigan, and its ravages at Detroit were so alarming that hundreds fled in dismay to the woods where many died or were devoured by wild beasts. The troops sent forward by steamboat to the scene of military operations died in such numbers that general panic prevailed, and the solemn custom of ringing the passing bell for the departed, which up to this time had been observed in Detroit, became so continuous and so fearful a message of warning in the ears of the people, and added so much to the general alarm that it was discontinued. Cases of cholera continued to occur for the next two years, and in July, 1834, Governor Porter himself died of it. President Jackson nominated Henry D. Gilpin of Pennsylvania to the vacancy, but the Senate refused to confirm him and no further attempt was made to fill the place.

Before the alarm caused by the cholera had

passed away, Detroit was excited by a negro riot which led to the most disquieting apprehensions of arson and general plunder. There were now considerable numbers of negroes in the town, some of whom were fugitives from slavery; and it was from an unsuccessful attempt to return two of these to their master that the riot arose. Some fires occurring near the time were attributed to a purpose by the negroes to burn the town; the mayor of the city, in alarm, called upon the secretary of war for military protection, and a company of soldiers was sent. But the alarm was probably without further cause than must always exist when a considerable part of the population is held in public estimation and treatment as degraded, and it soon died away.

At this time Michigan was enlarged by the addition of the territory west of the Mississippi and north of Missouri, as far west as the Missouri and White Earth rivers, and counties were laid out in that distant country. But the people were now becoming earnest in their desire for state government. A census was ordered in 1834, which showed that there were within that portion of the territory which by the Ordinance of 1787 was to constitute one of the five states 87,278 inhabitants; considerably more than were necessary to entitle it to admission as a state in the Union under the compact. Congress was, therefore, memorialized to set off the western territory from

Michigan; and in anticipation of compliance the people west of Lake Michigan were allowed to name one of their own number for a delegate in Congress. In April, 1835, an election was held of delegates to a state convention for forming a state constitution, and this convention met at Detroit in May and agreed upon a constitution which was submitted to the people and approved by them in October.

This action excited a boundary controversy with Ohio which threatened serious consequences. To understand its merits it is necessary to go back to the Ordinance of 1787. One of the Articles of Compact of the ordinance was that there should be formed in the Northwest Territory thereby organized not less than three nor more than five states, and the boundaries were designated. If three were formed, they were to be bounded on the east and west by lines which now constitute the east and west boundaries of Ohio, Indiana, and Illinois respectively, but continued north to the national boundary. But Congress reserved the right to form one or two states in that part of the territory which lay north of an east and west line drawn through the southerly bend or extreme of Lake Michigan. This was declared to be an article of *compact* " between the original states and the people and the states in said territory," and by the express terms of the ordinance was to " forever remain unalterable unless by common consent," and it never by common consent had been abrogated or changed. On the contrary, in the enabling act for the admission of Ohio to the Union, the northern boundary of that State had been made an east and west line drawn through the southern extreme of Lake Michigan, running east from its intersection with a due north line from the mouth of the Great Miami, to Lake Erie or the territorial line, and thence, with the territorial line through Lake Erie to the Pennsylvania line. The act providing for the organization of the Territory of Michigan had made this same northern boundary of Ohio the southern boundary of Michigan, and the setting off of that territory with a western boundary extending through the centre of Lake Michigan to its northern point and thence north to the national boundary, was regarded as conclusive of the election of Congress to form five states instead of three out of the Northwest Territory; the farther territory west of Lake Michigan having been afterwards attached to Michigan for merely temporary purposes of government. The people of Michigan had, therefore, two rights solemnly guaranteed to them by the ordinance, neither of which could be taken from them without their consent. These were, first, to have a line drawn due east from the southern extreme of Lake Michigan for their southern boundary, and, second, to be admitted to the Union as a state on reaching a population of sixty thousand. Up to this time the Territory had exercised jurisdiction to the line in dispute, had appointed officers, collected taxes, and granted charters to corporations which were now without contention exercising their corporate functions.

On the other hand it was said with truth by Ohio, that when the Ordinance of 1787 was adopted, the true location of the southern extreme of Lake Michigan was not known, and was supposed to be much farther north than it actually was; that, by some well-informed people, it was supposed, even so late as when Ohio was made a state, to be so far north that a line drawn due east from it would leave the Frenchtown settlement to the south of it and therefore within Ohio; but the convention which adopted the constitution for that state, under the enabling act of Congress, in order to provide for the contingency of the line running farther to the south than was commonly supposed, had accepted the northern boundary with the proviso "that if the southerly bend or extreme of Lake Michigan should extend so far south that a line drawn due east from it should not intersect Lake Erie, or if it should intersect said Lake Erie east of the mouth of the Miami river of the Lakes, then, and in that case with the assent of the Congress of the United States, the northern boundary of this state shall be established by and extend to a line running from the southerly extreme of Lake Michigan to the most northerly extreme of the Miami Bay, after intersecting the due north line from the mouth of the Great Miami River aforesaid, thence northeast to the territorial line, and by the said territorial line to the Pennsylvania line." Congress, after the constitution containing this proviso had been adopted, had declared Ohio a state in the Union, and this, it was claimed, was an implied consent to the proviso. Congress had since admitted the States of Indiana and Illinois to the Union, and in each instance had carried the northern boundary considerably to the north of a line drawn through the southerly bend or extreme of Lake Michigan; and this, it was insisted, as the supreme legislative authority of the Union, it had undoubted power to do, whatever view might be taken of the ordinance as a "compact." This last claim was disputed by Michigan, as being equivalent to a claim that one party to a compact may annul it at its own pleasure; but it was also denied that in the case of the boundary between Ohio and Michigan Congress had ever consented to any change. On the contrary, it was shown that Ohio had applied for the consent of Congress to the boundary as proposed by the proviso above given, and had not succeeded in obtaining it. The case between Ohio and Michigan stood, therefore, upon the Ordinance of 1787, unaffected by subsequent congressional action; and what had been done in the cases of Indiana and Illinois did not in any way complicate or affect it. Possibly those cases might become the subjects of legal controversy, and if they should, it would be time enough to consider them.

Such was the condition of the question when Governor Lucas of Ohio, early in 1835, procured legislation in his state for taking possession of the disputed territory, which included the present city of Toledo, for the election of officers for it, and for running and marking the boundary line according to the Ohio claim. Michigan responded with legislation making it highly penal to accept or exercise any public office within the territory, except under commission of the United States or of Michigan. It was not long before the militia were called out on both sides to enforce the respective claims. An armed collision being thus imminent, the president took notice of the controversy and called upon the attorney-general for his opinion. The attorney-general responded that until Congress should give express assent to the change in the Ohio boundary, the territory in dispute must be considered as belonging to Michigan. The position was an embarrassing one to the president. It would be his duty, under the opinion of the attorney-general, to restrain the proceedings of the Ohio authorities, and to employ for that purpose the military power if necessary. But this might lose the State of Ohio to the party of which the president was the head; and it was already a great state and might possibly hold the balance of power in the next presidential election. He might also displease the States of Indiana and Illinois, both of which were interested adversely to the Michigan claim. Here were three great states, with considerable votes in the electoral college, on one side, and a territory with no vote at all on the other; and John Quincy Adams might well say, as he did: "Never in the course of my life have I known a controversy of which all the right was so clear on one side, and all the power so overwhelmingly on the other; never a case where the temptation was so intense to take the strongest side, and the duty of taking the weakest was so thankless." The president, feeling the temptation and dreading the duty, sent Mr. Richard Rush and Mr. B. C. Howard as peace commissioners to arrange the difficulty, but their efforts were without avail. Toledo was the real subject of the controversy; it was indivisible, and there could be no compromise in respect to it.

Meantime the situation was greatly complicated by the organization of a state government in Michigan, and the assumption of state powers. At the same time that the constitution was voted upon, state officers, executive and legislative, were elected provisionally, who, on the adoption of that instrument, assumed their respective offices. Stevens T. Mason, acting governor of the Territory, was elected governor of the State, and Edward Mundy, lieutenant-governor; judges were appointed and courts organized; the legislature met and elected Lucius Lyon and John Norvell United States senators. Isaac E. Crary, at the general election, had been chosen representative in Congress. All this was done under the claim that, by the Ordinance of 1787, the people, now that the population exceeded sixty thousand, had an absolute and indefeasible right to form a state government; and the representatives of the State went on to Washington to demand admission to the seats in Congress to which they claimed by right to be entitled.

It was very certain, however, that though Michigan might have a right to recognition as a state, the right was not so far absolute as that its observance could be compelled. Congress alone could recognize a state as a member of the Union, and admit its representatives to seats in the two houses; and if it should refuse to do this, even in the plainest case of right, no means or method of compelling it to take the proper action could possibly exist. Michigan, if a state in fact, was, therefore, a state out of the Union, and must stay out of the Union until it should please Congress to grant admission. Nor was it at all probable that admission would be granted while the boundary controversy with Ohio remained undetermined. The president was known to be displeased with the action of Acting Governor Mason in respect to that controversy, and in September, 1835, he appointed to succeed him as governor John S. Horner of Virginia, a young man as ignorant of the territory and of the people as Mason had been when first appointed. When it is considered that Michigan, at this time, had a population of not less than a hundred thousand people, and that there could probably be found in every organized county many persons better fitted to be their governor than the man sent on to occupy that office, the abuse of the appointing power in the case is seen to have been most flagrant. The appointee came on and attempted to act as pacificator, but instead of being received with respect, he was treated with indifference or subjected to practical jokes, and in a public meeting held at Detroit it was plainly intimated that the people would not be displeased to see him relinquish the duties of his office and return to the land of his nativity.

It was evident that Mr. Horner was not acting governor of Michigan, whatever might be his legal right or title. The president directed him not to recognize the pretended state officers and state courts; but his action in this regard was of no importance; they were recognized by the people, and they proceeded in the exercise of the ordinary powers of sovereignty, while he, for all practical purposes, was an official nonentity. He was not long in becoming convinced that his official importance, if not his personal comfort, would be enhanced by removal beyond Lake Michigan, to the portion of the territory which, in organizing the State, had not been included within it; and he adopted that course and disappeared from Michigan history.

But the condition of things in which a state was exercising powers of sovereignty within the limits of federal jurisdiction but not in the Union was too anomalous for long continuance. The president desired to bring it to an end, and Congress agreed upon a proposition for the admission of the State on condition of its resigning the disputed territory to Ohio and accepting, instead, a much larger territory, since known as the Upper Peninsula, which included valuable mines of copper and iron. This proposition was submitted to Michigan to be acted upon by a convention of delegates chosen by the people for the purpose, and if accepted the State was to be immediately received into the Union. But the belligerent feeling was still too strong for this compromise; and in a convention of delegates held at Ann Arbor, September 4, 1836, it was rejected by an emphatic vote. Thus a settlement of the difficulty was apparently as far off as ever.

But the interests favoring admission were now daily growing more and more powerful. The president's wishes on the subject were well known to his active partisans, who constituted a strong and growing party and had chosen the state officers. A presidential election was pending and a very natural desire existed to participate in it. A distribution of the public lands or their proceeds was one of the issues of the day, and if it took place it would be unfortunate if Michigan should fail to receive its share. The senators and representatives chosen to seats in Congress were naturally anxious to occupy them, and politicians were equally anxious to be recognized in the distribution of federal patronage. And the state officers, though supported by the people and in the undisturbed possession of their offices, could not fail to realize the fact that acquiescence by the federal authorities in the present condition of things would only be temporary, and that the time must come when there would be a conflict in which the State could scarcely fail to be overborne. In short, it was manifest that Congress was master of the situation; and that however clear might be the right of the State, it must sooner or later accept such terms as should be dictated to it. A movement for another convention was therefore soon on foot, which assumed to represent the whole people, though in fact originating in the caucuses of the Jackson party, and representing that party almost exclusively. It suited the purposes of the movers in it to speak of their action as the "action of the people in their primary capacity;" a high-sounding phrase seeming to imply some right and often made use of when the purpose is to accomplish something of questionable nature by setting aside for the time the constitution or the laws. Delegates were accordingly chosen under the forms of regular election who convened at Ann Arbor, December 6, 1836, and with no more authority than any party caucus, assumed in the name of the State, the sovereign power of accepting the proposition of Congress. No pretense could be more baseless than this assumption of authority by the convention; people ridiculed its meeting and christened it the "frost-bitten" convention; but the dominant party in Congress found it convenient to accept its action as a solemn act in state government, and on January 26, 1837, the State was declared to have accepted the proposition of Congress and thereby to have become a member of the Federal Union.

The act which thus assumed to admit Michigan to the Union upon a false assumption of fact was one which it would have been idle to quarrel with or condemn. The State could not maintain its anomalous position, and for any wrong in its treatment only Congress could give redress. The courts, as the seceding states discovered in the reconstruction period, are powerless to control purely political action, or to call it in question for any purpose. The governor protested, but at the same time admitted the folly of allowing a bootless grief to delay admission to the Union. The grief was neither very deep nor very lasting. The State had maintained its honor in standing upon its rights, and the compromise which by a species of fraud was forced upon it gave more than it took away, and left the State a decided gainer in the transaction. The governor did not dismiss the subject without indulging in much rhetoric to show how greatly the State had been wronged, thus affording the opposition a fine opportunity for ridiculing "the hero of the bloodless plains of Toledo" for unbuckling his sword and coming down from his high horse so tamely; but if all his important acts had shown equal wisdom, there would have been little in his administration to remember with condemnation. The mock heroics put the people in good humor, and they turned with cheerful spirits to their peaceful avocations as citizens of the United States, readily forgetting and forgiving the wrong which was so far from having harmed them. The successor of Governor Mason went again over the grounds of complaint in his first message, but this was a re-threshing of old straw, and nobody took any interest in it.

The constitution under which the State was admitted to the Union was carefully restricted to prescribing the fundamentals of government and the general framework of official organization, and did not, as so many recent essays in that direction have done, enter the field of legislation. In this respect it may well be regarded as a model. Six month's residence in the State was made sufficient for the exercise of the elective franchise, but, with singular liberality, any white male inhabitant who was resident in the State at the time of the adoption of the constitution was given the ballot, even though not a citizen. This made many recent immigrants from Europe voters in both state and federal elections, and furnished a striking illustration of a sentiment very prevalent at the time, that the coming to America to enjoy the benefit of its institutions was of itself an evidence of fitness to take part in administering its government. It was much like the sentiment developed during the civil war, that the oppressed race which had been intensely patriotic when the life of the nation was threatened by its enemies might be safely trusted with the ballot when peace was restored.

Michigan was the thirteenth of the new states admitted to the Union " on an equal footing with the original states:" its acceptance of the constitution doubled the count of the states. It was a grand Union to which the State was admitted, and it was made such by a constitution which was worthy of everlasting regard and affection. But the time had not yet come when the people of the states were to look to the nation more than to the state as the government in which their interests were chiefly concerned. The tide of national feeling was just now flowing very strong, for Jackson by his proclamation and Webster by his masterly speeches against nullification had rallied the two great political parties to the sentiment with which

Jackson had begun his administration, — "The Federal Union; it must be preserved." But the original constitution was still maintained in its integrity, and the dispute over the right of nullification had done nothing to diminish or weaken proper state powers under it. It had only determined, so far as the expressed will of the people could do so, that the Union under the constitution of Washington and Hamilton and Madison was to be perpetual.

The states under that constitution were very far from being dependent provinces or inferior municipalities. Under the apportionment of powers as between state and nation, the people looked to the national government for very little that touched their every-day life. The general government had charge of foreign relations; but these only in a distant and imperfect manner interested the people at large, except when there seemed to be danger of unfriendly relations with other countries. The general government levied taxes for its own purposes, but for the most part it laid them as indirect taxes, and they were scarcely perceived by the people as burdens. It coined money, but in the early period of its history the major part of the coin in circulation was of foreign coinage, and nearly all of the paper currency was the bills of banks existing under state charters which had been authorized by state law. It passed bankrupt laws, but these were only for emergencies and were soon repealed. Only in the postal service did it appear before the people as a daily and hourly benefactor and friend. The whole subject of the domestic relations was left to the states: the subject of contracts and domestic trade; of wills and the descent of property; of land titles and the administration of estates; of the making of highways and of their use and control after being made; of providing schools and furnishing the means of education to the people; of granting charters of incorporation, and all that infinite variety of rules and regulations known as laws of police, which are ever present and all about the citizen, his business and his property, prescribing limitations and setting bounds to use and enjoyment even in respect to that which is unquestionably his own, that he may not unreasonably encroach upon the use and enjoyment of their own by others. State power and state law were thus present at all times, touching the citizen for his advantage and direction in all his relations: by his fireside as much as in his business; in his marriage; in the control, management, and education of his children; in the labor he employed; in the civil and religious organizations to which he attached himself; in the breaking up of the domestic relations if unhappily that should occur; in the final arrangement of his affairs for death; in the enforcement of debts for and against him in life and for and against his estate after death; in

THE STATE NEARER THAN THE UNION. 229

short, in nearly everything which had for him and those associated with him — whether in kinship or socially or in business — an every-day interest; it was only in respect to his mail that the state did not chiefly concern him. The federal government seemed a distant power, indispensable as a shield against foreign animosities or encroachments; and once in four years the citizen was likely to get warmed up in the course of the presidential campaign so as to feel a deep interest in the result, but this would be as often because he had inherited a place in one of the parties of the day as from any deep conviction that he had a personal concern in the choice the people would make. It was the state that was an ever-present beneficence, in whose doings he had a constant and immediate interest, and to whose provident arrangements he owed daily and hourly obligations. But he felt the state in its burdens also: the taxes imposed were considerable, and they were also direct; the citizen never paid them without knowing it, as he might pay customs duties, or other indirect taxes; and he had therefore an immediate interest in seeing that they were not levied for any but proper public purposes, and not expended dishonestly or wastefully. Almost all the local officers, except the postmaster, were also provided for and chosen, under state laws; so that in every way the state seemed vastly more important to the citizen than the nation; and the range of subjects over which it had supreme control was so vast, and the subjects themselves so important, that state sovereignty seemed to the fireside philosophers, as they discussed politics with each other, a more palpable and conspicuous constitutional reality than the sovereignty of the Union. It was somewhat different in the large commercial towns, where foreign trade was considerable, and also in towns where large expenditures were made for military and naval purposes, or land offices located; but the agricultural and laboring classes of the country naturally attached themselves to state interests; and as parties divided on the construction of federal powers, the majority tended to the party that proposed to maintain in all their integrity the rights of the states.

Then the courts for the administration of justice were, for the most part, state courts, and the state regulated civil rights and prescribed and punished crimes. The federal judiciary had under its control the subjects of bankruptcy and admiralty, of controversies between states, and controversies in which foreign countries or their people might be concerned; and citizens of different states might implead each other in federal courts; and there were a few other cases which might be there brought. But nearly all the litigation of the country was in the state courts: they were the courts in which neighborhood controversies were determined; they sat with a neighborhood jury and they were the courts whose doings were immediately before the people and enlisted their interest and attention.

The time had not yet come for great expenditures of money by the general government upon works of internal improvement, or for great gifts of land to aid in the construction of such works. The party of strict construction of federal powers was in the ascendency, and disputed the power of the nation to make highways in the states, except as for strictly national purposes it might become important. Neither had the time for high protective duties yet come to interest great numbers of people in the customs taxes, and bring great lobbies to Washington.

It may well be said, therefore, that it was something to be proud of, to be a member of a commonwealth possessing the sovereign powers which were possessed by the states of the American Union; and the people of Michigan accepted their place as citizens of the twenty-sixth state, not with pride merely, but with unbounded confidence in its future.

CHAPTER XII.

THE STATE AND ITS ELEMENTS.

The period of immaturity and tutelage was at last over, and the people who constituted the political society had become a state in the American Union with sovereign powers. They were well entitled to a recognition of this privilege of independent action, for their numbers were ample, the average of intelligence was high, and the elements of a vigorous and self-respecting state were to be seen on all sides in abundance.

The French-Canadian element was still conspicuous along all the eastern border of the state, and the increase was large and continuous, though the proportion relatively to the whole population was all the while diminishing. The grades of society among this people ran from highest to lowest: many of them boasted, with much pride, of aristocratic descent, and had inherited large wealth; and these constituted an intelligent and refined society into which the better classes of other nationalities were glad to be admitted. At the other extreme in the social scale were the *coureurs de bois* and *voyageurs*, who still were to be found in considerable numbers, though their occupations, except upon the upper waters, were for the most part gone; the fur trade in Michigan being no longer the large and profitable commerce it once was, and no considerable parties being now organized to conduct it. But these roving characters still gathered about the old French settlements, and took up, when they labored at all, such occupations as made their lives most nearly correspond to those they had been accustomed to lead. Many became professional fishermen; others got to be draymen and petty expressmen with little carts and ponies. And then above these lowest classes, the French in and about the towns were found in numerous employments; many being market-gardeners and hucksters, many others merchants in a small way; and whatever the business, women were not unfrequently the principals in carrying it on. But this people had their part in more extensive operations also; and some of the leading and most prosperous business men were of this nationality.

French farms may almost be said to have lined the river from the mouth of the Detroit to Lake St. Clair; their houses fronted upon the road which ran along the river bank, and there was only a narrow belt of cultivation behind them, bordered by dense forest, in which wolves, bears, and other wild animals still offered pastime to the sportsmen. The agriculture of the farmers was of the most primitive character; the plow, except the share, was of wood; with a wooden wheel on either side of the long beam, the one small to run on the land side, and the other larger to run in the furrow. Oxen were fastened to this plow by a pole which had a hinged attachment; they were not yoked, but the draught was by thongs or ropes fastened about their horns. A little two-wheeled cart into which was fastened a pony, or perhaps a cow or steer, was the principal farm vehicle. The early farmers did not appreciate the value of manure in agriculture, and removed it out of their way by dumping it in the river, but they were beginning now to learn in that regard better ways. The houses for the most part were of a single story with a plain veranda in front; and here in pleasant weather would gather the household for domestic labor and social recreation. The houses of the wealthier classes were of hewed logs, with a large chimney occupying the space of a room in the centre, and a garret hung with festoons of drying or dried fruits, pumpkins, garlics, onions, and medicinal and culinary herbs. The family washing was done at the river, and the pounding of the clothes was with a little hand mallet, after the method of their ancestors from time immemorial. Everywhere the spinning-wheel was in use, and the madam, with just pride in her deftness, made the clothing for the family. The kitchen was a common gathering-room for the family, who liked to see the cookery going on, with pots and kettles and spiders in an open fireplace. Around many of the old houses and yards were pickets of cedar, ten or twelve feet in height, which were originally planted for defense against the Indians; but the Indians who had their homes about the towns were no longer feared, and were generally nominal Catholics and well treated. The only fastening to the front door of the house was a latch on the inside, which was raised to open the door by a strip of leather or deer's hide run through a hole in the door, and hanging down on the outside. When the latch-string was drawn in the door was fastened; but so marked an indication of distrust or inhospitality was seldom witnessed, as no one — not even an Indian — would be guilty of so great a breach of propriety as to lift the latch and cross the threshold without permission of the owner. The family when leaving the house temporarily did not therefore deem it necessary to fasten the door.

The horse in common use was so small as to be considered and called a pony, and was reputed to be a cross of the wild Mexican horse with mares captured at the time of Braddock's defeat. The French had been long enough in the country to have old orchards of apples and pears: pear-trees fifty or sixty feet in height, and bearing in a season thirty or even fifty bushels of fruit were not uncommon, and the fruit, though not of the highest quality to eat out of hand, was unsurpassed for culinary purposes. There were crude cider mills, and much cider was made for domestic use. Peaches were raised, also, of a poor and common sort, and from these distilled in rum a drink was made which was much used.

The French, whether rich or poor, educated or ignorant, were always polite, light-hearted, gay, and buoyant, and always fond of sports in which old and young could participate together. Festivals were kept with unrestrained enjoyment: New Year's especially, when every child, whatever the age, was expected to kneel for the paternal blessing; when calls were made upon all acquaintances, presents exchanged between friends, and every lady was expected to submit to be saluted with a kiss upon the cheek. Mardi Gras and Easter were also festivals of great enjoyment, but Lent came with devotional aspect, and was scrupulously kept. They were a church-going people, and many religious customs were still kept up which were destined to die out. The christening and baptizing of the church bell was one of these, and so was the distributing of the blessed bread in church in commemoration of the love-feasts of the early Christians. But when church services were over on Sunday sports were in order, and the return home was likely to be a scene of boisterous merriment and of pony racing by the young men. The marriage of young people was a great occasion, for they understood well that the church did not allow of divorces, and the marriage was in fact what it purported to be, a binding for better or for worse for life. Regularly it was preceded by a formal contract before a notary; the bans were published for three successive Sundays in church, and the wedding festivities were kept up for several days. But man or woman who after losing the spouse married a second time, and especially a third time, must expect a *charivari*, with which no police officer would trouble himself to interfere. The average of education among the people was low, for many never went to school at all, and the church schools, in which most of the education was given, were not of a high order, and taught catechism more than grammar or arithmetic. The ladies were fond of gay and picturesque dresses and of flowers and other simple decorations for themselves and their homes, and in these particulars good taste was general.

Detroit in this year 1837 had become a considerable town, having now perhaps eight thousand people. Old wind-mills upon which the people formerly relied for the grinding of cereals were coming now to be disused, though some were still standing. The noble river in front of the town offered, at all seasons of the year, many inducements to sports and festivities, of which all classes of the people were eager to avail themselves. In the winter, when frozen over, it became the principal highway, and was gay with the swift-going vehicles. A narrow box upon runners wide apart made the common sleigh, and the ponies, sometimes driven tandem, seemed to enter into the spirit of racing almost as much as their masters. When there was no snow the little cart was the common vehicle of land carriage for all classes of the people; ladies went in it to church and to parties, and made fashionable calls, being seated on a buffalo robe spread on the bottom, and they were backed up to the door at which they wished to alight, and stepped upon the threshold from it. Now and then there was a family which had a *caleche;* a single carriage with the body hung upon heavy leathern straps, with a small low seat in front for the driver, and with a folding top to be raised in sun or rain. But the cart was a convenience which all classes could enjoy and appreciate, and it was especially adapted to a town like Detroit, which was built upon a clay-bank, and had as yet neither sidewalk nor pavement.

Many Scotch were now among the business men of Detroit, with a fondness for making money, and a shrewd knack at doing so. There were also some Irish and some English, but the major part of the people who were not French were of American birth. Among these there were now being established — what in fact had existed before, though not in much strength — societies for literary culture and enjoyment. The Detroit Young Men's Society was one of them, which for twenty years was to be an important institution in the town, and the training-school of governors, senators, and judges. At the barracks, though there was none now, there would shortly be a small military force to preserve peace on the frontier; and the officers and their families would constitute an important and valuable addition to the society of the place at all times.

Detroit during the territorial period had to a large extent monopolized political offices and influence, but though still the capital and the commercial metropolis, its political domination had dwindled to a disputed hegemony. Important towns were springing up all over the southern part of the State, and several of them were already prominent, and had public journals which were conducted with ability, and citizens who were well known abroad and whose influence was felt in other sections. Monroe, Ann Arbor, Marshall, Tecumseh, Pontiac, and Adrian were the largest of these, and none of them was without ambitious men who aspired to leading positions in state affairs, and with ability to justify the aspiration. Wealth was as yet an unimportant source of influence, for there were few men of special prominence in that regard. The merchants handled most money: they went once or twice a year to New York to buy goods, and in the country they were obliged to keep general assortments of dry goods, wet and dry groceries, hardware, and boots and shoes; but wants were moderate in those days, and the stock though general in kind was small in amount and cheap in quality. By far the larger part of the people were small farmers who were now busy in bringing their land under cultivation; their fortunes were in their farms, and they subordinated everything else to converting their own labor into substantial and permanent value in improvements. Many of them were of New England descent; all the New England States were represented among them, and Vermont especially had sent a large contingent who were tired of rocky hillsides. But the majority were one generation removed from New England, being descendants of those who settled in New York and Ohio. Western New York, especially, was largely represented; the purchasers by "article" from the great land companies of that district, having in many cases found themselves unable to complete their payments, had been glad to sell their "betterments" for enough to buy a lot of government land in Michigan and move with their families upon it.

It was a hard life which the pioneer farmers of Michigan had come to lead. A rude log cabin for a home, and the bare necessaries of life for their families contented them while they were clearing their lands; and the lessons of industry and econ-

THE SUPPLY OF FOOD. 241

omy would have been forced upon them by the situation even if they had not learned them before, as the most of them had. When the cheapness of land is taken into account, their farms must be deemed small, averaging perhaps a hundred and twenty acres; and hard labor and the chills and fever incident to the clearing of a new country gave them sallow complexions and made them prematurely old; but in coming to Michigan they had calculated not so much upon their own immediate advantage as upon giving their children an opportunity to "grow up with the country;" and they accomplished all they had counted on if they could see that year by year their possessions increased in value, and could rely with confidence upon giving their children the rudiments of education and a fair start in the world, and on being independent in their circumstances in their old age. Even now, though they could not supply all their wants from their farms, they contracted few debts, but postponed purchases when they had nothing to barter for the articles they desired.

Of meats salt pork was the staple, and many of the people rarely had any other, but all had wheat or corn bread and potatoes, and a hearty appetite need crave nothing better. Many orchards were planted, but few were as yet in bearing, and fruit was a rare luxury; the people had little money with which to procure it from the Eastern States, and none at all to expend in the extravagance of

Southern fruits, which in after years were to become so common. They were forced, therefore, to be content with the wild fruits of the country. Of the wild crab or wild plum a preserve was made which was palatable as a relish to the monotonous diet of pork, and if a few wild strawberries could be gathered in June, or blackberries later, they were great as well as rare luxuries. In the swamps cranberries could be found to a limited extent, and on sandy plains whortleberries, but the resources in all these directions were limited and exceptional. For a time there would be deer, wild turkeys, and other game in considerable quantities, but the pioneer farmers of Michigan had little time to give to sport, and those who engaged very much in it were likely to become so far fascinated with its excitements as to fall gradually into the life of thriftless wood-rangers. On the prairies wild bees were abundant, and in the fascinating pages of Cooper one may read how men became skillful in following them to their homes and robbing them of their delicious stores. In some parts of central and northern Michigan the maple-tree furnished sugar orchards, and the Indians who still lingered in the State were sugar makers to a considerable extent. They also gathered berries in their season for barter with the white settlers, camping in temporary colonies for the purpose.

Few of the pioneers had brought their spinning

wheels with them, for as yet there were but few sheep in the State, and by the time wool had become abundant, the old ways of working it up had passed away. For a while the material for garments, which in rural New England and New York were home-made, must be bought; but cheap, coarse cloth answered the purpose, and the wives and daughters made it up for use. The pioneers could not be particular about other qualities of their cloth than those of wear and comfort, and nobody would criticise the style or the fit. Silks for the woman and broadcloth for the man were rare extravagances; many a bridegroom destined to become an important personage in business and political circles went to the altar in Kentucky jean, and received his bride in calico; and the wedding journey from the bride's home to the husband's was made with an ox-team which was prized more than would be a chariot and four because of what it promised in farm improvement. If it was winter the vehicle might be a home-made sled with bent saplings for runners; and nothing could be better, for nothing could be more suited to the times. There was little sentimentality in this, but there was New England hard sense, and good promise of domestic virtues and contentment.

In early times pioneers sometimes made meal of their corn by pounding it in a hollow stump, but this was seldom done at this time. Other contrivances, however, which were nearly as primitive, were sometimes resorted to. One ingenious person had constructed a mill, which answered an admirable purpose, by felling a tall tree and excavating a trough the whole length of it on the upper side as it lay. The trough was a foot in width at the top, narrowing as it deepened; a small quantity of corn was poured into it, and was then ground into meal by means of a heavy wooden wheel rolling over it. The wheel was a section cut from the butt of the tree, and shaped to fit the trough, and was rolled back and forth by two persons who took the ends of a pole which was run through the centre of it. The use of the mill was free to all, and it was a great neighborhood convenience. But wheat, rather than corn, was the staple bread food in Michigan, and these rude contrivances would not make flour. The grist mill must be resorted to; and that might be a day's journey away, and the farmer who went that distance with his small grist was never quite sure that he would not find the mill out of repair, or not running from want of water, or because the miller was prostrated by one of the fevers incident to a new country; and then he might be compelled to go farther to another mill, or to retrace his steps and repeat his tedious journey at another time.

Except in southwestern Michigan where there were prairies, the first necessity of the time was to get rid of the forest, and the short way to get rid of it was to cut and burn it without discrimination. For none of it was there a market, and many a great black walnut, the growth of centuries and fit for the adornment of a palace, was given to the flames because it cumbered the ground. In clearing up the farm the whole family could take useful part; the man chopped and piled the logs, the woman piled and burned the brush, leaving the babe, if there was one, in some convenient shade where it would be kept quiet in watching the busy proceedings. The pine country was not as yet much invaded by settlers, and the tulip-tree or white-wood, which was light and easily worked, was the favorite tree for lumber. Saw-mills of the primitive sort were common, and the farmers, as fast as they were able to do so, put up a "framed" house and moved into it, leaving the log cabin as a common store-house and workshop for rainy days. The moving from the old house into the new was the second stage of pioneer life, and there was likely to be a "house-warming," of which a dance was the chief feature.

Of the religious condition of the people little need be said. Though there were many excellent and sincerely religious persons among them, religion had not been a motive with them in coming into the wilderness. They had come to better their temporal condition, and the hardships and privations of every sort which are incident to life in the woods they had expected to submit to cheerfully. The Canadian French had their priests and maintained regular church services, but as to the main part of the population Michigan might be regarded as missionary ground. Many devoted Christians were for years without opportunity to attend church services; and some so greatly longed for the society of their brethren in Christian communion that they would go a day's journey, or even farther, to attend a meeting. The several denominations sent missionaries hither who came expecting to undergo great hardships and submit to many privations, and none were disappointed in that regard. The Methodists were commonly first in gathering congregations in the new settlements, and the circuit rider was often a character of note; rough and unlettered and ready to boast, perhaps, that the Lord had been his teacher from the Bible, and not the school-masters with their foolish grammars. But such men were often sincere and earnest, and being all things to all men, gathered considerable churches and laid the foundation upon which others more competent afterward built. This was the day of camp-meetings and revivals, and strange scenes were sometimes witnessed when people had "the power" and fell to the ground helpless. Rough characters gathered at such meetings for excitement and mischief, and they often became scenes of wild disorder and pugilistic encounters.

But it sometimes happened that those who came to scoff remained to pray. At this time there were many churches of other denominations; of Baptists and Presbyterians especially, and, in some places, of Episcopalians; and these, except the Episcopalians, had their occasional revival or protracted meetings. In the country districts, the school-house was generally the place for religious meetings, and perhaps the same house would be occupied by two or more denominations alternately, morning and evening, or on successive Sundays. But church edifices began to multiply rapidly. Said hopeful Abi Evans, in a letter from her solitary cabin in Tecumseh in 1824, "Perhaps I may see the day when the gospel may be preached at our place." It was now but thirteen years since her letter was written, and there were several churches near enough to her home to be reached by an early morning walk on Sunday. But this was an exceptional case; many of her sisters who were not so fortunate in their locations would live longer than she and yet pass away without having similar aspirations gratified.

In southeastern Michigan were many people of the society of Friends, commonly called Quakers, who dressed in sober drab and took off the hat and applied title of honor to no one. These had their plain meeting-houses without spire or bell, in which they gathered, and, discarding all music, listened to words of wisdom from the elders, if the spirit should move them to speak. The speakers at these meetings were perhaps as often as otherwise women, who seemed to have special gifts. The Friends were a sober, industrious, steady, and thrifty people, and their general integrity and fidelity were so well known that they were often invited by their fellow citizens to serve in important public stations. They were the first of the people to raise their voices against slavery, and the fugitive slave was always befriended and protected by them. The first " wood-notes wild" which caught the ear of the world from Michigan were the anti-slavery poems of Elizabeth Margaret Chandler; and these were well worthy of being listened to and of being held in lasting remembrance. Some of the few negroes in the State were fugitives from slavery, but they felt safe so far back in the woods with sympathizing friends about them, and Canada was a convenient refuge in case attempts were made at their recapture.

Michigan had its full share of lawyers, many of whom were well trained in their profession, and would be a credit to it anywhere. Others were untrained, unlettered, and unkempt, and their vulgarity and insolence would be tolerated nowhere but in the woods. They tried small cases for smaller pay on still smaller knowledge, and were never so well satisfied as when they gained a suit by a trick. Doctors there were in plenty, too, who rode the country on horseback, with medicines in saddle-bags, and dealt out such doses of calomel and jalap as would seem to render impossible the survival of any but the fittest. But in those early days the calls upon the doctor bore small proportion to the number of cases of disease; the people doctored themselves with various decoctions of bitter herbs and other simples which were popularly supposed to have healing qualities. The women were midwives to one another as occasion required.

The postal facilities of the people were as yet very primitive. The railroad from Toledo to Adrian brought a daily mail, but this was as yet the only railroad in operation in the State, though considerable had been done on the roads from Detroit to Pontiac, Detroit to Ypsilanti, and Palmyra to Jackson. But the daily mail was not now limited exclusively to the railroad; one was sent out also in coaches on some of the leading territorial roads. A few years before it was made subject of complaint in the "Detroit Gazette" that the driver of the coach was not provided with a horn to announce his coming; but he had one now and he sounded it vigorously as he approached a mail station, and brought his horses up smoking, with a brisk trot, if the state of the roads was such as to admit of it. But from the time the fall rains set in until the roads became dry in the spring there was little brisk movement of stagecoaches, and the driver must be content if he could go over the roads at the rate of three or four miles an hour without any breakdown. And much of the mail service of the State was done with considerably more modest conveyances than coaches; to some extent with lumber wagons, but much more largely on horseback. A horse and a boy going over the road perhaps twice a week were sufficient on most routes. Congressional documents were not at this time sent into the State by the ton, the people took few papers, and the correspondence by letter was too expensive to be much indulged in. The postage on a letter from the old home of most of the people was twenty-five cents, and money was not so plenty as to admit of frequent communication. The post-office was likely to be a box in one corner of a store or tavern, and the postmaster, when a letter was called for, turned over the whole pile until he found it.

The backwoods pioneers were not without their sports and pastimes. The State paid a bounty for the scalp of the wolf, and this furnished sufficient inducement to make the people eager to trap him. A whole neighborhood sometimes turned out to hunt a troublesome bear which had been carrying off swine, and once a year or so they would divide into two parties and engage in a great contest, to see which should bring home the most game of all kinds, estimating the animals from bears and wolves down to squirrels, according to importance. A raccoon heard of in the corn-field always gave occasion for extemporized sport, and the young farmer was seldom so much fatigued by his day's labor as to be disinclined to turn out for a 'coon hunt which might extend far into the night and require the cutting down of one or more large trees. Husking-bees, after corn harvest, and raising-bees when a new house or barn was to go up, were occasions for general merriment, and something to drink of a stimulating nature was expected on these occasions, for the day of total abstinence had as yet come to very few. Still, although nearly all persons drank occasionally, an habitual drunkard at this early day was rarely met with. In the winter, if snow fell to the depth of two or three inches, a sleighing party might seem to spring up spontaneously, and the home-made sleigh was amply good enough for such diversion. An old furniture box or a crockery crate filled with straw made a good body for it, and as many rode as could manage to find sitting or standing room. Every tavern had its ball-room, where dancing parties were given, to which any one might come who could purchase a card of admission; for there are no gradations of society in a new settlement, and every man and every woman is presumptively respectable. These parties were very simple affairs, but they were not for that reason the less enjoyable by the hard-working pioneers. The spelling-school furnished great sport also: whole neighborhoods, young and old, gathered and chose sides in a spelling contest, and the youthful prodigy, perhaps, spelled all the rest down, not excepting the doctor or the merchant who were educated at the academy. The amusement reached a climax when the master himself was caught tripping and was obliged to take his seat in confusion. The morals of the people at this time were better than appearances might indicate. Coarse profanity and vulgarity were heard so often that they failed to shock the hearer, and treating at a public bar was common when friends met and on all sorts of occasions. But domestic scandals were exceedingly rare, and divorces almost unknown. Society was very primitive and there was little courtesy and less polish, but there was no social corruption and parents had faith in each other and little fear for the morals of their children. The general standard of business integrity was high, and as the time had not yet come when great funds were needed for the purposes of political campaigns, elections were honestly conducted.

On the whole, it must be said of the pioneers of Michigan, that in character and aims, in what they were, what they did, what they suffered, and what they accomplished, they deserve, and should have, the grateful remembrance of those who, coming after them, reap the harvest of their sowing.

THE PATRIOT AGITATION.

This year began in Canada the "Patriot" agitation, which led in 1838–39 to partial insurrections, and to some acts of violation of neutrality by American citizens in crossing to Canada to assist the insurgents. The most lamentable of these was a crossing from Detroit to Windsor in December, 1838, and a fight resulting in the loss of a number of lives. The occurrence is noteworthy here only as it evidenced the intense sympathy of the people with the struggle of any other people for greater liberty. The international complications which followed were settled by the treaty of 1842 under the admirable management of Mr. Webster, which reflected new honor upon American diplomacy, already so illustrious.

CHAPTER XIII.

MONEY IS MADE ABUNDANT IN THE NEW STATE.

The new State was now in the Union, and it was enjoying the benefits of an immigration almost unparalleled in the history of mankind. It was not the movement of men in tribes or aggregate bodies, impelled by necessity or by political considerations to abandon their country for another; but it was an immigration of individual families, influenced by motives which affected them severally, and by an expectation that they would benefit their condition in so doing. Yet the aggregate number was enormous, and it seemed like the migration of a nation coming with radiant hopes to take possession of a land of promise. Their coming seemed to make the State rich; for though very few of them were persons of considerable means, the most of them came as producers, and if they brought nothing else they brought a capacity for labor and an expectation that by labor they were to make their fortunes. Their coming had rendered necessary many new facilities for travel and business; and the legislature had been prompt to recognize the fact.

LAND SPECULATIONS. 255

During the short period while Michigan had been a State but not in the Union, there had been legislation providing for the organization of fifty-seven townships, and the laying out of sixty-six state roads; eleven railroads had been chartered and nine banks; and permission had been given to construct thirteen dams upon navigable waters for manufacturing purposes. Much of this legislation was premature, as we can very plainly see now; but it did not then seem so to the people. General causes were inflating prices and inciting to speculation all over the country; the market values of land were rapidly increasing, and the imaginations of men were so far excited by the great changes which were taking place on every side, that it seemed impossible to suggest a scheme so wild or so improbable that it should be without plausibility in some minds. Speculators were eagerly making entry of all the government land for which they could raise money; and in illustration of the spirit in which this was done, an instance is given in which two brothers made purchase together in a single day of upwards of two hundred and forty quarter sections of land, without even taking the precaution to have them first visited and examined. But sales by individuals were quite as active as sales by government; the great majority being made upon small payments down and the purchasers expecting to make fortunes from the rapid rise in prices. Thus everybody seemed to be growing rich; and though much of the appearance was fictitious, even the coolest heads could see that the apparent prosperity had some foundation, and that in the rapid settlement of the State there was reason for a steady and considerable increase in values.

The currency of the country naturally and necessarily demanded early attention. At this time it consisted almost exclusively in issues of state banks. President Jackson's famous specie circular had made it necessary that payments for government lands should be made in gold and silver, but what was made use of for this purpose did not readily find its way into the channels of trade, and if it had done so, the amount of coin in the country would have been found wholly inadequate to the demands of business. Nearly all financial transactions were therefore necessarily carried on with bank paper, and the most of this had its origin outside the State. A hasty glance at the condition of the currency in territorial times seems a necessary introduction to any account of early state legislation.

The people of Michigan had had an experience in currency as extensive and diversified perhaps as that of any other people in the world. Much of the earliest trade was with wampum; and when this proved insufficient for the wants of the trade, furs and peltry became a substitute, — the beaver and other skins commonly dealt in having each a

CONDITION OF THE CURRENCY. 257

recognized value in the market, by which flour and other provisions, liquors, etc., were bought and sold. But these primitive devices were found quite insufficient to meet the demands of trade during the period of the American Revolution, and merchants made their due-bills which were received as change in business transactions, under an expectation that they would pass from hand to hand as currency. In 1779 an appearance of legality was given to this practice by the governor, who permitted the merchants to issue bills expressly designed for currency; the quantity issued being limited to the estimated value of their stocks on hand. The merchants all received each other's bills, and had a set time in which to make their exchanges; and though losses sometimes occurred from bankruptcy, the percentage was not great, and the system answered for the time a very good purpose. All the while there was some coin in circulation; and this consisted largely in Spanish dollars, which for convenience in change were cut into halves, quarters, and eighths. The subdivision invited cheating, which became after a time so general and so serious that in 1798 the grand jury presented the cut money as a nuisance, and it was driven out of circulation.

The attempt made in 1806 to establish a bank at Detroit has already been referred to. The men concerned in this scheme and who were to supply the capital had ample means, and there is no reason for the belief that anything fraudulent, or which seemed to them improper, was contemplated. But the local needs required no such bank; and if it acquired a circulation at all commensurate to its capital, it must find it in distant parts of the country. Congress disapproved of the charter, and the bank was forced to discontinue business, which it did without, so far as we know, any considerable loss to creditors. A few of the bills failed to be returned for speedy redemption, and Judge Woodward, the first president, was annoyed some years afterwards by threats of suits upon them. He was more annoyed by bitter and unscrupulous newspaper attacks upon him for his connection with the scheme, which, though published at Pittsburgh, circulated freely among his enemies in Detroit.

The presence of the army in Detroit caused a considerable expenditure of government money, which ceased with the capture by the British. Colonel Proctor, the British civil governor, then undertook to supply to some extent the want of local currency by issuing a proclamation making army and commissariat bills legal tender, under penalty of two hundred dollars for refusal to receive them as such; but this was in the nature of a forced military loan, and the bills disappeared when the British occupation ceased. After the war much money was brought in from other states to meet government expenditures, but there was no specie in circulation, and merchants and other individuals and corporations issued small due-bills for change; and these were of all denominations from five dollars down to one cent. Even churches contributed to the wants of trade by this "shinplaster" currency, which was easily counterfeited, as Father Richard found to his cost when his bills issued for St. Anne's began to come in for redemption.

In 1817 it seemed to the business men of Detroit that the time had come for a local bank, and in December of that year a charter was obtained, and the bank put in operation the next season. But the principal circulation in the territory was now Ohio bank bills; and of the banks which issued them little was or could be known. Some were supposed to be good and some doubtful, and in 1819 the merchants of Detroit appointed a committee, which may be styled a vigilance committee, to give warning of danger in respect to this currency as occasion should arise. But Ohio currency continued to be more abundant than any other for many years, and serious complaints were made that the disbursing officers of the general government made their payments in it. The wrong in this was very considerable; for though the bills were nominally received at par, they were really at a discount of from twenty to twenty-five per cent. Merchants could not make use of them in New York or Boston where their purchases were principally made, and a large sacrifice upon them was inevitable. As the banks had a great temptation to hold out inducements to the circulation of their bills at a distance from the point of redemption, their payment by officers on public demands was always open to a suspicion of official corruption, and the suspicion generally found voice among those who felt that they were wronged by being forced to take the paper. But for this there seemed to be no remedy: the general fact was that the people took in their ordinary business transactions whatever they found in circulation as money, and if they distrusted it for any reason, they were only the more prompt in passing it off. By the year 1822 small coins had again found their way into circulation to an extent that left no excuse for the fractional currency issued by individuals, and in a public meeting it was resolved no longer to receive it. New York, New England, and Kentucky bank-bills were now to some extent circulating in the territory, but the need of local banking facilities was becoming urgent, and five years later two banks were chartered, only one of which, however, was organized. In 1829 two more were chartered and went into operation, in 1832 another, and in 1835 five. Of these last one was located west of Lake Michigan, and two were railroad corporations with liberty to organize for banking purposes also. Eight banks were in existence when the state government was organized, and seven more were established within its limits under state charters before the State was formally admitted to the Union. For the most part they were in good hands and managed honestly, but the charters were almost entirely wanting in provisions for the protection of bill-holders or other creditors. A "safety fund" was provided for by general law, through the payment annually to the state treasurer of one half of one per cent. upon the capital stock paid in, and it was to be applied to the payment of the debts of any bank that should become insolvent. A bank commissioner was also provided for, with full powers of examination of books, papers, and securities, and with authority to take steps to enjoin any bank which was proceeding illegally or improperly.

It would seem that fifteen banks, which was an average of one for less than ten thousand people in the State, ought to have been ample for the transaction of its business; but at the very next session of the legislature the number of new charters applied for was so great that it was determined by general law to provide the means whereby any association of persons who could furnish the necessary means, and give proper securities for the protection of the public, might by voluntary action assume banking powers. The cry of monopoly was already in the air; and this general provision for converting everybody at pleasure into a banker was adopted "upon the plausible principle of introducing a free competition into what was considered a profitable branch of business heretofore monopolized by a few favored corporations." The common belief was, that in banking, as in other kinds of business, demand would regulate supply, and that banks would come into existence only when and where there was need for them, and where capital was available for the purpose. Then if it was found on trial that a bank was not needed, it would simply wind up its affairs and go out of existence, as a merchant might close out his business and engage in something else; and the experiment, if the public was sufficiently protected by the law of organization, would harm no one. Let the law be carefully framed, it was said, and under proper supervision everything might be left to the ordinary operations of trade and business. With sentiments like these prevailing, a general law was passed March 15, 1837, under which any ten or more freeholders of any county might organize themselves into a corporation for the transaction of banking business, with a capital of not less than fifty nor more than three hundred thousand dollars, on furnishing the required securities.

The provisions made by the law for the protection of the public were: that no bank should commence operations until thirty per cent. of the stock should be actually paid in, in specie; that securities in bonds and mortgages on real estate, or in bonds executed by resident freeholders and approved by the county treasurer and clerk, should be given for the payment of all debts and the redemption of all bills; that the banks should be subject to the safety fund act, and that a failure to pay the bills and notes on demand, or within thirty days thereafter, in lawful currency, should operate as a dissolution. And when, added to these, the banks were made subject to the constant supervision of the bank commissioner, it seemed to the public of that day that a banking system of exceptional security had been established.

The legislature which passed this act adjourned March 22, 1837, to November 9th following, but long before that day events had happened which rendered a special session imperative. The wild speculations of the country had been rapidly approaching a climax. Money, during the preceding winter, had commanded exorbitant rates of interest, ranging from two to four per cent. a month to persons in good financial standing and in regular business, and it was impossible that this state of things should long continue. In the spring business houses in the leading cities of the country began to fail. So many suspended that a panic was started, and at the beginning of May there was a run upon the banks of New York. A great meeting in that city besought the president to rescind the specie circular, as a necessary relief to the business pressure, and the "Washington Globe" responded that "there is no pressure which an honest man should regret." But the pressure was greater than the banks could sustain, and in a few days the banks of New York, Philadelphia, Boston, and Baltimore suspended specie payments and the suspension became general throughout the country. The banks paid out each other's bills, and the people, unable to get other currency, were compelled to take and use them, but every one of the banks was, in a legal sense, in a condition of practical insolvency. Legislatures were called together to devise a remedy for the consequent evils, and, under a belief that the banks had assets sufficient to meet all demands upon them when the present stringency should be over, the temporary suspension of specie payments was legalized.

The Michigan legislature was convened in special session June 12th. Up to this time no banks had been actually organized under the general banking law, though preliminary steps had been taken in several cases. Governor Mason in his message, after depicting in vivid language the financial and commercial embarrassments of the country, proceeded to point out as their causes overbanking, over-trading, and extravagance among the people. He spoke particularly and strongly of excessive bank issues, which he declared to be a violation of the simplest principles of political economy. The evil effects were depicted in detail and in strong colors, and his views were emphasized by a review of the present condition of the country and with some prophecy of the immediate future.

How far the governor, in what he was saying, was expressing settled convictions in his own mind, and how far he was merely repeating the current talk in the political circles to which he inclined, it would be difficult now to determine. If he believed all he said of the evils of excessive bank issues, and if he saw a financial crisis approaching, as his message would indicate that he did, it would naturally be expected of him that he would recommend such legislation as would remove the causes which were still active in the multiplication of the evils he pointed out: especially might it be expected of him that he would recommend the repeal of the general banking law, so far, at least, as it authorized corporations for which proceedings had not already been originated. But the truth probably is, that he comprehended very imperfectly the actual crisis. In this regard he was no more lacking in foresight than the community in general. Everything about him was still excited and speculative; values were nominally maintained; dealings in wild lands and town property at fancy prices were still active though mostly on credit, and the notion floated vaguely in people's minds that there was wealth in land as such, independent of labor and improvement. But as the State was still rapidly settling, any one could see that land must continue to be bought and sold, and as private and public improvements spread over the State, the hope that the market value would continue to go up did not seem wholly chimerical. The same legislature which had passed the general banking law had authorized the governor to borrow five millions of dollars for railroads, canals, and other improvements, and it was plausibly argued that when these improved highways had been made to penetrate every part of the State, as was proposed, farming lands would approximate in value to those in western New York, and prosperous villages would rise up all along the lines of internal communication. The governor, therefore, so far from recommending the repeal of the general banking law, expressed his strong opinion that the banks of the State were generally in a sound condition, and that what was to be feared was, that as a consequence of specie suspension, elsewhere, runs would be made upon Michigan banks which, notwithstanding they had ample assets, would force them to suspend operations. He, therefore, recommended the passage of a law legalizing the temporary suspension of specie payments, and the legislature, adopting his suggestion, authorized the suspension until May 16, 1838; the banks in the mean time being prohibited from paying dividends while in a state of suspension, and also from selling gold or silver at a premium and from buying their own notes at a discount. An amendment to the bill, taking from the banks the privilege of collecting their own demands in specie while not paying specie themselves, was defeated.

This was the most important outcome of the special session, and it was certainly very extraordinary legislation. It left the general banking law in force, with full authority to organize banks under it, and to begin the business of issuing bills *in a state of suspension;* to flood the State with an irredeemable currency, subject only to the condition that the associates should give security for the ultimate redemption of their bills and the payment of their other debts, and that they should pay in thirty per cent. of their capital stock in specie before commencing business. Wild lands that had been recently bought of the government at one dollar and twenty-five cents an acre were now valued at ten or twenty times that amount, and lots in villages that still existed only on paper had a worth for banking purposes only limited by the conscience of the officer who was to take the securities. Any ten freeholders of a county must be poor indeed if they could not give sufficient security to answer the purpose of the general banking law. The requirement of the payment of thirty per cent. of the capital stock in specie was more difficult to be complied with. But as the payment was to be made to the bank itself, the difficulty was gotten over in various ingenious ways, which the author of the general banking law could scarcely have anticipated. In some cases, stock notes in terms payable in specie, or the certificates of individuals which stated — untruly — that the maker held a specified sum of specie for the bank, were counted as specie itself; in others, a small sum of specie was paid in and taken out, and the process repeated over and over until the aggregate of payments equaled the sum required; in still others, the specie with which one bank was organized was passed from town to town and made to answer the purposes of several. By the first day of January, 1838, articles of association for twenty-one banks had been filed, making, with the banks before in existence, an average of one to less than five thousand people. Some of them were absolutely without capital, and some were organized by scheming men in New York and elsewhere, who took the bills away with them to circulate abroad, putting out none at home. For some, locations as inaccessible as possible were selected, that the bills might not come back to plague the managers. The bank commissioners say in their report for 1838, of their journey for inspection: " The singular spectacle was presented of the officers of the State seeking for banks in situations the most inaccessible and remote from trade, and finding at every step an increase of labor by the discovery of new and unknown organizations. Before they could be arrested the mischief was done: large issues were in circulation and no adequate remedy for the evil." One bank was found housed in a saw-mill, and it was said with pardonable exaggeration in one of the public papers, "Every village plat with a house, or even without a house, if it had a hollow stump to serve as a vault, was the site of a bank." The suspension act, which under these circumstances gave free license to scheming parties for frauds which the general banking law sufficiently invited, was very justly characterized as "a high crime against society."

The governor, when he delivered his annual message in January, 1838, still had confidence in the general banking law, which he said "offered to all persons the privilege of banking under certain guards and restrictions," and he declared that "the principles upon which this law is based are certainly correct, destroying as they do the odious feature of a banking monopoly, and giving equal rights to all classes of the community." But he thought there had been abuses of the system for which the legislature should provide remedy, and he reiterated his opinion of the evils of excessive paper issues. He recommended a law for the withdrawal of small bills, that gold and silver might take their place as currency, and he expressed the opinion that it would be wise to create a state bank with a capital limited to the amount of the state loan he had been authorized to make. A most extravagant recommendation, which if adopted might have involved the State itself in the bankruptcy which was then impending over so many of the people.

The aggregate amount of private indebtedness had by this time become enormous, and the pressure for payment was serious and disquieting. Property on the market was as abundant as ever, but sellers were numerous and eager, while buyers were few, and conversion into money was almost impossible. Wheat, which was worth two dollars and a half a bushel in 1836, had now gone down to a dollar, and other agricultural products in like proportion, and the depression affected all other prices. The people must have relief; and what relief could be so certain or so speedy as more banks and more money? More banks therefore continued to be organized, and the paper current flowed out among the people in increasing volume. The legislature, in December, had undertaken to improve the banking system somewhat, and had provided for the appointment of three bank commissioners who should inspect every bank at least once in three months, and had also prohibited the suspension of specie payments by any bank which might be organized after the first of January following. But the prohibition was of no moment. Twenty-eight banks were organ-

EVASION OF THE LAW.

ized after that date, and succeeded in getting their issues afloat, which was all that in many cases the promoters expected or cared for. The banks created under the general banking law were appropriately christened by the public "wild cats," and it was easy for any one to obtain their bills who could give reasonable assurance that he would circulate them at a distance and keep them afloat.

The bank commissioners when they entered upon the duty of inspection encountered, as was to be expected, a combination, organized and vigilant, to deceive and mislead them. The specie found by them at one bank was sent by hurried journey ahead of them to be counted at the next; "gold and silver flew about the country with the celerity of magic; its sound was heard in the depths of the forest, yet like the wind one knew not whence it came or whither it was going." It was found in some cases that large packages of bills sent to a distance for circulation were not entered on the books or reported; that the books were intentionally prepared for deception; that kegs of specie kept for show and credit were kegs of nails with a little silver on the top; and that every conceivable device had been resorted to, in order to make that appear sound and worthy of trust which was rottenness and fraud in its very birth. But distrust had come to be universal. Whoever took the bills of the banks did so intending to pass them off at the earliest possible moment. They were at a great discount as compared with Eastern bills; the issues of one bank were at a discount as compared with those of another; merchants kept couriers by whom they hurried off to the banks of issue the bills they were compelled to take, that they might if possible exchange them for something in which they had more confidence. No "circulating medium" ever before circulated so rapidly. The commissioners were vigilant in taking steps to wind up the concerns of banks which had been demonstrated to have no soundness, but new banks still continued to be formed. When a bank failed it was of course that laboring men and farmers should be the principal losers; for they had neither the means of keeping well informed concerning the condition of the banks, nor the facilities for putting off doubtful bills which were possessed by the merchants. At the beginning of 1839 the bank commissioners estimated that there were a million dollars of bills of insolvent banks in the hands of individuals and unavailable. Yet the governor, in his annual message delivered in January, found it a "source of unfeigned gratification to be able to congratulate [the legislature] on the prosperous condition to which our rising commonwealth has attained," though he thought there should be a correction of abuses in the banking system, but of what nature were the abuses, and how to be remedied he failed to be specific in pointing out.

He was careful to say, however, that there ought to be no war upon the banks, for "the banks have their rights and should be protected in them," but he added at the same time, as if to warn them against any possible inclination to misbehavior, that "they are not above all law, both human and divine."

How far the actual fact corresponded to this last remark, there might possibly be differences of opinion. It was very certain that in the management of the affairs of many of the banks no moral obligations whatever had been recognized; and it was equally certain that from first to last their operations had contemplated the circumvention and defeat of all such laws of the state as had protection of the public in view. And the general fact was that the mischief was done before any legal remedy could be applied. The hopeful governor reiterated his opinion in favor of a great state bank, but he had acquired no converts to his plan, and it received little attention. The insolvent banks were rapidly passing out of existence; by the end of 1839 forty-two of them were in the hands of receivers, and only two of the chartered banks and four of those which were organized under the general banking law were still keeping open doors for business. A very large share of all the currency of the State had become absolutely worthless in the pockets of the people, and was as much lost to the owners as though it had been committed to the flames. Market values of merchantable property had depreciated in proportion to the reduction of currency; there was no sale for lands and little for anything else except the bare necessaries of life; distrust in business circles was universal, and business was utterly prostrate. Distress had taken the place of the unnatural excitement, extravagance, and elation of fictitious wealth. It was a natural sequence to this condition of things that a revolution should take place in the political control of the State, and that the Jackson party, which had held undisputed sway to this time, should be deprived of power. The Whigs in the fall of 1839 chose a majority of the legislature, and elected William Woodbridge governor. The revolution was the result of general causes, operating throughout the country, though every state had an experience of its own, with peculiar features.

But no political change could stop the vicious consequences of the wild-cat banking, which were attributable to no one party, and which were continued by suspension laws through several years. All the important legislation of the State for some time, and especially all that concerned public improvements and the collection of debts, was shaped in view of the depression which followed the financial dissipation. But the measures of relief only aggravated and prolonged the evils of a worthless currency: "a compound," as a writer of the day justly said, "of folly and wickedness." " Of course the people were swindled out of a million or two of property, — and this was a lesser evil than the frightful inroads made upon their moral principles, for a doubtful currency contaminates all hands that touch it." Then came stay laws, and laws to compel creditors to take lands at a valuation. They were doubtful in point of utility, and more than doubtful in point of morality and constitutionality. The federal bankrupt act of 1841 first brought substantial relief: it brought almost no dividends to creditors, but it relieved debtors from their crushing burdens and permitted them, sobered and in their right minds, to enter once more the fields of industry and activity.

The extraordinary history of the attempt to break up an "odious monopoly" in banking by making everybody a banker, and to create prosperity by unlimited issues of paper currency, was brought at length to a fit conclusion. There had always been in the minds of sound lawyers serious doubts of the constitutionality of the general banking law; and in 1844 the matter was brought to judicial test. The constitution declared that "the legislature shall pass no act of incorporation unless with the assent of at least two thirds of each house;" and this provision it was believed contemplated that each proposed corporation should be considered and determined upon separately. It was not in the minds of the people that a great number of corporations should be created or provided for by a single act, by a legislature which, if considering the necessity or expediency of any single one of them, might disapprove of it altogether. The provision was restrictive, having its origin in a distrust of corporations which was prevalent among the people, and was meant to impose an important and effective restraint upon their easy and free multiplication. This was the view taken by the court, and the law was held void in its inception. The banks were consequently illegal institutions; the securities given for the payment of their debts were void; the obligations they had taken from individuals were nullities. Even the receiverships which had been created for winding up their concerns were of no legal importance further; for the banks having never had existence could have no creditors to account to, and such receivers as were in possession of assets which they could make available, pocketed them. But in many cases there were no assets to pocket. Such were the fruits of the experiment of giving equal and practically unlimited rights in banking to everybody who wanted a shorter road to wealth than that trodden by labor and honest industry.

The new State, under the bold but inexperienced guidance of its youthful governor, disdaining the lessons of history, had determined to try for itself the experiment of manufacturing riches by the

SUBSIDENCE OF THE BANKING MANIA. 277

printing-press. The condition after the experiment might be compared to a forest after a cyclone: everything was prostrate, and everything was in confusion. The State was now paying the cost of its lesson in the destruction of credit, the loss of all the fictitious and much of the actual wealth of the people, the bankruptcy of great numbers, and several years of stagnation of business. General and forced economy was a necessity of the situation; but this was a blessing. After 1841, the few chartered banks which survived were able to maintain their position as specie paying, and by their legitimate assistance the people patiently and with steady industry addressed themselves to the development of the resources of the State and to the improvement of their own condition. Thousands never recovered from the bankruptcy and discouragement which followed the financial collapse; but the State at large was soon rapidly accumulating substantial wealth, and acquiring an independent and self-respecting population.

Thereafter wild-cat banking was a by-word in the State; but the lessons it taught needed to be learned at some time, and were not likely to be learned except with experience as teacher. One of its lessons was that neither real estate nor anything else not immediately convertible into money can support the credit of bank currency. But for the experience of the several States in banking, in the years 1837–39, who shall say that the national currency act, when it came to be passed, might not have been as little guarded against dangerous schemes as some of its state predecessors?

CHAPTER XIV.

THE STATE ENTERS UPON INTERNAL IMPROVE-MENTS.

The years 1835, '36, and '37 were years for the building of air castles everywhere, but especially in the new West. Nowhere were the imaginations of the people more active, or more excited with visions of great prosperity than in Michigan, and nowhere was there greater excuse for it. Every steamboat on Lake Erie was loaded with people on their way to the Peninsular State, and the road through the Black Swamp from Cleveland to the Maumee exhibited a continuous moving caravan of emigrant wagons slowly and laboriously dragged along. The Erie and Kalamazoo railroad, with its little cars of stage-coach fashion, was doing what it could to help the procession move on into Michigan: it carried "baggage at the risk of the owners," but its speed was not such as to put life at much risk, except perhaps when a broken strap rail ran a "snake head" up through the car floor. In the interior might be heard on every side the sound of the woodman's axe and the crash of falling trees; new houses, very primitive but each sheltering a family, were being put up everywhere; and crops were being gathered where only the year before all was wilderness and solitude. A magical transformation was going on before the eyes of the people, which had been rendered possible through the construction of the Erie Canal, whereby De Witt Clinton, Myron Holley, and their associates had added so vastly to the wealth and importance of the Empire State, and won for themselves immortal renown. It was a striking evidence of what improved means for the transportation of persons and property might do for a state; and the proof that the people were awake to its importance is seen in the fact that in forming their constitution, preparatory to admission to the Union, they took pains to impose upon the legislature the duty of following the example of New York. The provision to this end was the following: "Internal improvements shall be encouraged by the government of this state; and it shall be the duty of the legislature as soon as may be, to make provision by law for ascertaining the proper objects of improvements, in relation to roads, canals, and navigable waters; and it shall also be their duty to provide by law for an equal, systematic, and economical application of the funds which may be appropriated to these objects." As this section neither gave power to the legislature nor undertook to set bounds to power otherwise possessed, it was obviously out of place in the constitution, where only the outlines and fundamental principles of government are looked for; but it was indicative of prevailing thoughts and aspirations, and had no little influence upon subsequent state action. It may therefore be regarded as a significant landmark in the history of the State.

The laudable ambition of the first governor to distinguish his own administration and to advance the growth and prosperity of the State would naturally lead him to act promptly upon this mandatory provision. The surface of Michigan was such as to admit of easy and economical construction of both railroads and canals, and it might well be deemed a reproach to the State should it be behind the rest of the Union in these great and now indispensable conveniences. Accordingly the governor in his annual message reminded the legislature that "the period has arrived when Michigan can no longer, without detriment to her standing and importance as a state, delay the action necessary for the development of her vast resources of wealth. Nature has bestowed upon us the highest advantages of climate, a fertile soil and peculiar facilities for commerce; and with a prudent and wise forecast to be exercised by the legislature and the people, we cannot fail soon to reach that high destiny which awaits us." It is impossible to mistake the spirit of this message: the emphatic words are words of action: we cannot *longer delay :* we must *soon* — not by steady and measured steps, but immediately — " reach that high destiny which awaits us," if we have the " prudent and wise forecast " which perceives the opportunity for greatness, and embraces it without hesitation or faint-heartedness.

Accordingly the governor recommended surveys to determine how and by what routes the waters of Lake Michigan might be connected by canals with the waters of the eastern part of the State; and he suggests a series of state railroads, and the purchase by the State of certain roads which had already been begun by corporations. The legislature responded promptly to this action. An act was passed for the location and construction of three lines of railroad across the State: one from Detroit to the mouth of the St. Joseph River; one from Monroe to New Buffalo, and one from the mouth of the Black River to the navigable waters of Grand River or to Lake Michigan. The sum of five hundred and fifty thousand dollars was appropriated to begin the construction, and further sums were voted for the survey of a canal route from Mount Clemens to the mouth of the Kalamazoo River, and of a canal around the falls of the St. Mary, and for various minor projects which may now be suffered to rest in the oblivion to which the State long since very properly consigned them. To provide funds for these purposes, the governor was authorized to borrow on the credit of the State the sum of five million dollars, at an interest which should not exceed five and a half per cent., and to issue state bonds therefor. The sum borrowed was to constitute an internal improvement fund, and it was declared that the proceeds of all railroads and canals constructed by the State, the interest on all loans which might thereafter be made by the State from the internal improvement fund, and the dividends arising from all bank stock owned or which might thereafter be owned by the State, so far as necessary, should constitute a sinking fund for the payment of the principal and interest of this loan. The bonds were not to be sold at less than par. The sum to be borrowed was subsequently increased by two hundred thousand dollars, that the State might advance to each of two railroad companies then engaged in building roads the sum of one hundred thousand dollars.

Five million two hundred thousand dollars was a large debt for a state whose people, less than two hundred thousand in number, were still struggling under the hardships and privations of pioneer life; and a little more experience in the manner in which public moneys are expended in state works would have satisfied any considerate person that this amount would be only the beginning of what would be required to complete the magnificent system of public works which the legislature had planned. This, however, was not generally understood at the time: the calculations of cost were low; it was only the calculation of returns that was magnificently large. The committee of the legislature that reported the scheme had no difficulty in demonstrating, by facts and figures, that the income from the railroad from Detroit across the State must be thirty per cent. annually upon the cost; a most splendid and satisfactory result, as all must admit, to flow from acting promptly with proper confidence in the future of the State. The cost of the road, it is true, with all its station houses and other buildings, was estimated at only a million and a half; but this was for a single track only, and the surplus earnings, after providing for the interest of the cost and paying off the principal, were expected to be ample for the building of an additional track as fast as needed. Such were the crude and ignorant calculations upon which, in the early days of railroads, states were induced to plunge into debt and to peril their credit and good name, sometimes almost beyond hope of protection or rescue.

In his annual message for 1838, the governor was able to say that under the act authorizing the five million loan he had made such arrangements as would enable the State readily to command any portion of the amount, and that five hundred thousand dollars of the bonds had already been sold in the American market at the very handsome premium of six per cent., and the remainder

PRUDENCE CREEPING BACK.

had been put upon the European market. He also reported that the improvements which had been entered upon were progressing to his satisfaction. But there were indications that the governor was becoming circumspect, and perhaps beginning to fear that the State had entered upon undertakings which were likely to test its powers unduly. He questioned whether the sum the State had undertaken to borrow would be sufficient, even with the most rigid economy, to provide for the construction of the works undertaken, and he submitted the propriety of leaving the minor works to individual enterprise; the State constructing the great and leading communications only. The minor enterprises, however, as well as the greater, were already entered upon, and as nobody was proposing their construction as individual enterprises, it was not at all likely that state expenditures upon them would be suffered to stop while the larger works were progressing. When a great system of internal improvements is entered upon, sections and localities have claims they will not suffer to be ignored; the questions involved are largely questions of local advantage, and the state, in the distribution of its favors, must consider all, and be impartial to all.

In his message for 1839 the governor still speaks in hopeful terms of the progress of public improvements, but the information he has to communicate respecting the loan is not agreeable. The sale of bonds to the amount of five hundred thousand dollars had fallen through after two hundred thousand had been paid for, and he was obliged to look elsewhere for a purchaser. He had found one in the Morris Canal and Banking Company, for a part of the sum required, and that company as agent for the State had closed out a sale of the remaining bonds to the Pennsylvania United States Bank. The terms were not what the State had expected to make: the sale was in fact below par, but was made nominally at par by an allowance under the name of commissions. One million three hundred thousand dollars had actually been received into the state treasury, and the governor, while not satisfied with what had been accomplished, assured the legislature it was the best that was possible in the existing state of the money market. This was a great disappointment to the State, and subjected the governor to serious criticism. But worse news was to come: it was soon to be a question not of the loss of a percentage merely, but of the loss of the major part of the loan. The Morris Canal and Banking Company failed; the Pennsylvania United States Bank failed; the two had possession of all the state bonds and had paid for some of them; upon the remainder only a small percentage had been paid, but the bankrupt institutions, without right or authority, had hypothecated the bonds for their own debts. Only about one half the face value had been received by the State.

This was a startling condition of things. The State not only had urgent need of the whole amount of the loan for the works already begun, but it had now become manifest to the most sanguine that a much larger sum would be necessary for their completion. Nothing, it was now seen, was to be realized from earnings which could be applied to construction. If the loan failed even in part, progress upon the works must be stopped, or at least greatly delayed. But it now appeared that while the State was to receive scarcely half the expected loan, the whole amount of the bonds was in the hands of parties who would insist that they were purchasers for value, and demand full payment. The State must then pay, or it must expect to be classed in the money market of the world in the ranks of repudiation. Repudiation is the lowest depth of state degradation; it had already brought some states into disgrace; and a people might justly be sensitive to its imputation, even when their purpose was right and honorable.

To narrate in detail all that took place afterwards would make a long and dreary story which may well be left untold. The results are all that are now important. The bank crash came with its attendant ruin and bankruptcy, and the State was soon in condition rendering it impossible to pay the interest on even the full-paid bonds. Work on the state railroads was likely to come to a stop, and it was only kept in progress by means of an issue of state script payable in lands, of which half a million acres had been donated by the United States to the State for internal improvement purposes. The sacrifice upon this script was necessarily very great, and its use was a wasteful expenditure of state resources. The ordinary expenses of government could not be met without borrowing, for it would have been impossible to raise by taxation sufficient to meet all demands without causing great distress. As the amount payable on state bonds was now in controversy, the interest was necessarily in dispute, and no part of it was provided for, or was likely to be until the controversy was in some manner determined. To add to public embarrassments, it was now made known that the details of the negotiation for the loan had not at first been fully communicated, and that some of the terms were so unusual and so detrimental to the interests of the State as justly to call for censure.

Regarding the bonds which had been intrusted to the Morris Canal and Banking Company, and which were now in other hands, the State took at the outset a position which was deemed just, and maintained it firmly. The bonds which had been bought and paid for should be paid in full, principal and interest. There should be no repudiation; and if payment of interest was delayed, interest should be paid upon the deferred payment. But as to bonds not sold in fact, but upon which something had been paid, the State would recognize an obligation to the extent of the payment, but no farther. It was not believed the holders of those bonds were entitled to claim the rights of *bonâ fide* holders: they stood in the shoes of the Morris Canal and Banking Company, and of the Pennsylvania United States Bank, neither of which could have equities against the State entitling it to demand upon the bonds more than it had paid for them with interest; and the State, even at the risk of misconstruction, would refuse to go, in recognizing the bonds, farther than equity and the rules of law as between individuals would require. On the part-paid bonds being surrendered, the State would issue full-paid bonds for the sum equitably due upon them. More than this it was not believed that justice could demand. The proposition of the State was not immediately accepted by the bond-holders, but it was not long before the part-paid bonds began to come in, and in the end all were retired. The episode was a disagreeable one for the State, but when it was over the state credit was good, and the debt was not beyond its ability to pay in due season.

The works of internal improvement still remained on the hands of the State, and in the day of its poverty and trial they were continually calling upon a depleted treasury for money to keep them in progress. But now that the great bubble of speculation and inflation was burst, it became plain to the comprehension of the dullest that some of the state projects were wild and chimerical, and they were abandoned altogether. Such was the case with the projected canal from Mount Clemens to the mouth of the Kalamazoo River, which it was now seen would be worthless if constructed. The only works of much promise were the central and southern of the three railroads, which were now very well under way. But doubts were arising in the minds of the people whether the State had been wise in undertaking the construction and management even of these: whether it was possible for the State to do either the one or the other with the same prudence and economy as could private owners. These doubts soon matured into a settled conviction that the management of railroads was in its nature essentially a private business, and ought to be in the hands of individuals. By common consent it came to be considered that the State in entering upon these works had made a serious mistake; and the legislature, in an act for funding the loan bonds, invited proposals from state creditors for the purchase of the state railroads. The times were not then propitious; but in 1846 the Central and Southern Railroads, so far as they were then constructed, were sold by the State to corporations which had been chartered for the purpose of purchasing. The aggregate price was two million and a half, a sum very much below what had been their cost to the State. But the people felt that the roads were well off their hands, and as has been said by one familiar with the whole history, "Here virtually ceased to exist all our works of internal improvement. Nothing but the débris of our airy castles remained, and that only to plague our recollections." The two great railroads when taken up by corporations went rapidly forward to completion, and they soon became great national highways whose utility to the State was quite equal to the highest expectations ever formed concerning them.

Having all their bitter experience with internal improvements fresh in mind, when they formed a new constitution in 1850, the people resolved to put it out of the power of the legislature again to involve them in extravagant projects. And here we reach another landmark, significant in itself, but especially notable when contrasted with the provision respecting internal improvements which has already been quoted from the constitution of 1835. In 1850 the people deemed it necessary to prohibit what in 1835 they commended; and they now provided that " the State shall not subscribe to or be interested in the stock of any company, association, or corporation," and also that "the State shall not be a party to or interested in any work of internal improvement, nor engaged in carrying on any such work, except in the expenditure of grants to the State of land or other property." These were very positive provisions; and by adopting them the people believed they had rendered it impossible that projects of doubtful wisdom and utility should be engaged in at the public cost.

But diseases in the body politic, like those in the human system, are likely to take on new forms from time to time, and they are not to be exorcised by words, or kept off by constitutional inhibitions. The mania for internal improvements at the cost of the public, when it returned fifteen years later under the administration of Governor Crapo, took on the form of aid to railroad corporations by the several municipal bodies in the State. Such aid was being given in other states, and railroads as a consequence were being constructed with a rapidity never paralleled. Michigan was lagging behind the rest of the country: Why should this be so? Every town which should subscribe to the stock of a railroad would immediately receive a full return in the enhanced value of its landed property, and would have the stock besides. This was what was commonly said and commonly believed; and the legislature, well reflecting the common desire, passed a general law under which townships and cities were to be permitted to vote aid to railroads. The railroads, under another general law, might be laid out anywhere by the projectors at pleasure; so that monopoly in these public conveniences seemed to be effectually provided against. The governor vetoed the railroad aid act, but the legislature passed it over his veto. The business of voting aid to railroads was soon active; and the most visionary scheme was found as likely to receive aid as any other: perhaps more so, for more work would be done for it. Nothing is so easy as to build railroads if it can be accomplished by dropping votes into a box. Only fossils and croakers will disturb the public mind by reminders that the sums voted must at some time be paid, and that the roads when built may pay nothing towards them. The State in detail by its corporations was fast plunging into indebtedness which had already reached an aggregate of several million, when the process was arrested by a decision of the state Supreme Court that the act under which the voting had taken place was unconstitutional. The decision was a bitter disappointment to many, and the public clamor for a time was loud and earnest; but a movement to obtain an amendment to the constitution which would permit such municipal aid to railroads was unsuccessful, and the excitement soon died out. The people had taken the "sober second thought," and had become convinced that municipal corporations in their power to contract debts or to expend public moneys should be confined closely to proper municipal purposes. And this conclusion may be taken as a third conspicuous landmark in the history of internal improvements in Michigan.

CHAPTER XV.

ECONOMY, RECUPERATION, AND PROGRESS.

THE ascendency of the Whig party in the State came to an end in the great reaction which followed the death of President Harrison, and the quarrel of his successor with the party which had elected him. In 1841, John S. Barry, the Democratic candidate for governor, was chosen, with a legislature of the same political faith to support him. The new governor was a man peculiarly adapted to the station in the present condition of state affairs. The State was just beginning to recuperate after its wild and disastrous financial extravagances, and an executive was needed who would bring the most careful and rigid economy into the administration of government. In Barry the State found such an executive: his New England hard sense had been strengthened, solidified, and broadened by pioneer life, and he was a fitting leader to bring the State back to ideas and practices of economy and frugality, without at the same time lowering its character or tainting its administration with meanness. He had been much in public life, but without at any time neglecting his business as a merchant, and he had accumulated what was thought in those days a considerable fortune, by strict attention to business in all its details, and by prudent foresight and frugality in expenses. His honesty in public life was scrupulous, and it was a matter of course with him that he should expect, on coming to his new office, to give practical effect in state affairs to the prudential rules and principles which he knew must be sound and wise for the public, because they were profitable and expedient when applied to the business of individuals. He was much lacking in popular manners, but he had been chosen governor in the belief that he would give the State a safe and economical administration, which above all things was what the people desired and the State needed at this time. The public expectation was fully justified: the public economy was rigid and well maintained during his administration; and when men whose projects he frowned upon went off calling him a bear, and circulated by way of ridicule the story that he mowed the state house yard to sell the grass and put the money in the state treasury, the hard-working farmers of the State knew instinctively he was the proper executive for the time, and proceeded to give him a reëlection. A bear before the treasury seemed quite in proper place just now, and no economy was ridiculous which pointed a moral. In spite of the governor's cold and repelling demeanor, he acquired a popularity to which few of his successors attained ; and it may be said of his four years' service, that no other period of four years in the history of the State has been more useful to the people, who were now slowly but steadily and surely laying the foundations of a solid and permanent prosperity. The works of internal improvement were managed with prudence and economy, and the offer which had been made to state creditors to sell them and receive in payment the outstanding state obligations was before the public, and preparing the way for the sale that soon afterwards took place.

Emigrants continued to come into the State in considerable numbers, and the process of clearing off the forest and improving the land went on rapidly, but the people were able to add to their possessions only slowly and for the most part by hard labor and strict economy. Following Governor Barry came Alpheus Felch, who resigned in the second year of his service to accept the seat to which he had been elected as senator in Congress, and was succeeded for the remainder of the term by William L. Greenly. Then came Epaphroditus Ransom, elected in 1847, in whose term the capital was removed from Detroit, where it had hitherto been, and located in the woods of Lansing forty miles from any railroad. In this same term are to be noted two exceptions to the general fact that the emigrants to Michigan came singly or in families, and not in organized bodies of colonists. In 1847 a party of Hollanders, coming from their native land for greater religious liberty, under the leadership of Rev. Albertus C. Van Raalte of the Dutch Reformed Church, founded the village of Holland and also Hope College; and they were followed from year to year by many others who also settled in the same part of the State, where they had schools and publications in their native language and established many churches. They were sufficiently numerous to give a distinctive character to the population of many localities in that section of the State. But it was a good character and the people were not incongruous with the existing population of the State.

A colony of a very different character settled on Beaver Island, led by James J. Strang, who had been a Mormon elder at Nauvoo and high in the confidence of Joseph Smith, the first prophet. After his superior was murdered, he claimed to have been designated as his successor, but he was defeated in his aspirations of leadership by Brigham Young, and driven off by excommunication. He went first to Voree, Wisconsin, where he started a colony on the community plan, but in 1846 removed to Beaver Island, where he founded a settlement which was called after himself, St. James. Over this settlement he assumed the authority of high priest and king, and he made laws for it which were implicitly obeyed. He established and enforced rules of strict morality, prohibited entirely the sale of ardent spirits and enforced the prohibition, observed the seventh day as the Sabbath, built a tabernacle, and collected a tenth from the people for religious and all other public purposes. For two successive terms he was elected a member of the legislature, and performed the duties with ability, and for the most part to general acceptance. But in 1849 he introduced polygamy, and though it never spread much among his people, it led to some secessions, to continuous trouble thereafter with the "gentiles," and to some armed collisions. In 1856 he was assassinated by renegade Mormons and the colony scattered, leaving behind it no trace in Michigan of this strange delusion.

Governor Barry was reëlected in 1849. Up to this time the constitution of 1835 had remained in force, and been satisfactory to the people. But now radicalism was in the air the world over, and discontent with existing institutions was rife in every civilized country. In France, Italy, Hungary, and Germany there were revolutions, or attempts at revolution with considerable success, and everywhere the aspiration of the people was for greater liberty and more privileges to the individual and less power to the rulers. For the overthrow of existing governments there could be no excuse in the United States, but uneasiness and a desire for change was general, and existing conditions in law and in society encountered sharp and persistent criticism. The current of anti-slavery agitation was particularly strong and uncompromising, and in 1848 the Democratic party of the country temporarily went down under its blows. An agitation in favor of greater rights and more distinct individual recognition of married women in the law went to some extent hand in hand with the agitation against slavery, but it found advocates in every party, and a general concession that some of its demands were proper. The governor's power of appointment under the existing constitution was particularly complained of: he appointed the judges and all the heads of department; and this seemed an imputation upon the judgment of the people. To most persons there seemed to be no good reason why they should not elect all of their officers as well as a part of them.

That the various questions in government then agitating the public mind might be properly considered, a constitutional convention was called, which met at Lansing on the first Monday of June, 1850, and proceeded to revise the constitution of the State with much thoroughness, under the influence of the prevailing radicalism. A few of the more important provisions it will be interesting to notice. A married woman, it was declared, shall hold her property, whether acquired before or after marriage, to the same extent as if single, and may dispose of it by contract, deed, or will at pleasure. No more charters of private incorporation shall be passed; but corporations shall be formed under general laws, which shall at all times be subject to legislative control and repeal. By this provision the doctrine of the Federal Supreme Court in the Dartmouth College case, that the charter of a private corporation is a contract, — a doctrine from which there had always been much dissent, — was meant to be altogether excluded in respect to corporations thereafter formed. Aliens were given the liberty to hold real property with the same freedom as citizens. Judicial officers from highest to lowest were required to be elected by the people, and so were all the heads of department and all other important officers. And various provisions were adopted to bring the exercise of power as near as possible to the people concerned, and to make the responsibility constant and direct. Representatives in the lower house of the legislature were required to be elected for one legislature only, and in single districts. The county board of supervisors was made an important body, with considerable powers of local legislation, and with authority to pass finally and exclusively upon all claims against the county. The old abuses of the Court of Chancery in England were remembered, and inspired a provision for abolishing the court, and handing its jurisdiction over to the courts of law. The temperance sentiment found expression in a provision that licenses for the sale of intoxicating drinks should not be granted. The evils of unrestricted banking were still fresh in mind, and it was declared that no banking law should be passed without submission to the people, nor without individual liability on the part of officers and stockholders; and the legislature was to have no power to authorize a suspension of specie payments. The grand jury was done away with as cumbrous and generally unnecessary, though one might be ordered for special cases. A very important and humane provision was that a homestead should be exempted from execution for debts, and also not less than five hundred dollars of personal property. And the legislature was required to make the public schools free.

Many restrictions were imposed on the legislative power of the State, but the most notable of these were such as concerned the finances. The State was now in debt, but its credit was good, and it was determined that this should be sustained and the debt paid as speedily as possible. The legislature was therefore required immediately to provide a sinking fund, which should be increased annually at least five per cent. until the whole debt was extinguished. The State was to be at liberty to contract debts to meet deficits in revenue, but not to exceed at any one time fifty thousand dollars; and also to repel invasion, suppress insurrection, or defend the State in time of war. The issue of state script was prohibited. These provisions, with a prohibition against the State loaning its credit to individuals or corporations, or engaging directly or indirectly in works of internal improvement, were thought ample to give protection against the consequences of a return of the mania under which the five million loan had been contracted.

The provisions respecting salaries of state officials are deserving of notice, as indicating the tendency of public thought at the time. It is first to be remarked that the convention determined to fix the salaries, so that it should not be in the power of the legislature to increase them under the influence of extravagant ideas or of lobby pressure. Next it is to be observed that the sums named were very small; small even for the time, and soon to appear ridiculously so when the expenses of living should be greatly increased, and the State become populous and wealthy. The salary of the governor was fixed at one thousand dollars; that of the circuit judges, who were then also judges of of the supreme court, one thousand five hundred dollars, while the other state officers were to receive, some of them a thousand and some eight hundred dollars. The people of that day, who were only through the most rigid economy and by slow and patient steps advancing to a condition of financial independence in their private concerns, thought these salaries sufficient. They were equal to the average expenditure of well-to-do people; and provision to that extent, it was thought, should content the public servants. At these figures the salaries, with the exception of those of the circuit judges, which have been raised to twenty-five hundred dollars, have remained ever since. It has been deemed, by many, a reproach to the State that this has been the case. The opinion is often and very strongly expressed, that to secure the best talent in the service of the State, the compensation must be equal to what the best talent secures in the various branches of private business. There is some degree of truth for this opinion; at the same time it is probably true that no citizen of Michigan ever declined one of its leading offices for the reason solely that the salary fixed by the constitution was inferior to what he might reasonably look for in private life. And it is also probably true that the low compensation for public services has had a powerful tendency to keep alive ideas of economy and frugality in official circles and in all branches of state expenditure, and even among the people at large; and that we may justly attribute to it some influence in securing the remarkable exemption from official peculations and legislative scandals and corruption which the State for the most part has enjoyed.

The constitution was adopted, and it has continued to be the fundamental law of the State, with slight amendments, to the present day. One of its provisions is that every sixteenth year the question of a revision shall be submitted to the people. It was so submitted in 1866, and decided in the affirmative; but when a revision was prepared by a convention elected for the purpose, the people rejected their work. In 1882 the question of revision was negatived by popular vote. Thus since 1850 no disposition has been manifested to tinker the constitution, but conservative ideas have steadily prevailed. The most important amendment was made in 1875, in the repeal of the provision forbidding licenses, which was adopted in order to make way for heavy taxation of the liquor traffic, after prohibitory legislation had been in existence for twenty years. Now and then complaints are made of the system which makes the judges elective, but these are based not so much upon experience as upon theory, and no considerable disposition has at any time been manifested among the people to change the system. Those who note carefully the results have not perceived that the people have shown less inclination to be independent of party or of improper influence in the choice of judges than have been executive officers when vested with the appointing power.

A brief paragraph will bring us to the time of the great civil war. Robert McClelland was elected governor for one year in 1851 and was reëlected for two years in 1852, but resigned to

REPUBLICAN ASCENDENCY.

become a member of the cabinet of President Pierce. Andrew Parsons, the lieutenant-governor, was left to serve out the unexpired portion of his term. Up to this time, from 1841, the Democratic party had been in power in the State, but in 1854 the newly formed Republican party obtained the ascendency and maintained it unbroken for twenty-eight years, electing Kinsley S. Bingham governor in 1854 and 1856, and Moses Wisner in 1858. Austin Blair was elected in 1860 and became the "war governor" of the State; a title which by his integrity and patriotic vigor he made one of lasting honor.

CHAPTER XVI.

THE STATE PROVIDES FOR UNIVERSAL EDUCATION.

The founders of a state soon pass away; but in their aims and purposes, and to some extent in their personal characteristics, they build themselves into the structure they create, and give to it a character and individuality of its own. Ages afterwards it may be found that the germinal thoughts which took root under their planting are still growing and expanding, and that the ideas with which they quickened the early polity are dominant in the life of the mature commonwealth, though possibly those who act upon and give effect to them may have lost the recollection of their origin.

If the general education of the people is important to the state, Michigan was fortunate in the persons to whom the destinies of the territory were committed in its early days. In their minds, as we find them expressed in the laws they adopted and the institutions they founded, two ideas appear to have been dominant from the earliest period. These were, that the means of rudimentary education should be placed within the reach of every child in the political society; and that the opportunity for thorough culture should be given as speedily and as completely as the circumstances of the people would permit. And these ideas were never lost sight of until full effect was given to them after the admission of the State to the Union.

The early schools in the territory were of course French, and connected with the church. Their main purpose was to give religious instruction, and they were attended to some extent by Indian children. But private schools in which English was taught were in existence from the time of the outbreak of the Revolutionary war; poor affairs, and scarcely worth remembering now. When Father Richard came, he made an endeavor in the direction of better church schools, and with considerable success. In 1804 he established a school for girls, with four young ladies as teachers, and also a Latin school for young men. Both of these were broken up by the great fire of the next year, but schools of less ambitious character were established shortly afterwards, and Father Richard in 1808 reports six of such schools, three of which were taught by Indian teachers. The instruction in the schools for girls embraced sewing, spinning, knitting, and weaving, and to the Indian children this part of the instruction was probably the most valuable. Father Richard thought his schools ought to receive public assistance, and he applied to the legislature for the grant of a lottery franchise; but though the evils of lotteries were not so well understood then as now, his application failed of effect, and his schools continued feeble and of low grade.

The future promised better things. Before the territory was detached from Indiana, it had become the settled policy of the United States to reserve from sale the sixteenth section of every surveyed township, and to set it apart for the use of the township for the support of common schools. It had also become customary to make some smaller donation of public lands for the endowment of a university, and one township of such lands had been appropriated to Michigan, in contemplation of its becoming a separate government. But for a long time these donations must of necessity be of little value: value must be given to them by the settlement and improvement of the country, and in the mean time they would constitute the promise of an endowment for education rather than the endowment itself. All early education, if any was given at the public cost, must therefore be provided for by direct taxation of the people.

In 1809, while as yet the population of the territory was under five thousand, an act was adopted which provided for the laying off into school districts of all the settled portions of the territory, and for an enumeration of the children between

THE EARLY SCHOOLS. 309

the ages of four and eighteen in each of the districts. From these districts annual reports were required of the moneys expended in the support of schools and the construction of school buildings, and the territory was to levy an annual tax of not less than two nor more than four dollars for each child reported within the ages above mentioned. The sum collected was to be apportioned among the districts; not, however, in proportion to the number of children in them respectively, but in proportion to the sums they had expended in the year preceding for school purposes. The gift of the territory was thus made in aid of schools, but was so apportioned as to invite and encourage liberality on the part of the people in making provisions from their own means for them.

The schools which were established under this act must have been very few in number, and very primitive in all their appointments. Eight years afterwards, however, something in the direction of higher and better education was attempted. Rev. John Monteith, a well-educated Presbyterian clergyman, had come to Detroit in 1816, where he had collected a congregation composed of various denominations of Protestants, to whom he preached on Sundays. He soon formed the acquaintance of Father Richard, and friendly intercourse between them brought out the fact that both were greatly concerned at the want of means of education for the youth of the territory, and willing and desirous to assist in supplying them. From Governor Cass they found ready and hearty coöperation, and the eccentric chief justice also lent assistance. The latter in August, 1817, drew up and secured the adoption of "An act to establish the Catholepistemiad or University of Michigania," in which an elaborate plan for a university was marked out. The plan was crude and pedantic, but its author had grasped certain principles which were of the very highest importance, and which from this time became incorporated in the polity of the territory, and subsequently of the State also. In every state, as he believed, the education of the people is important to the state itself, and should be assumed as a state duty. It should not be restricted to elementary education merely, but the state ought to place within the reach of its youth such higher education also as is commonly given in the colleges of the land. And this education should be non-sectarian. In recognition of this duty the act provided that fifteen per cent. should be added to the regular territorial taxes, to be appropriated to the support of the university. Students entering the university should pay small fees if able, but if not able to pay, the fees should be a public charge. Sectarianism in the university was not expressly legislated against, but its absence for the time was most effectually secured by the appointment of Mr. Monteith as president and Father Richard as his

A UNIVERSITY IN NAME. 311

principal assistant in instruction. The Presbyterian and the Catholic, it was very certain, would not coöperate in sectarian work.

This was an ambitious project for the young and feeble territory, which as yet was almost wholly without available means, and whose few schools were only of the most primitive character. It must have been very plain to every one that the complete realization of such a project could only be accomplished after many years; but the earnest and enthusiastic parties who had taken hold of it determined to do immediately whatever should be found within their power. The people of Detroit were solicited for contributions towards the erection of a university building, and the foundations of the building were soon laid with appropriate ceremonies and public rejoicings. But though a school was soon begun, the education given in it was necessarily of the most elementary character. A building and a high-sounding name could not make a university: there must be students competent to receive collegiate instruction, and as yet there were no such students in the territory. But it is something to have high aspirations, and to have made an effort in the direction of their realization.

Nor while leading men among the white people were thus engaging in the preparatory work of education, were the Indians found indisposed to contribute some share to so important an object.

The same article in the fundamental ordinance for the government of the territory which enjoined that "the utmost good faith shall always be observed towards the Indians," had also affirmed the necessity of religion, morality, and knowledge to good government and the happiness of mankind, and required the encouragement of schools and the means of education. This immediate association of religion and learning with good faith to the Indians was emphasized by the fact that the teachers of the Indians were also their religious guides; and these had always been found to be their best friends, and their most reliable protectors against the rapacity and greed of their white neighbors. Possibly in the great conference of Governor Cass and General McArthur as commissioners on the part of the United States with the chiefs of the Ottawa, Chippewa, and Pottawatamie tribes of Indians, held at Fort Meigs on September 29, 1817, the governor may have ventured with diplomatic skill and caution to bring freshly to their minds the labors of their priests and teachers for their good; and possibly the Indians, who were seldom justly chargeable with forgetfulness of kind treatment, may have needed no reminder to incline them to make suitable acknowledgment. But whatever the fact may be as to the incentive, the value of religion and learning are found recognized by the treaty in a grant of six sections of land in equal shares to the Church of St. Anne at Detroit and to "the College at Detroit." The Indians made the grant, as they say in the treaty, because of being "attached to the Catholic religion, and believing they may wish some of their children hereafter educated." The gift to the college was not a large one, and it would have seemed insignificant if made before the Indians had alienated the principal portion of their domain to the government; but its merit must be estimated by what they had retained for their own use, rather than by the extent of their original possessions. The gift, moreover, was fully equal in positive value and prospectively superior to the gifts for like purposes which made John Harvard and Elihu Yale immortal, and quite as justly entitles Tontagini and his associate chieftains to grateful remembrance among the founders of colleges.

The act for the organization of the university was revised in 1821, and relieved of its pedantic features. To obtain preparatory schools, trustees were empowered to establish from time to time "such colleges, academies, and schools depending upon the said university as they may think proper, and as the funds of the corporation will permit;" and the name was changed to the University of Michigan. In the same act religious distinctions in the governing board, the board of instruction, and in the privileges of students were forbidden.

But the university was still but a plan: beyond its name there was as yet but little to it. The practical development of the common school system was much more rapid, and gave promise that at length the University idea would be realized. Early in 1826 Congress was induced to grant an additional township of land towards the endowment of the university; and Governor Cass, in calling the attention of the legislative council to this grant in the following November, strongly urges the establishment of schools to be supported by taxation. In no other way, he thinks, will provision be made sufficiently extensive and sufficiently permanent to embrace all who require instruction, and who have not the means of obtaining it. The governor specially emphasized the political aspect of the subject, and urged the importance that all who were to be rulers of the State should be given the means of acquiring fitness for their duties.

These wise views were quite in advance of any then prevalent in any part of the country. The legislative council responded by making such changes in the school laws as seemed to the members to tend in the direction recommended. In 1829 the laws were completely revised, and a department of education was established, at the head of which was to be a superintendent of common schools appointed by the governor. The legislation does not, however, appear as yet to have been entirely satisfactory to the governor, and he again recurs to the subject in his message of the following May. No wiser or juster tax, he argues, can be levied than one devoted to the education of the poor; and he reiterates and amplifies his view, that political institutions whose foundations rest upon public opinion can never be secure unless the people are educated. "Public opinion, to be safe, must be enlightened."

It cannot be important to follow in detail the subsequent legislation of the territory, and it will suffice to say that it was in the direction pointed out by the governor, and that provision was made whereby schools were required to be kept in every district for at least three months in each year by teachers of approved competency, in which the children of the poor were to be instructed free of charge or tax. The rate bill was not abolished for those who were able to pay it; but the door of the school-house was set open to the poorest, and the people united in the expectation expressed by President Monteith in his first annual report, that "thus the public will be benefited by genius and talent which would otherwise have died in obscurity."

But the schools at the time state government was established were still very primitive affairs. There were as yet no professional teachers. Some farmer or mechanic, or perhaps a grown-up son or daughter, who had had the advantages of the common schools of New York or New England, offered his or her services as teacher during the dull season of regular employment, and consented to take as wages such sum as the district could afford to pay. A summer school taught by a woman, who would be paid six or eight dollars a month, and a winter school taught by a man, whose compensation was twice as great, was what was generally provided for. But in addition to wages the teacher received his board; "boarding around" among the patrons of the school, and remaining with each a number of days determined by the number of pupils sent to the school. If we shall incline to visit one of these schools in the newer portions of the State we shall be likely to find it housed in a log structure, covered with bark, imperfectly plastered between the logs to exclude the cold, and still more imperfectly warmed by an open fire-place or by a box stove, for which fuel is provided, as the board for the teacher is, by proportional contributions. The seats for the pupils may be slabs set upon legs; the desks may be other slabs laid upon supports fixed to the logs which constitute the sides of the room. The school books are miscellaneous, and consist largely of those brought by the parents when emigrating to the territory. Those who write must rule their paper with pencils of lead of their own manufacture, and the master will make pens for them from the goose-quill. For the most part the ink is of home manufacture. There are no globes; no means of illustration; not even a blackboard. Even President Monteith, it is said, drew his mathematical figures in sawdust for want of anything better; but in the common schools the higher mathematics are unknown, and the pupil who has mastered vulgar fractions and the rule of three is likely to be the best of the school. Order is the first law, and the rod the accepted means of enforcing it. The pupils are classified according to attainments, but not unfrequently the master has little competency to do more than give out the lessons as he found them in the book, and to hear recitations without comment or explanation. Such in many cases was the Michigan school. Better school buildings were now springing up, with better furnishing; but as a rule nothing could seem more dreary or dispiriting than the average district school. Nevertheless, many an intellect received a quickening in these schools which fitted it for a life of useful and honorable activity. The new settlers made such provision for the education of their children as was possible under the circumstances in which they were placed, and the fruits of their labors and sacrifices in this direction were in many cases surprising.

The territorial council granted charters for academies, but the name in most cases indicated rather an aspiration than an existence. In two or three places good service was being done; notably at Ann Arbor by Mr. O. C. Thompson, a graduate of

Princeton, sent out for missionary work by the Presbyterian Church. But farther back in the woods, a young graduate of Brown, while threading his devious way through the forest from one lonely cabin to another, by trails that required the fording of rivers and the crossing of treacherous marshes, that he might minister in sacred things to those in need, was at the same time considering the means of popular education, and making it the subject of deep and earnest thought. He was quite in accord with the governor as to the duty of the State to provide for the education of its youth, and the questions he dwelt upon were questions of methods and means.

John D. Pierce had been sent out in 1831 by the Congregationalists as a home missionary, and had held the first religious meetings in the counties of Jackson, Calhoun, and Eaton. He had also solemnized the first marriage and officiated at the first funeral ever taken in charge by a Protestant clergyman in western Michigan. He was an enthusiast in his work, but his enthusiasm was tempered and controlled by thorough practical sense, and he joined to the earnestness and self-abnegation of the devoted missionary the levelheadedness so essential to success in the ordinary walks of business life. He had brought with him into the wilderness as a bride an intelligent and refined lady whom he had married in the State of New York, and we catch occasional glimpses of her as she is conveyed in an open ox-cart from Detroit to distant Marshall, often drenched in rain and sometimes fast in the mud, catching at night as best she may such unrefreshing rest as a bed of boughs or a blanket on the floor of a log cabin may afford. It is a time when emigration comes by caravans; and though at nearly every house may there be found entertainment for man and beast, the accommodations are meagre and quite below the demands upon them. To the bride, delicately trained and unfamiliar with hardships, the log cabins of Michigan, in which many of the ordinary comforts of home life were as yet unknown, must have seemed sufficiently forbidding; but she was not long permitted to share her husband's labors and privations, for in the very next year the Asiatic cholera in its devastating march across the country sought her out in the wilderness and made her its victim. The missionary was left alone with his labors; but he had devoted his life to the work to which he had been called, and he addressed himself with patience and trust to his laborious and absorbing duties.

The constitutional convention of 1835 had recognized the supreme importance of education, and had made the position of superintendent of public instruction a permanent constitutional office. It had required a school to be kept in each school district for at least three months in every year, and had pledged the faith of the State to the preservation of all donations for schools or for the university, as permanent funds for the purposes for which they were given. But as yet the State was not admitted to the Union, and it was not known what form any donation by the federal government would take. General Isaac E. Crary, a neighbor of the young missionary, had been a member of the constitutional convention, and the two had frequently discussed together the subject of state education, and had enlightened their understandings, so far as the books of the day would enable them to do so, by information respecting what was being done in Prussia and other countries. They agreed that education ought to be an independent department of the state government; and it was made so by the constitutional convention. They also agreed that the lands granted by the general government for school purposes ought to be granted directly to the State as trustee, instead of being given to the townships as had been customary. With the State as trustee of the lands, there would be reason for hope that the endowment for schools would be carefully preserved and utilized, but in the hands of the townships the experience of other states had not been such as to justify confidence in like preservation. Fortunately for the State, General Crary was its first representative in Congress; and through his prudent and cautious management the grant by the general government was so shaped as to meet his views. This was a great and lasting advantage, and the ultimate results were equal to the highest expectations of those who had secured it. The State faithfully observed its duty as trustee; no part of the school-fund grant was ever lost; none of the funds derived from it were ever squandered or misappropriated.

But the services of General Crary to education were not confined to those performed at Washington. On his way to the seat of government he had called upon Governor Mason at Detroit, and had taken the liberty to urge upon him the importance of placing the subject of education in competent hands. He had gone farther than this, and recommended the young missionary as the suitable person for superintendent of public instruction. The governor was favorably impressed with his views, and sent for Mr. Pierce, with whom he had a long and satisfactory interview. The result was his appointment to the office, and the commitment to his control of the whole subject of state education, with the charge and management of a million acres of land. The legislature called upon him to prepare and report a system of common school and university education, and the report was made, approved, and adopted the very year the State entered the Union. The system reported has in the main been in existence ever since.

It would not be important to enter here upon

an examination of the state common school system in detail. It will suffice to say that it contemplated the establishment of a primary school within the reach of every child in the State, and that it gave full power to the voters of every school district to establish free schools if they should see fit to do so. The time had not yet come for making the maintenance of free schools compulsory: public opinion in some quarters was not yet educated up to it. But the law then adopted was a long step in that direction; and the distribution to be annually made among the school districts, of the income derived from moneys received on sales of school lands, would do something towards encouraging them to make the schools free, and towards lightening the burden of doing so.

The plan for the organization of the university was not so readily accepted as that for the primary schools. Mr. Pierce encountered at the outset a prejudice against state universities, and a disbelief in their success, based upon the failure that had generally attended the effort to establish them. He encountered also, to some extent, the opposition of the several religious denominations, each of which wanted a college of its own, and was also jealous lest some other might obtain control of a state institution. But the superintendent had faith in himself and faith in the people; and he proceeded to mark out a plan which he proposed to put in operation on a non-sectarian basis, and with a curriculum of studies not inferior to that of any college in the land. The government of the university was to be in a board of regents of executive appointment, with the state officers as *ex officio* members, and its support was to come from the income derived from the sale or leasing of university lands. No more than ten dollars was to be demanded for admission to the university, and residents of the State were to be charged nothing for tuition. The plan contemplated a department of literature, science, and the arts, a department of law, and a department of medicine, to be established successively as the funds at the control of the regents would permit. In the appointments to the several chairs of instruction it was intended that the leading religious denominations should be suitably represented, and that no just cause of complaint should be open to any one on the score of religious partiality in the governing board.

This was the general plan. But obviously it was a plan whose complete realization must be postponed for some considerable period. It was not proposed that there should be in the university any preparatory department; and the old difficulty, that there were no students prepared to receive the higher instruction, was still as apparent as ever. In the whole State, also, there were not more than one or two schools in which the necessary preparatory training could be had. Preparatory schools seemed, therefore, to be the first necessity; and partly to provide them, and partly to give agricultural education, the regents were empowered to establish branches of the university when their means would allow of it.

The department of literature, science, and the arts was shortly established, with beginnings which were very humble. But its five students for the first year were added to in each successive year, until the department attained the dimensions of a respectable college. In 1850 the department of medicine was established, and something of the university form began to appear. By the new constitution, adopted that year, the organization of the board of regents was popularized by giving the election to the people by direct vote. The term, moreover, was made a term of eight years, and the board was given complete control of the university and its funds, to the exclusion of legislative dictation. This was felt to be a most valuable and important change: it secured steadiness in plan and conservatism in management, and it placed the university beyond the dangers that might spring from popular excitements and prejudices, and from political overturns. A few years later was founded the department of law, giving symmetry to the university, and bringing strength to the other departments.

Meantime the curriculum of the university was being enlarged and liberalized in many ways, and especially in giving to students a latitude in the choice of studies quite beyond what had before been allowed in similar institutions. The fact was recognized that the needs of intellectual training and acquirement were not the same in different occupations and different walks in life, and that to prescribe the same course of instruction for all was to compel a waste of time and effort by many, when the same time and effort might usefully be employed in the acquisition of knowledge that would have special importance and value. Many parallel courses of instruction were therefore marked out, and a liberty of choice given that was greatly to the advantage of those who desired to avail themselves of university training. New schools were also established: the school of pharmacy, the school of homœpathic medicine, the dental school, the school of music, and the school of political science; so that the university came to have many departments, instead of the three originally contemplated. To give all these schools due support, the income derived from the sale of university lands was found quite inadequate, and the State by taxation supplied the deficiencies, though observing in doing so the same rigid economy that had always characterized its expenditures for services rendered to the public. The regents also, disregarding antiquated prejudices, and the prophecies of evil with which ultra-conservatism was so ready, threw open the doors of every school to women, and thereby offered to them every opportunity for liberal education which was placed within the reach of the other sex. This was a measure of justice, and its advocates soon had the satisfaction of knowing that none of the prophesied evils followed from it. It was adopted as soon as the demand for it was sufficient to justify incurring the necessary additional expense, and it had from the first and has retained the popular approval.

The branches of the university which the regents established were not long maintained, for the sufficient reason that they were not long needed. The common schools of the State came in time to do admirable work, and in the leading towns they grew into high schools, with numerous teachers, where the classics were taught, and where young men and women could be and were prepared for college. Admirable work was done by some of them in this direction; and one — the school at Ann Arbor — annually for the ten years preceding 1884 graduated an average number of pupils, with full preparation to enter upon a regular university course, greater, it is believed, than is fitted for college in any other public school in the country. These high schools are the academies of the State; the work they do is of the most satisfactory and substantial character, and the State is justly proud of them.

The constitution of 1850 made it the duty of

the legislature, within five years from its adoption, to make provision in every school district for free instruction at least three months in the year. The duty was only in part performed within the time prescribed; but the high schools as a rule were soon for the most part made free, and the rate bill is now at last abolished throughout the State. Free instruction in the common schools has thus become the right of every child of proper age in the State.

Such in brief has been the progress of instruction in the common schools, which are the foundation of the state system of education, and in the university which crowns and completes the structure. But between the common school and the university are other institutions, each of which has its appropriate place in the system, and is necessary to complete it. Foremost of these are the State Normal School at Ypsilanti, and the State Agricultural College at Lansing. A school for the deaf and dumb at Flint and another for the blind at Lansing are liberally supported by the State, and make ample provision for such education as those unfortunate classes are capable of receiving. In 1874 a state school for dependent children was opened at Coldwater. Into this school are gathered orphan children who are without means of support, and children who become inmates of county almshouses, and they are not only given the ordinary instruction of schools, but the benefits of family life as well. It is a part of the plan of the school that suitable homes where they may be adopted, or places where they can receive remunerative employment, shall be found for the pupils. In this way many who would be in danger of drifting through want and neglect into vice and crime are saved to useful and honorable lives.

Such is the educational system of Michigan. Its founders took position in advance of the thought of their day, and those who followed them have endeavored to give effect in full measure to their views. No commonwealth in the world makes provision more broad, complete, or thorough for the general education of the people, and very few for that which is equal. It has been the settled conviction of the people for many years, that there can be no more worthy expenditure of public moneys than in the training of men and women in useful knowledge; and they have acted upon that conviction. The newer states of the Union in framing their educational systems have been glad to follow the example of Michigan, and have had fruitful and satisfactory success in proportion as they have adhered to it. And for all that has been accomplished, Michigan is indebted to the intelligence, the unselfishness, and the far-seeing wisdom of some of its own eminent citizens, who with the public confidence for their support have not waited for older but more provincial states to point the way, but have trustfully moved on from step to step in the direction of an ideal excellence which was early in their minds, and has been steadily adhered to since.

No feature of **the educational work** of Michigan is more satisfactory **in the retrospect** than the unity **of** effort in prosecuting it; all classes, **as a** general fact, having given it liberal support. This is true of the immigrant as well as of the native born citizen; and of the Germans, who were most numerous of the later immigrants, it may justly be said, they were as active and helpful in support of the schools as they were industrious and thrifty in their private business.

CHAPTER XVII.

THE WAR IN DEFENSE OF THE UNION.

A GREAT war was now about to convulse the Union, of which slavery would be the occasion, but which would present issues far transcending in importance any which were involved in the further continuance of that institution, great as were the evils which necessarily sprung from it. The states of the Union, which at the time of the separation from the mother country were thirteen in number, had added other commonwealths one by one until the whole number had become thirty-three, united under a constitution which gave to the weakest for all purposes of protection the strength and resources of all, and which, by providing for the peaceful consideration and adjustment by regular tribunals of all controversies, which might otherwise give occasion for appeals to force, gave to the whole family of states the best security for amicable and profitable relations, and to civilization the best protection that it is possible for statesmanship to devise. The same constitution, while it insured peace to the states, diminished immensely the danger of hostilities with foreign nations, not only because it made the states thus united sufficiently powerful to command respect, but also because it left international relations exclusively to the federal government, and put it out of the power of any single state, or even of any number of states, to disturb the peace of the world without the general consent given through the federal Congress. Under the influence of the passions excited by the controversy over slavery it was now proposed to break up the Union into sections. That great evils were likely to flow from this was certain; only the number and extent were in doubt. It would be a distinctively retrogressive step, taken in a century when civilization was progressing more rapidly than ever before; it must abolish, as between the states, in different sections, the methods provided for the peaceful determination of controversies; if it could be accomplished peacefully, which was more than doubtful, it would still multiply immensely the dangers to peace among the states, and would make the very proximity of states friendly in union a continual menace and danger. And the claim of a right to disrupt the Union was planted upon a principle of disintegration whose very acceptance would not only be justification in advance for further separations, but would be a constant and tempting invitation to discontented parties to reject the adjustment of controversies by regular tribunals, and substitute the arbitrament of the sword. The proposed disruption of the Union must therefore, irrespective of its effect upon the institution of slavery, be a distinct loss to civilization, in that it would destroy or at least diminish the securities which statesmanship had contrived for the peace of the world, and especially for the peace and prosperity of the American world. It would also, in its demonstration that the written constitution of the leading federal government of the world was inadequate to the strain and crucial test of a heated domestic controversy, tend to weaken very greatly the popular tendency towards free institutions, and the harmonious coöperation of free states which was characteristic of the age.

But slavery was an element of discord in the Union which it was daily becoming more difficult to deal with peacefully. It had had its origin at a time when it was not condemned as it now was by the enlightened conscience of the civilized world. There were slaves in Virginia when the Pilgrims landed at Plymouth; and every American colony became slaveholding, and continued to be so when, by their declaration of Independence, the united colonies declared liberty to be an inalienable right. When independence was acknowledged by Great Britain, only one state had as yet become non-slaveholding. So accustomed were the people to the institution, that its rightfulness was seldom questioned, and only now and then did any one venture to remark upon the inconsistency of a people fighting for their own liberties while holding others in bondage. The first damaging blow to slavery may almost be said to have been inadvertent: it was when the people of Massachusetts, without chattel slavery in mind, declared by the constitution of 1780 that "all men are born free and equal, and have certain natural, essential, and inalienable rights; among which may be reckoned the right of enjoying and defending their rights and liberties." This, as the courts decided, of its own force put an end to slavery within the state. The second and far more important blow was given when Congress incorporated in the ordinance of 1787 the anti-slavery proviso. This was a great and notable event; and was prophetic of others, for it was a precedent for putting the government distinctly on the side of freedom. And then in 1820 came the Missouri Compromise legislation, by which slavery was prohibited in all the territory then belonging to the Union lying to the north of latitude thirty-six degrees and thirty minutes.

It seemed at the time that the Missouri Compromise insured to the non-slaveholding states an eventual preponderance of power in the Union; but this was put in peril by the large acquisitions of territory from Mexico at the conclusion of war with that republic. In the justice of the war with Mexico there had not been entire unaminity of opinion on the part of the American people. Many had believed it was begun and carried on solely for the purposes of an extension of slavery, and for obtaining territory which would eventually become slave states; and they deemed it their duty, while the war was still in progress, to render such a result impossible, by annexing a condition to any appropriation for the acquisition of territory, that in whatever should be acquired there should be no slavery.

General Cass was at that time in the Senate of the United States, to which he had been elected in 1845. He opposed the condition, on the grounds, among others, that it would probably defeat altogether any acquisition of territory from Mexico, and also that at most it would be a mere declaration of present legislative intent on the subject, and would bind no subsequent Congress when practical legislation came to be adopted. A little later he wrote his famous Nicholson letter, in which he laid down the doctrine that no power had been granted to Congress by the constitution to legislate generally for the territories, and that its authority must be limited to the establishment of territorial governments when needed, leaving to the people of the territories the regulation of their own domestic concerns, in subordination to the constitution. This would leave to the territorial legislature the full control over the subject of slavery. Upon the platform of this letter General

Cass was nominated for the presidency in 1848, but was defeated. He returned after the election to a seat in the Senate, which he had vacated pending the canvass, and took part in the adoption of the compromise measures of 1850, which it was hoped would put an end to an exciting and dangerous controversy.

But the compromise of 1850 was not even a truce between hostile and opposing forces: it was rather an agreement by parties assuming to stand between such forces that there should be no more contention, while at the same time the real belligerents remained as hostile as ever, and awaited the opportunity for an encounter. The opportunity was not long delayed: the Kansas-Nebraska bill in 1852, and the state of civil war in Kansas which resulted, created the most intense excitement throughout the country, and strengthened very greatly the anti-slavery sentiment in all the Northern States, while intensifying in the Southern States the opposite sentiment. In Michigan a political revolution took place in 1854, one of the results of which was that General Cass failed of a reëlection to the Senate, and Zachariah Chandler succeeded him.

In the presidential election of 1856 the question of setting bounds to the further extension of slavery was the paramount issue, and it continued to be the leading and almost the sole issue in national affairs until after the election of 1860, when the party which avowed its determination to preserve the territories for freedom, while disclaiming any purpose to interfere with the institution of slavery in the states, succeeded in electing Abraham Lincoln to the office of president. But parties, as was inevitable with the issue which was made, had divided on sectional lines.

Immediately after the election, distinct and authoritative announcements began to be made in the Southern States that it would not be submitted to. It was declared that the election of president by a party hostile to slavery was a wrong and a menace to all the slaveholding states, which neither their interests nor their honor would permit them to acquiesce in. It was declared further that the states, which had assented to the constitution and become members of the Federal Union, had an undoubted right to withdraw that assent at any time and to secede from the Union; and several of the states in a short time had called conventions composed of delegates chosen by the people, by which ordinances of secession from the Union were adopted. These states assumed to be thereafter no longer under the federal jurisdiction, and they formed among themselves a confederation and adopted a provisional constitution.

The people of the Northern States, as a general fact, neither agreed that the slave states had been wronged in the election of an anti-slavery president, nor assented to the right of a state to secede from the Union. Assent to the constitution they regarded as irrevocable: it made the states a nation, and imposed upon the nation the obligation to enforce its laws in every state regardless of any action the state or its citizens might take to the contrary. The border slave states took a position different from those taken to the north and the south of them. The people for the most part sympathized with their Southern brethren, both in their view of the wrong that was done them in the election, and in their belief in the right to secede; but they deprecated the action which the extreme Southern States had taken, as being calculated to lead to civil war. How to avert such a war now that the action had been taken was the question. It was assumed in the border slave states that those states, occupying as they did a position between the others, both geographically and politically, were entitled to speak with some authority as pacificators, and that it belonged to them to propose some compromise, whereby the hostile sections by mutual concessions could be brought again to their ancient harmony. Accordingly Mr. Crittenden, one of the senators from Kentucky, took the lead in proposing a compromise; but its concessions were not such as to satisfy the extreme South, while at the same time they were more than the North would consent to make. When this result became certain, a peace conference, as it was called, to be composed of commissioners from each of the states, was invited to convene in Washington in February, 1861, to consider and if possible agree upon and report to Congress some plan of compromise and conciliation, by the adoption of which the seceding states might be won back to the Union. What was desired was that each state would send its most eminent and conservative citizens as commissioners; and it was then hoped that their aggregate wisdom would be sufficient to devise a plan of conciliation and harmony adequate to the emergency, and that the influence of their united counsel would secure its adoption.

Certain concessions by the North it was generally supposed would be absolutely essential. Among these was a provision by constitutional amendment for the more effectual return of fugitive slaves escaping to Northern States, and for payment of their value when they escaped by reason of assistance given them. But one of more importance was that the territories should be open to settlement by slave owners with their slaves, and that all power in Congress to legislate against slavery in the territories should be taken away by express constitutional provision. It was in respect to this last feature of the proposed concessions that the chief difficulty was likely to be encountered, for it was a concession of the very principle on which the recent election had been won.

Nevertheless the Union was in peril, and twenty-two states sent commissioners to the conference.

Michigan by the deliberate act of her legislature refused to participate in it. The name of peace conference seemed to the people of the State a misnomer: the conference was to be held under an implied threat of war unless one section of the Union surrendered altogether its leading political principle. Mr. Buchanan in his annual message had declared that he found in the constitution no authority for coercing states withdrawing from the Union, but his conclusions found little support in Michigan. Governor Wisner, who had just left the executive chair, had said. in retiring: "Michigan cannot recognize the right of a state to secede from this Union." If individuals, whether as private citizens or as officers, attempted to take their state out of the Union, the nation must deal with them, not by way of coercing the state, but to compel individuals to obey the laws of the United States, and to perform national obligations. Austin Blair, the new governor, had repeated and amplified the sentiments of his predecessor. "Safety lies in this path alone. The Union must be preserved and the laws must be enforced in all parts of it at whatever cost. . . . Secession is revolution, and revolution in the overt act is treason, and must be treated as such." These utterances expressed the sentiments of the State. The Union had not been formed on any understanding that it might be dissolved at will by dissatisfied parties, and to concede the right would be destructive of all its advantages. If constitutional obligations had been violated in the election other considerations would be presented, but the voters of the State had done nothing but exercise their undoubted right in taking part with others in the election of a constitutional officer in a perfectly constitutional way; acting, in doing so, upon matured convictions and according to the dictates of their consciences. They therefore had nothing in their action to regret, nothing to withdraw, nothing in point of principle to compromise away. They were at peace now without the aid of the peace conference, and they would remain at peace unless war should be opened upon the Union of which the State was a part; and if war should thus come, all the grand results which had been anticipated in the formation of the Union and which so far had been realized would be at stake, and nothing would remain but to put forth such effort to save the Union as might be within the compass of state power and resources. Such were the views which found expression at Washington through the representatives of the State in Congress. Senator Chandler in a speech in the Senate said: "The people of Michigan are opposed to all compromises. They do not believe that any compromise is necessary; nor do I. They are prepared to stand by the constitution of the United States as it is; to stand by the government as it is; to stand by it to blood if necessary." And a little later he said it would be more reasonable to join a tribe of savages than to live under a government that had not power to enforce its laws.

The peace conference was abortive, and on Friday, April 12, 1861, war upon the Union was inaugurated by the attack on Fort Sumter. On the following Sunday the officer in command lowered his flag in surrender, and the captors marched in with rejoicings as for a great victory. The victory was a fatal one for slavery; any earnest and prolonged contest for the preservation of the Union necessarily involved the existence of that institution. It also necessarily referred to the arbitrament of war the dogma of the right of states to secede from the Union. On the same Sunday that Sumter was evacuated, the people of Michigan in their several localities were gathering after church services, in parks and other public places, to counsel together respecting the alarming crisis that was now upon them, and to prepare for the responsibilities which were involved in a struggle for national existence. The most eminent and trusted citizen was in every place the speaker. At Ann Arbor, the seat of the state university, Dr. Henry P. Tappan, its eminent and respected president, addressed the assembled people, impressing upon them with great force and earnestness the necessity of the Union to the peace, prosperity, and happiness of the people of all the states, and the duty of every citizen to defend it at any necessary sacrifice. Slavery as the occasion of the war was rarely alluded to in these meetings; the issues of the opening contest rose far above any question of domestic policy, constitutional law, or party politics.

When Sumter surrendered, Lewis Cass, who in the cabinet of President Buchanan had done all that was in his power to hold every state to its place in the Union, was living in retirement at Detroit. A great public meeting was convened in that city on one of the dark days which followed, and he was called upon as its most distinguished citizen to preside. Naturally his mind reverted to the day, nearly fifty years before, when near the very spot where the meeting was being held, an American general, who had lost the courage and vigor of his youth, had subjected the people to dishonorable capitulation. The venerable statesman was himself now old and feeble; youthful ardor had given way to some degree of despondency; but he had lost nothing of his attachment to the Union, and he thanked God as he took the chairman's seat that the flag of the Union still floated unmutilated above him. His remarks were brief, but they expressed the general sentiment and determination of the people of the city and of the State. "It is the duty of all zealously to support the government in its efforts to bring this unhappy civil war to a speedy and satisfactory conclusion, by the restoration in its integrity of that great charter of freedom bequeathed to us by Washington and his compatriots." The address was brief but significant, and there was inspiration for others in the fact that the venerable statesman did not tolerate the thought of a divided country.

The history of Michigan in the war is part of the general history of the country, and nothing need be said of it here but that the State did its full duty, putting more than ninety thousand men into the field, of whom many thousand were left to rest in soldiers' graves. The four years' war was unsettling and demoralizing, as all wars necessarily are, and its effects were perceived in a speculating feeling in business circles which gradually extended so as to bring within its mischievous vortex classes of persons who had never ventured before. They were perceived also in a weakening of the sense of the sacredness of life and of private property; and in some degree of the family sentiment also; and in a great increase of crimes of all sorts, but especially of crimes of violence. Nowhere in the Union were the rejoicings more hearty when the news came that Richmond was in the hands of the federal authorities, and that the preservation of the Union was made certain. A task which had seemed to other nations too desperate to be undertaken had been accomplished, and in the process of accomplishment the great domestic evil that had been the occasion of the war had been overthrown completely and forever.

CHAPTER XVIII.

THE STATE AND THE NEW UNION.

The great civil war had been fought on the part of the government to preserve the Union, and for no ulterior purpose whatever. "The constitution as it is and the Union as it was" was the rallying cry of the people, and the platform upon which Mr. Lincoln in his inaugural address proposed to found the policy of his administration. The acts of secession being deemed altogether void, the government would endeavor to hold, occupy, and possess the property and places belonging to it in all the states, and to enforce everywhere its laws, and thereby bring the people everywhere to a recognition and observance of federal authority and of their duties in respect to it. The political departments of the federal government disclaimed altogether the right to interfere with any constitutional exercise of state authority, even in respect to the institution of slavery, though slavery had become the occasion of civil war. Loyal parties, whatever had been their political affiliations before, agreed in pledging devotion to the constitution as it had been formulated and adopted at the

VALUE OF A WRITTEN CONSTITUTION. 345

beginning, and their purpose to maintain it unimpaired.

The peculiar excellence of the American constitutions was supposed to consist in the fact that they had been deliberately framed as written charters of government, so that they expressed all that was within the intent of the framers, and would stand as agreed upon without being subject to that gradual modification and change which is an inherent quality when the constitution is unwritten. In the latter case, as in the conspicuous instance of the constitution of England, there will be gradual building up and growth, which may at the time be wholly imperceptible, and only apparent in results; but the written instrument comes into existence with the understanding and purpose that its several paragraphs and provisions shall mean forever exactly what they mean when adopted; and if a change is to take place in the constitution, it must be brought about by the steps which in the instrument itself are provided for, and must consist in such modification of the language and provisions of the instrument, or of such emendations or additions as shall be formally and deliberately made. By this means we are supposed to have at all times a written instrument which embodies the whole constitution; and when we reach a proper interpretation of the powers it confers and the limitations it imposes upon those powers, as they stood in the minds of the people when adopting it, we are to give effect to that interpretation, in whatever may be done under the constitution at any time in the future.

Such is the theory underlying American governments. But the theory can be true only in the most general sense. No instrument can be the same in meaning to-day and forever, and in all men's minds. Its interpretation must take place in the light of the facts which preceded and led to it; in the light of contemporaneous history, and of what was said by the actors and the ends they had in view. And as men will differ upon facts and differ in mental constitution, so will they differ in interpretation; and in the case of a written constitution, the divergences are certain to increase when it comes to receive practical application. And if at any time the people are subjected to a great constitutional crisis, they are not thereafter precisely the same in ideas, sentiments, desires, hopes, and aspirations that they were before: their experience works changes in their views and in their habits of thought, and these may be so radical that they seem altogether a new people. But as the people change, so does their written constitution change also: they see it in new lights and with different eyes; events may have given unexpected illumination to some of its provisions, and what they read one way before they read a very different way now. Then the logic of events may for all practical purposes have settled some questions before in dispute; and nobody, in his contemplation of the constitution, can separate it if he would from the history in which its important provisions have had a part, or be unaffected in his own views by that history.

In constitutional countries there must be schools of interpretation and construction, in which men will range themselves according to the spirit and intent which they respectively discover in the charter of government. In the United States these have existed from the first; and they have been given the names of Hamilton and Jefferson, because those great statesmen, when called to the performance of important functions in government which involved a construction of the constitution, discovered respectively a different spirit and tendency in that instrument. Hamilton discovered in it a purpose to create and give vigorous energy to a great nation; and in so far as the administration of the government fell to him, he deemed it his duty to give effect to this purpose. He was the ablest man of the day holding these views; and being eminently endowed with the qualities of a leader, he became the natural head of the great national party. Jefferson read in the constitution a purpose to preserve the states in their integrity with all their powers, so far as was consistent with the existence of a confederacy having such authority as a strict construction of the constitution would give it. He also was a natural leader of men, and became the head of the state-rights school in constitutional interpretation. Holding such antagonistic views, it was natural and perhaps inevitable that these great leaders should suspect each other's motives and actions; and that while Hamilton should come to think it was the purpose of Jefferson to set the states above the nation to the destruction of effective unity, Jefferson on the other hand should believe that his great rival was endeavoring to do whatever should be possible, in perverting the constitution to a concentration of power in the federal government which the states had never agreed upon, and which if deliberately proposed would never have had their assent. From them the mutual suspicions extended to their friends and followers; and their several public measures were regarded with jealous eyes as having purposes in view which their authors would not venture to avow. The funding schemes of Hamilton for federal and state debts were not, in the eyes of Jefferson, so much vicious in themselves, as vicious in their purpose and tendency to concentrate power and rob the states of their due importance; and when, under the administration of John Adams, affairs with France assumed a threatening aspect, other persons besides Jefferson were ready to suspect that Hamilton was willing war should result, not so much because the conduct of France seemed imperatively to require it, as because he expected from the necessary concentration of power and expenditure in the general government, as a result of war, a great extension of its relative importance.

The war of 1812 was attended by some peculiar circumstances, which had the effect to neutralize tendencies that might otherwise have appeared. The administration of the government was at the time in the hands of the state-rights party; and its avowed principles would restrain it from taking centralizing ground. A much more important circumstance was that some of the most influential states were in control of the party which had opposed the war, and the general government was from that cause hampered and weakened through the whole of it. But afterwards and long before the great crisis of 1860, the construction of the constitution in its leading features had been determined by successive decisions of the federal Supreme Court in accordance with the views held by the school of Hamilton. The views of Mr. Jefferson had also in a measure become discredited with the people, mainly through the nullification episode and the patriotic fervor at that time inspired in defense of federal authority. But as the legislative and executive departments of the government had generally been in the hands of the party most strenuous for the preservation to the states of all their powers and rights, the tendency to centralization was kept perhaps as much in check as in the nature of things was possible.

State sovereignty and national unity was a favorite phrase which was supposed to be a terse expression of the leading ideas and purposes of this party in government. If a doubt at any time arose respecting the relative province of state and nation, the principles of this party afforded an easy and simple test for its solution; for presumptively all power was in the state until it could be shown how and in what provision of the constitution it had been given to the Union.

The change when the great civil war came on was very great. The revolution of parties would account for some of this; for the party which had succeeded in the recent presidential election was for the most part of the school of Hamilton. Jefferson had now been further discredited by the fact that those who were endeavoring to disrupt the Union claimed to be his followers and disciples, and quoted papers prepared by his hand in justification of their disintegrating doctrines. And it was easy to do this; for under the strain of intense political feeling, when the federal government was adopting legislation of the most questionable character, and which he believed was not only unwarranted by the constitution but subversive of liberty, he had secretly formulated for his followers the famous resolutions of '98 and '99, which seemed on their face to contain the germ of nullification if not of secession. But the Abolitionists might, with quite as much reason, have claimed him as their prototype and leader; for his condemnation of slavery had been planted on the highest ground of morality and natural justice, and he had been prompt to legislate for freedom on the very first opportunity. Nevertheless, Jefferson for the time being was discredited in the public mind, and the correctness of Hamilton's views of government was thought to be demonstrated by the attempt at secession, and by the need of extraordinary powers in the government to prevent it. It seemed to be the duty of patriotic citizens to strengthen the federal government in every possible way, and remonstrances from any quarter, however well they might be grounded in constitutional law, and however honest their purpose, were listened to with impatience. The party of secession had claimed to found their dogmas upon constitutional state rights, and to represent such rights in their rebellion; therefore, as the war progressed with its intense excitements and varying phases, the very term "state rights" became obnoxious to patriotic ears as one which represented principles and interests standing in antagonism to the tremendous national interests, in defense of which the people were now so freely expending blood and treasure.

Under the influence of sentiments like these, many clear infractions of the constitution were excused by the public as being justified by an overruling necessity; such, for example, as the interference by federal forces with state elections in Kentucky. The longer the war continued and the more numerous were the excesses of power, the more they came to seem in the minds of many persons to be in harmony with the spirit of a constitution which was designed to insure the perpetuity of the Union, and might therefore be supposed to contemplate the doing of whatever was essential to that end. "We break the constitution that we may save it," was sometimes said: a paradox, the mischief of which was not universally perceived until calmer times brought cooler heads. It was the opposite view — that the constitution might be appealed to for protection even by those who were seeking to destroy it — that seemed at the time preposterous. When, therefore, men were tried and condemned for treasonable practices before military tribunals in Indiana, the proceedings were approved by a prevailing contemporary sentiment, which held that the protections to liberty incorporated in the constitution were subject to an implied exception, and might rightfully be set aside when great emergencies required it.

Many such things are inseparable from a state of civil war; and they are recorded afterwards not so much for the purpose of fixing the responsibility for them upon individuals, as to guard against their being accepted as lawful, and thereby leading to mischief in the future. But in this connection they are to be noted also as accounting in some degree for the rapid strengthening of federal power while the war was in progress. A violation of the constitution, even when disapproved by public sentiment so that it fails to become a precedent, may nevertheless have important influence upon the public mind, in accustoming it to accept as quite in order other questionable acts which before would have been promptly condemned. A wholly baseless claim vigorously insisted upon, especially when the power of present enforcement exists, may be as likely in public affairs as in private business to lead to compromise by concession of some part of what is claimed.

But the centralizing forces which raised no question of constitutional right or authority were now powerful. The government was making vast military expenditures; it was giving out enormous contracts in which the profits might be large, and the birds of ill omen gathered about the departments in great flocks, as eager for their feasts and as reckless of anything else as the vultures upon the fields of battle. The government was all the while drawing in and paying out large sums of money; and the financial currents were to and from Washington, not to or from the state capitals except as the states were acting as subordinate auxiliaries in the war. With a new administration, according to the vicious custom still prevalent, came an expectation of an entire change in the civil force; and from every part of the country men flocked to Washington demanding recognition of political claims, and forgot the impending peril of their country in their eagerness to turn others out of office and obtain their places. Many new offices were now necessarily created; and for the time being the national government was the great dispenser of favors, privileges, valuable employments, and profitable contracts, whose executive, by a dash of the pen, was giving offices which gratified the ambition of a life-time, while heads of departments by their favors were enabling others to lay the foundation of enormous fortunes. All these things not only for the time affected the relative interest of the people in their state and national governments, but they greatly and permanently affected the imaginations of the people; diminishing the states and their rights and powers relatively to the Union, and making them appear in a constitutional point of view less and less like sovereignties, and more and more like subordinate sections of a state. It was also natural while this process was going on, and while the needs of the government and the demands upon its strength were so great, that the people should come to look upon the constitution as an instrument which a just regard to its purpose required should be liberally construed, in order that it might accomplish the ends for which it was established, and that it should no longer be looked upon as an instrument in which the grants of power to the federal government must be found expressed; as even Marshall, the great expounder of the preceding generation, had conceded was the case. The attempt of states to break up the Union had put everything at stake in a life and death struggle on the battle-field. For all these reasons a rapid and very radical change was going on in respect to the view to be taken of the constitution; so that even when the letter remained unchanged, the change in spirit and practical expression made it almost a new instrument.

Nothing in this regard affected the imaginations of the people more than the destruction of the institution of slavery in a considerable portion of the Union by executive proclamation enforced by the army. It had been from the first agreed by all schools of constitutional construction that the federal government had no power over the institution of slavery in the states, except in the matter of the reclamation of fugitives, or perhaps as slaves became the subject of interstate commerce. The states, by the constitution, had been left to regulate their own domestic institutions in their own way; that of master and servant as much as that of marriage. But Mr. John Quincy Adams had advanced the idea, which at the time appeared to most persons unworthy a moment's serious thought, that the fact would be otherwise in time of war; for the general government might then deal with slavery as any existing emergency might seem to require. The people of the United States would have scouted this notion even at the time of the breaking out of the civil war, and the most of them for a year thereafter. The conservative portion of the people, including Mr. Lincoln himself, showed a readiness to avoid as far as possible anything which could injure the institution of slavery, and even the army was for a time to some extent made use of for sustaining it. But the time speedily came when it seemed that it might become necessary to choose between slavery and the Union; and with the supreme purpose in view to save the Union, the effect upon slavery began to be discussed chiefly in its bearings upon the accomplishment of that purpose. Mr. Lincoln in his open letter to Horace Greeley, written in August, 1862, put in a few epigrammatic sentences his policy and purpose at that time.

"I would," he said, "save the Union. I would save it in the shortest way under the constitution. The sooner the national authority can be restored, the sooner the Union will be 'the Union as it was.' If there be those who would not save the Union unless they could at the same time save slavery, I do not agree with them. If there be those who would not save the Union unless they could at the same time destroy slavery, I do not agree with them. My paramount object is to save the Union, and not either to save or destroy slavery. If I could save the Union without freeing any slave I would do it; if I could save it by freeing all the slaves I would do it; and if I could save it by freeing some and leaving others alone, I would also do that. What I do about slavery and the colored race I do because I believe it helps to save this Union; and what I forbear I forbear because I do not believe it would help to save the Union. I shall do less whenever I shall believe what I am doing hurts the cause, and I shall do more whenever I believe doing more will help the cause. I shall try to correct errors when shown to be errors, and I shall adopt new views so fast as they shall appear to be true views."

It will thus be seen that the question in Mr. Lincoln's mind, how slavery should be dealt with, had become one of mere expediency; and when he decided, as he shortly did, that the destruction of slavery would conduce to the restoration of the Union, he gave the fatal blow. It may have been an act of questionable constitutional right, but it was irreversible when done, and it went a long way in strengthening the growing impression that in time of war whatever in government is found expedient must be legally admissible.

Then Congress undertook — what it had never attempted before — to provide the whole currency of the country. It had power by the constitution to coin money; but coin had always constituted a small percentage of the whole currency, the most of which had been the bills of state banks.

Twice a national bank had been chartered as an expedient agency in government, but the constitutional power had always been contested, and, though affirmed by the judicial, had been denied at last by the political departments of the government under the lead of Jackson, and the judgment of the people might be said to stand recorded against the judgment of the court. But now Congress assumed to give corporate powers not to one national bank merely, but to banks in every quarter of the country, sufficient in number for all the demands of business; and the question of power to do so was scarcely made in any quarter. Congress did not stop at authorizing national banks; it undertook to destroy the state banks to make place for them. It was not claimed or pretended by any one that this might be done directly and avowedly; for state power to create banks of issue was unquestionable, and what the states had lawful power to create, Congress could not have lawful power to destroy. If the state banks were destroyed it must therefore be done by indirection; the purpose must not be avowed even though it might be evident and palpable. Chief Justice Marshall had said, in overruling state taxation of the national bank, that "a power to tax is a power to destroy;" meaning and intending by this epigrammatic phrase, that the power to raise a revenue from a subject might require to be exercised over and over again to the degree of absolute exhaustion. But Congress availed itself of the expression, and by its action said in substance, "We desire to destroy state banks of issue; we have the power to tax them and we will put forth that power for their destruction. We will impose upon their circulation a burden under the name of tax which it will be impossible for it to bear, and thus compel withdrawal." The obvious comment upon this is, that the power to tax is a power to raise revenue, existing in government for that purpose and for no other; and this legislation was not adopted for purposes of revenue, for no revenue was expected or desired from it. The law, therefore, was not a tax law, but in its essence it was a law prohibiting under penalty the issue of bills by state banks. The legislation was made to assume the form and take the name of taxation, because under its true name its adoption would confessedly have been incompetent. A further very obvious comment is, that if one class of state corporations may constitutionally be thus legislated out of existence by Congress, that body must have the like power to destroy at pleasure other state corporations; and it might perhaps, on some view of national expediency, tax out of existence all corporations for insurance purposes except such as Congress itself might charter for the District of Columbia and other territories and places within its exclusive jurisdiction; thus taking to itself this whole subject as completely as if control over it had been expressly conferred. This would be making the power given to Congress for the purposes of revenue a power of destruction irrespective of revenue. But the tendencies of the times were such that the legislation was sustained with little question and less opposition. The feeling was general that the country was well rid of state bank bills which in times past had been infinitely mischievous, and nobody troubled himself with the question whether a dangerous precedent was not being established in the process of getting rid of them.

The government also issued bills of its own, and declared that they should be legal tender as between individuals; not merely for such debts as should be thereafter contracted, but for preëxisting debts contracted when gold and silver alone were legal tender. Then came the question, Whence did the government derive the power to give this effect to the evidences of its own indebtedness? It is not to be found expressly conferred by the constitution: there is nothing in the debates of the convention which framed that instrument indicating a purpose to confer it. Legislators and lawyers looking for it in the constitution suggest that it may be referred to the power to borrow money, or the power to coin money, or to some other specified power; but at any rate it may be referred to the war power, which is so tremendous in its scope that those wielding it can alone set bounds to it. If in their opinion the issue of legal tender currency is a necessary expedient when war puts the existence of the Union in peril, then the issue must be as lawful as the employment of men or artillery in the field. Such was the reasoning of many at the time. But when it is once determined that the power of Congress may be grounded in necessity, it logically follows that it cannot be limited to the time of war. The necessity that makes for itself the law, knows no times; it is conceivable that it may be slight in time of war and urgent in time of peace; and when the groundwork of right is admitted, the power which passes upon the necessity cannot be restricted in the occasions. And necessity under such circumstances can mean only expediency. We thus reach a stage when Congress on its own view of expediency may exercise the tremendous power over contracts, of making them payable in something besides the money which the parties understood they were bargaining for: something which may or may not be of equal value; though if it were of equivalent value, there could in general be no occasion for imparting to it the legal tender quality.

The nation also during the war began to extend in various directions the jurisdiction of the federal courts. To some extent this was made necessary by the confiscation acts and the great increase in the revenue system; but much of the legislation for the transfer of cases from state to federal courts was based on reasoning which was only plausible; and it was as often adopted for the purpose of increasing the number of courts and making desirable places to be filled by federal appointment as for any other reason. One of the immediate and necessary consequences was to cast upon the federal Supreme Court an amount of business quite beyond its power to deal with, to the great detriment of suitors and of the country. Lawyers and legislators now busy themselves with the problem how to relieve the court of last resort, and various plans are suggested every one of which its opponents can show has fatal defects; but the easy, simple, and effectual plan of retracing all steps which were improvidently taken, and all steps for which the reasons have now passed away, is suggested by no one.

But that which perhaps at the time seemed most of all to belittle the states and to swell to greatest proportions the central power, was the process of reconstruction of states which began with Virginia, soon after the war opened, and was continued for several years. The theory of the government at all times was that the seceding states were never out of the Union: their constitutions and laws remained notwithstanding secession; and what was needed was that the people should be brought back to the performance of national duties. But in bringing them back they

THE TARIFF A PROTECTIVE ONE. 363

were for a time subjected to military rule, and terms were dictated as conditions to their readmission to their places in the Union. The most important of these conditions were the distinct negation of slavery and the elevation of the freedmen to the dignity of citizens and voters. Giving the elective franchise to the freedmen was a great and confessedly a hazardous experiment, and few if any of the states would willingly have consented to it; but the country was supposed to be still in the grasp of an imperious necessity, and the states had no choice but to accept the terms. The blacks had been freed, and now they must be protected; and the best and only effectual means of self-protection seemed to be the ballot. As the constitution had not contemplated the extraordinary circumstances in which the country was now placed, and therefore had not provided for them, reconstruction presented a problem in legislation which was unique, and, as the power of Congress was irresistible, its judgment upon the problem was necessarily final.

The war made heavy taxes a necessity; and the government, following its ordinary course, raised these for the most part as indirect taxes. In so far as they were levied upon imports, the levy afforded opportunity to discriminate for the protection and encouragement of American products. The heavy tariff thus became in large degree a protective tariff. When the war was over, a fearful load of national debt remained, and the war taxes were continued for the gradual extinguishment of this debt. But when the debt had so far diminished that the heavy taxes could no longer be defended on that ground, the protected interests were found to be so numerous and so powerful, that they were quite able to prevent success in any attempt at considerable reduction. The tariff thus became distinctively a tariff for protection; and all the protected interests looked to the federal government as being at once, to some extent at least, the source and the protector of their prosperity.

It will be interesting now to note the position of Michigan relative to this form of taxation. For this purpose the year 1880 may be taken, up to which time the heavy taxes had been maintained.

Michigan had now become, in all that goes to the making of great states, conspicuous and powerful in the Union. From having been the twenty-sixth State at the time of admission, it has now in point of population become the ninth. In wealth, prosperity, and promise, it is entitled to still higher rank. Only New York, Pennsylvania, Massachusetts, Ohio, Illinois, Connecticut, and New Jersey have more capital invested in manufactures; only Illinois, Indiana, and Ohio produce more wheat; only Ohio, California, and Texas raise more sheep. In the production of iron ore and copper, and in the manufacture of salt and lumber, Michigan is preëminent in the Union, and the shipments from its mines and forests determine the markets for the country. The State has thus become a grand and noble commonwealth; the little settlement so weak and so far in the wilderness when Cass was sent to govern and foster it, has grown to mighty dimensions. Its agriculture is excellent; its manufactures are greatly diversified and generally profitable; its channels of commerce are all that can be desired; its people are intelligent, hardy, industrious, and thrifty, and in natural resources it is unsurpassed by any state. State pride may surely find ample gratification in the contemplation of so magnificent a presentation of happy circumstances.

But some of the facts which have been named are calculated, while the protective system is continued, to concentrate the attention upon the nation rather than upon the State. The pine forests of Michigan, which challenge comparison with any in the world, border upon lakes and rivers which furnish easy avenues to market. But only a few miles away, Canada, also, has vast forests quite as favorably situated for transportation to market, and the Canadian lumberman would compete successfully with the lumberman of Michigan at every leading mart in the country, if he were suffered to do so on equal terms. If, therefore, other manufacturers are to be favored by discriminating duties, the manufacturers of lumber may point to the contiguity of their competitors as constituting a reason for favoring them, also, in like manner.

Whether for the permanent interest of the State it is best that the lumber interest should be thus favored, is a question about which the owners of forests and mills will not very much concern themselves. Protective duties enable them more quickly and more profitably to convert their forests into money, and they therefore favor them. But the duties operate as a premium to a speedy conversion of that which, in its natural condition, is yearly growing more and more valuable; and perhaps if Canada were suffered for the time being to supply in part the American market, the permanent interest of the State would be subserved thereby. But when wealth is coming in, every one wishes "the golden stream" to be "quick and violent."

The salt manufacture of Michigan finds its chief competition in New York, and cannot be protected against it. But the same duty on foreign salt which would favor the manufacture in New York would favor it in Michigan; and, though the interest needs no protection to make it remunerative, being generally profitable without, yet as the business employs a considerable number of men, and protective duties are supposed to foster labor and increase its compensation, the reasons for protection to salt are the same which support protection in the case of many other industries.

It perhaps goes without saying that the iron interest will be favored by protective duties if any is; and the protection when compared with others has generally gone to the verge of liberality. Of the copper mines of Michigan, one has been the most productive and profitable on the globe; and, if that alone were to be considered, protective duties for the purpose of adding to the already enormous profits would seem monstrous; but many other mines have never made fairly remunerative returns, and their abandonment might be a necessity unless copper also received some degree of protection.

Great quantities of cheap foreign wools are imported into this country, and the impression is common, if not general, among the wool growers of the United States that these coarse wools so far compete with the finer and higher priced wools of this country as to affect the price. Whether this impression is true or false, it has had its influence upon sheep growers in inducing them to demand protection, and upon Congress in acceding to the demand.

And so these great leading Michigan interests, of lumber, salt, iron, copper, and wool, to say nothing of many less important interests which are also favored by protective duties, have sufficed to rank the State with those favoring the protective system, and, while influencing the political course of the people, to make them feel at the same time that very much of the prosperity of the State was dependent not upon what the State could do to foster and protect them, but upon what could be done and was being done by the general government.

The superabundant revenue that has come to the government as a result of heavy taxation has made Congress over-liberal in the matter of expenditure. Schemes of doubtful public utility have easily found support; proper national works have readily obtained extravagant appropriations; and sometimes it has seemed that money was voted without discrimination, so many of the persons who cast the votes appearing to look for the benefit in the tax from which the money came, rather than in the purpose which was to be accomplished by its expenditure.

The geographical position of Michigan is such that the State has had an interest quite as great in the expenditure of the moneys realized from protective duties as in the duties themselves. With its two peninsulas it has, in proportion to area, a longer coast line of navigable water than any other state. The rivers St. Clair and St. Mary are great national highways, but the passage of the one is impeded by shallows, and that of the other by rapids, and a considerable expenditure of money has been necessary to make safe and sufficient channels for commerce. The State has numerous other rivers flowing from the interior with

THE INFLUENCE OF PENSIONS.

harbors at their mouths, some of them of large importance, and some that only the most optimistic could see value in; but such of them as are important have needed improvement, and in the river and harbor bills Michigan has been able on plausible claims to secure extensive recognition, and the claims have been allowed to an extent that has seldom left ground for complaint. And to every locality that has received a grant from the general government, the grant has somehow seemed like a mere gift, as if in some providential way the money had come to the national treasury without cost to the people, and the nation was distributing it in benefactions. The State would be powerless to make such benefactions except at a cost of direct taxes; and the people of the State would never assent to the levy of taxes for such purposes. In fact, they have prohibited it by their constitution.

An overflowing national treasury has also encouraged liberal pensions, and gradual additions to the classes of pensioners, until the number of persons dependent upon the nation for bounty of this nature has become enormous. The coincidence of interest between these classes and those in whose behalf heavy taxes are laid seems direct and close; and the more their number is increased, and the greater their interest, the more in their minds is the nation elevated, and made continually present as an entity of power and importance at the expense of the State.

The nation has also since the war made gifts of vast areas of land for the construction of railroads, and loaned large sums of money which might almost as well have been made gifts. It has added to its postal service something of an express business, which has within it the prophecy of greater things to come. The question of annexing the telegraph to the postal service is being urged, and the question of the nation assuming the regulation of railways has for some time been before Congress, and is certain to receive at some time in the near future an affirmative solution.

Then the number of federal office-holders has increased until they constitute a mighty army: an army greater in number than that with which Wellington at Waterloo changed the history of the world; greater than that with which Meade won the decisive victory at Gettysburg in the crisis of the civil war. It has been deemed necessary to legislate to prevent elections from being improperly influenced by the labors and pecuniary contributions of so large a body, directed and expended as they are likely to be by the political machinery of the party in power.

After all these important changes, these great additions to federal power, federal activity, federal beneficence to individuals and localities, and federal agencies and servants, it needs scarcely be said that it is not state action and state legislation that most attract attention, even when the citizen in the quiet of his own home or in neighborhood gatherings is discussing public affairs. Everything gravitates to Washington; the highest interests and the most absorbing ambitions look to the national capital for gratification; and it is no longer the state but the nation that in men's minds and imaginations is an ever present sovereignty. And this is as true of the states of which Jefferson and Calhoun have been the idols as it is of Massachusetts or Michigan.

"The constitution as it is and the Union as it was" can no longer be the motto and the watchword of any political party. We may preserve the constitution in its every phrase and every letter, with only such modification as was found essential for the uprooting of slavery; but the Union as it was has given way to a new Union with some new and grand features, but also with some engrafted evils which only time and the patient and persevering labors of statesmen and patriots will suffice to eradicate.

CHAPTER XIX.

MICHIGAN IN THE TWENTIETH CENTURY.

The opening of the twentieth century finds the State of Michigan practically out of debt; and the settled policy of the people in municipal as well as state affairs is to bear to-day the burdens of the hour, rather than to mortgage the future, which will have its own imperative needs in ever increasing ratio. Nor has this rule prevented the State from maintaining a foremost position in education, in charities, in improved reformatory and penal systems, and along those other lines which mark an advancing civilization. For example, of the half million dollars and more that make up the income of the state University, more than three fifths of the amount come from direct taxation; and a million and a half of dollars are annually distributed among the counties towards the support of primary education. To the many charitable institutions has been added recently a home for the feeble-minded and epileptic, which now accommodates five hundred inmates.

During the past quarter-century certain marked changes have taken place in the economic development of the State; there have been gains and losses; new industries have been developed, and the era of concentration has had its effects. The changes in the production of copper, iron, and lumber, which form the chief industries of Michigan, call for particular attention.

Before history began on the Western Hemisphere, the predecessors of the Indians came from the south to Lake Superior for copper. Such was their degree of expertness as miners, that on the site of the Minnesota mine they lifted a copper mass weighing six tons, supporting it on a cobwork frame of wood five feet in height; and at the Mesnard mine they moved a boulder of eighteen tons forty-eight feet from its original bed. Springing from the débris covering these ancient pits, have been found hemlock trees having annual rings showing that they began to grow nearly half a century before the coming of Columbus. The Indians were never miners; but the float pieces of copper which they found and gave to French explorers and missionaries induced the Intendant Talon to dispatch Joliet to the great lake in search of copper deposits. Neither the French nor the English,[1] however, achieved success in the quest. In 1819, Governor Cass, while making the first explorations in the Lake Superior region undertaken by the United States government, turned aside to visit

[1] Alexander Henry's *Travels and Adventures in Canada*, 1809, p. 231.

the then famous copper rock lying in the bed of the Ontonagon River. After many futile attempts this boulder was removed in 1843, and comprised the first shipment of copper from the Lake region. The government, however, laid claim to the rock, and it now reposes in an obscure corner of the National Museum at Washington.[1]

Public attention was called to the mineral riches of the upper peninsula by the reports of Dr. Douglass Houghton, who, in order to accomplish a geological survey for which there was no appropriation, had taken the contract to make linear surveys for the general government. Within a few months after the publication of Dr. Houghton's first report in 1841, Fort Wilkins at Copper Harbor was thronged with prospectors and explorers eager to gain a War Department permit to occupy mineral lands. Nine hundred and sixty such permits were speedily granted. One mine on Keweenaw Point produced returns in twenty-two years, of over two thousand per cent. on the investment; while from a mine in the Ontonagon region a single mass of pure copper of nearly a million pounds in weight sold for more than $200,000. Unhappily the vast majority of the claims turned out to be simply pits in which fortunes were sunk; and the usual history of mining ventures was repeated in the Lake Superior region. More than half the copper produced in Michigan now comes

[1] Report of the U. S. National Museum for 1895, pp. 1021-1030.

from the Calumet and Hecla properties on Keweenaw point. This rugged peninsula juts into Lake Superior about midway along its southern shore. From the great lake on the north, a government ship canal now occupies the route of the portage that Radisson found well traveled in 1661. From the canal vessels pass into the red waters of Portage Lake, its deep basin shut in by high hills from whose precipitous sides the cities of Hancock and Houghton face each other. In summer the mid-day heat scorches the scanty vegetation of the narrow valley; in winter the frequent snows are whirled through the narrow gorge by winds that cut like knives, while the mercury shrinks into a solid ball. Such is the heart of the copper country — a region always gloomy, but never grand. The Calumet and Hecla vein, discovered in 1861, after eight years of search by Edwin Hulbert,[1] was until 1876 the largest producer of copper in the world; and even now is without an equal as a profitable mining property. Each year it can be made to yield ninety million pounds of copper, so tough and so free from arsenic as to make it unrivaled as a conductor of electricity. Ore containing only from three to four per cent. of pure copper, is mined a mile or more under ground, is separated from the rock in vast stamp-mills, is cast into ingots, and put upon the world's markets at a profit.

---

[1] "The Copper Conglomerate," a series of letters by E. J. Hulbert, reprinted from the *Ontonagon Miner*, 1893.

Until 1876, the Michigan mines produced ninety per cent. of the copper output of the United States; now they yield but twenty-five per cent. Yet while the relative product is smaller, the number of pounds in the output is on the increase; new mines are being discovered, and old ones are being reopened with improved machinery.

On September 19, 1844, one of Dr. Houghton's surveying parties, under the leadership of William A. Burt, was engaged in running township lines and making geological observations between the Chocolate and the Carp rivers in Marquette County. On reaching the hills south of Teal Lake, the compass-man noticed decided fluctuations in the variations of the magnetic needle. The party was using the solar compass, which Mr. Burt had then but recently invented, and when the needle began to traverse several degrees south of west, the excited inventor exclaimed, "Now, boys, look around to see what you can find." Eagerly the surveyors scattered for the hunt, returning with specimens of iron ore gathered from the out-crop. Tales of the marvelous richness of the iron deposits quickly spread through the lower peninsula, and the next year citizens of Jackson organized a company and put an exploring party in the field. Reaching the site of the present city of Marquette, they started inland under the guidance of Marji Gesick, a sub-chief of the Chippewas. On reaching the spot where

DISCOVERY OF IRON ORE.

the Burt party had discovered traces of iron ore, they found a high hill sloping to the north, and at its base and along its sides was an outcrop of the finest quality of gray granular iron ore, standing out to view like a quarry of granite. Having located, under the Federal statutes, a mining claim one mile square, they built a forge to test the ores; but so unsuccessful were the first ventures that until 1861 the entire shipments of iron ore from Lake Superior did not reach one hundred tons a year. From the Jackson, however, nearly four million tons of ore were taken before the mine was worked out; and when recourse must be had to low grade ores, this original mine promises again to assume leading importance.

The iron region of Michigan now occupies the western half of the upper peninsula and comprises the Marquette, the Menominee, and the Gogebic ranges. On the Marquette range, the workings of the Barnum mine lie directly under the main streets of Ishpeming, whose citizens, transported in steam and electric cars, and busy with their daily vocations, give small heed to the fact that hundreds of feet beneath them is yet another city with electric lights burning incessantly, and with regular streets crowded with electric cars and thronged with busy miners. Forty miles south of the Marquette range is the Menominee iron region, whose famous Chapin mine, during the twelve years following its opening in 1880, produced sufficient ore to load a train of cars that would reach from Chicago to New York City. In the Gogebic range, on the extreme west, the Norrie was first among iron mines to attain a record of a million tons; and in 1900 the iron production of Michigan reached ten million tons. Stupendous as are these figures, they are excelled by those of the Vermillion and Mesaba ranges in Minnesota, from the latter of which, in 1900, nearly eight million tons of ore were taken from the surface of the ground by steam-shovels. The Michigan product, however, being hard ore, is essential for mixing with the soft friable ores of the Mesaba range, in order to make the latter work well in the furnace; and while, for the time being, Minnesota may claim a greater production, when the not distant day comes to resort to lower grades of ores and to delve under ground, the enormous deposits in Michigan will probably restore to our State the old-time supremacy.

The development of the iron industry has concentrated the ownership of the properties in few hands. The members of the Standard Oil combination, with seemingly unlimited means at command, began to acquire ore properties, to build railroads to the ore-fields, to operate lines of steamships, and finally to monopolize the iron industry of the country, until to-day the United States Steel Corporation controls the market. Such is the economy of working, that the ore is handled but twice from the mine of Lake Superior to the pig-iron of Pennsylvania, machinery and gravity performing the other operations. From mine to market the ownership is not changed. Economy is studied so closely that he who discovers a means of saving a cent a ton in ore production increases profits by $200,000 a year. Consequently, the highest salaries are paid to an army of explorers and scientific men engaged in the work of the great corporation. Steadiness of production, also, has been gained by concentration, and the labor market is no longer subject to violent fluctuations alternating between feast and famine. A few independent corporations, like the Cleveland Cliffs Company, have been able by superior management and the possession of valuable properties to maintain themselves, and even to wax strong. What the Calumet and Hecla is to the copper country, the Cleveland Cliffs is to the iron region, — a beneficent institution conserving its properties, putting into operation plans for the preservation of natural beauties and the reforestation of its lands, and developing among its army of employes a sense of loyalty to the company.

It is not altogether comforting to state pride that the vast mineral wealth of Michigan is owned and operated by corporations having their head offices in Boston, New York, and other cities of the east. From these mines the State derives only a comparatively meagre revenue; and such is the solidarity of the Lake Superior mining interests that low valuations have been the rule. In fact, the upper peninsula has always been treated as a region quite by itself. Its population is composed largely of Swedes and Finns; its wealth is concentrated in the hands of a few corporations and their representatives; and its soil is but slowly and partially coming under cultivation. In matters political there are certain offices and positions which go to that district as a matter of course; no other single congressional district is so largely influential in the affairs of the State.

The slowness of the early development of the Lake Superior mines, both iron and copper, and the remarkable production in the years since 1860, are explained generally by the rapid progress which this country made after the Civil War, and the consequent demand for materials of all kinds; and in particular by the building of the canal and locks to overcome the barrier to navigation formed by the rapids of Sault St. Marie. Shortly before the year 1800, the British Fur Trading Company constructed, on the Canadian side of the river, a sluiceway for the passage of their batteaux;[1] but during the war of 1812 a force of United States soldiers demolished the locks and burned every building in the vicinity. In his first message, Governor Mason urged the necessity of a canal, for he saw clearly

[1] The little old lock now performs the part of a fountain in the Lake Superior Corporation grounds.

that without such a waterway the gift of the upper peninsula would be valueless to Michigan. The legislature appropriated $50,000 for the work, but when, in 1839, the contractors began operations by filling a mill-race on the military reservation, a company of regulars from Fort Brady drove the laborers off. In vain the legislature protested to Congress against the outrage; and Senator Norvell's bill making a grant of government land to aid in the construction of a canal was defeated largely by reason of Henry Clay's speech, in which he referred to the rapids of Sault Ste. Marie as "beyond the remotest settlement in the United States, if not in the moon." In 1852, after sixteen years of importunity, Congress gave to Michigan public lands to the value of $750,000 to aid in building a canal with locks to be at least 250 feet long, 12 feet deep, and 50 feet wide. Michigan, as was then believed, lacked the constitutional power to grant charters to construction companies. Therefore, an organization, with a capital stock of one million dollars, was effected at Albany, N. Y., and work began on June 2, 1853. In twenty-two months the canal was constructed at a cost of $875,000, being within the estimates both as to time and expense. At the date of its completion, the lock was the largest in the world; it was built on the outskirts of civilization; the machinery for submarine excavation was invented on the spot, and all adjacent Canada was scoured on snow-shoes by men in search of blacksmiths' bellows for use in making forgings. The blasting-powder came from Connecticut and Delaware; the laborers were immigrants sent in gangs from New York City; the nearest telegraph station was at Detroit, 450 miles away; and much of the work was done in winter with the mercury often at 35° below zero, and with only eight hours of daylight. When the cold became intense a man was stationed at each runway, and as often as he saw a face frost-bitten he would rub it with snow until circulation was restored, so that the barrowman need not leave his work. Several enormous fortunes were made from the sale of the canal lands, and there is a case on record where an Englishman invested $100,000 in the Company's stock and in twenty years received $500,000 as a part of his reward. In 1881 the canal was transferred to the Federal government, and the same year the Weitzel lock, constructed by the United States at a cost of $2,180,000, was opened. The State lock continued to be operated until 1886, when the government began to construct the Poe lock, now the largest in the world, with a length of 800 feet, a width of 100 feet, and a depth of 21 feet. Within its granite sides vessels 540 feet in length and carrying 10,000 tons of freight are lifted in eight minutes from the level of Lake Huron to that of Lake Superior. In the two American locks, supplemented by the one constructed by the Canadian government, ninety vessels a day on the average are passed, and during the seven months of the navigation season, one eighth of the commerce of the United States goes through St. Mary's River. Canadian or American, each vessel in its turn, without discrimination as to nationality or the payment of a penny in tolls, glides into the great stone pit, is silently lifted or lowered, and goes its way.

To supplement the improvements at the rapids, the government has straightened the tortuous channel of the St. Mary's River, by cutting through islands and shoals a perfectly straight course twenty miles long, thereby making a saving of eleven miles in distance, and permitting night navigation of the river. At St. Claire Flats, where La Salle's little Griffon with difficulty found a channel, the government has made a broad passageway protected by wooden walls two miles long; and is now constructing a second one, so as to prevent collisions. Near the mouth of the Detroit River, also, is a long cut made by our government entirely in Canadian waters, for the accommodation of the rapidly increasing lake commerce. The Great Lakes and their connecting waters, one thousand miles in length, have become the greatest internal waterway in the world. At an average cost of six tenths of a mill per ton a mile, the vessels on this commercial thoroughfare carry two fifths as much freight as do all the railroads of the

United States, notwithstanding the fact that ice closes the waters from the middle of December until the first of April; and this commerce might be increased largely by reciprocal trade relations with Canada, which would encourage traffic across as well as along the natural waterways. Michigan in particular would be benefited by as free trade with Ontario as she now enjoys with Ohio, Indiana, Illinois, and Wisconsin.

The growth of commerce within the borders of the State was long delayed by lack of means of communication. The St. Mary's Canal indeed opened, during eight months of the year, a commercial highway to the upper peninsula; but for the remaining four months ice locked the Straits of Mackinaw, so that the only means of reaching the towns of the Lake Superior region by rail was by way of Chicago and Milwaukee, a recourse neither convenient in itself nor yet comforting to state pride. Indeed much of the once large and lucrative Lake Superior trade had been taken from the merchants of Detroit by their Chicago rivals; and the upper country had begun to agitate the question of political independence, when, urged by both commercial and patriotic considerations, a number of Detroit capitalists, headed by James McMillan (on whom the burden of the undertaking afterwards devolved), formed a syndicate to build a railway to connect the upper peninsula with the lower. The work involved an international bridge across the St. Mary's River to give a connection with Montreal by the old route of Indian missionary and explorer; and also a means of forcing a winter passage across the Straits of Mackinaw, a distance of seven miles. This was finally accomplished by means of a powerful steam car-ferry, with a small wheel under the bow to draw the water from beneath the ice while the big wheel at the stern forces the heavy vessel upon the broken ice-cakes, a principle afterwards borrowed by Russia for like service along the Siberian railway. As the agricultural lands of the upper peninsula come into use, and the country becomes more thickly settled, this means of winter communication will become more and more important; and since the connection was first made, the bonds of steel have been typical of the closer political relations between the two sections of the State. It was not until so late as 1885, however, that the city of Sault St. Marie, the first settlement within the borders of Michigan, was reached by the railroad builders, and the dog-sledge ceased to be used for the transportation of mails.

Within the past decade the waters of Lake Superior have been tamed and put to the service of manufacture. An American company first opened a short canal on the Canadian side of St. Mary's Rapids, developing twenty thousand electric horse-power; and afterwards the same corporation, succeeding where others had failed, constructed through the American town of Sault St. Marie a canal, three and a half miles in length and two hundred feet in width; and at its outlet built a power-house, capable of developing forty thousand electric horse-power. At the same time the level of Lake Superior is preserved for traffic by a system of automatic compensating-works in the nature of a partial dam placed at the head of the rapids, — a method which probably will come into use throughout the Lakes, to maintain for commerce levels disturbed by deepened channels. Evidently the day is not far distant when the greatest of fresh water lakes will become but a vast mill-pond, and the leaping waters of the Sault will be a beauty passed away.

When settlers first came to Michigan, their greatest enemy was the trees that kept the sun from the lands. To clear the fertile acres it was necessary to fell the great oaks and maples, and the superb trees of beech, walnut, and ash; and because there was no market for lumber and no mills in the interior, burning and burying were resorted to as means of extermination. Although lumber mills were in operation along the Detroit and St. Clair rivers long before the Americans took possession of Michigan, yet so late as 1854 there were in the whole State only sixty-one mills in operation, and the annual product was scarcely more than a hundred million feet, most of which came from the Saginaw valley. Among the settlers who came to Michigan about the time the State was admitted to the Union, many were reared on the banks of the Kennebec or the Merrimac; and their experienced eyes quickly saw in the white pine that covered more than half of the lower peninsula, the opportunity to make large fortunes. Buying great tracts of this pine at government prices or at a small advance, these far-seeing ones quietly bided their time; and when the cities of the west began to build themselves up, Michigan's forests fell at the rate of thirty-three thousand acres a year, yielding in 1871 two and a half billion feet of sawed pine, and increasing the output to over three and three-quarters billion feet in 1892. On each side of the State, the refuse from the lumber mills was used to evaporate salt brine, until in the production of both lumber and salt Michigan came to lead all other States; a supremacy that, so far as lumber is concerned, has now passed to Wisconsin.

In 1889, the State of Michigan placed in the Capitol at Washington a statue of Lewis Cass, thus setting its seal upon his work and worth. The successor of Cass in political power and influence was Zachariah Chandler. Judge Cooley has left on record a comparison of the two men: —

Mr. Chandler was a merchant of Detroit, and like his predecessor, a native of New Hampshire. He had strong native sense, easily adapted himself to all classes of men and all grades of society, was quick in decision, fearless in action, uncompromising in principle, and inflexible in purpose. . . . He was less learned, courtly, and polished than his predecessor; he knew much less of literature and history, of foreign countries and our relations to them; but he resembled Governor Cass in integrity and thrift, while in his nature he was far more combative and persistent. When the time came for the life and death struggle of the nation, no defiance rang out clearer and stronger; no courage was less doubtful of results; no vote was more unhesitatingly or more emphatically given for radical measures than were those of Zachariah Chandler. For twelve years he spoke the voice of the State in the Senate, and on the main questions of the day his utterances were never of doubtful import.[1]

The mantle of political leadership in Michigan, dropping from the shoulders of the dead Chandler in 1875, came to be worn easily by James McMillan, a Canadian by birth, but a resident of Michigan after he reached the age of seventeen. Lewis Cass represented the exploration and settlement of the northwest; Zachariah Chandler was the war spirit incarnate; and James McMillan typified the age of commercial development. Mr. McMillan's first success was as a builder of freight-cars in Michigan and several other States; to this he added the construction and operation of railways and of steamships, both freight and passenger; so that

[1] *Semi-Centennial Addresses*, 1886, p. 93.

he became preëminently Michigan's captain of industry. First and almost alone among the public men of the State in well-considered gifts to education and philanthropy, his unbounded energy found scope in every portion of the commonwealth. Elected to the United States Senate in 1889, he was twice reëlected, and served until his death, in 1902. In the long struggle for the establishment of the gold standard his good judgment and persistence counted largely; in the legislation for the deep-water channel to connect Duluth and Chicago with Buffalo he had a large share; and in the adjustment of matters growing out of the Spanish War he bore an influential part. His most conspicuous service, however, was rendered in the regulation of the affairs of the District of Columbia during the thirteen years of his senatorial service. The large and comprehensive plan for the improvement and beautification of the national capital, as formulated by the Park Commission, owes to him its conception and beginning; and the project was the culmination of labors that embraced every department of municipal economy in relation to the seat of the federal government. To the task he brought an intense interest in the problems presented, and a mastery of them; the quiet persistence necessary to legislative success, and an integrity of motive recognized and appreciated in both houses of Congress. It was his aim to restore the plan of the Federal city as outlined by

L'Enfant under the direction of Washington and Jefferson, and to have that plan carried to its ultimate conclusion in a manner befitting the wealth and power of this nation.[1]

Mr. McMillan's immediate predecessor in the Senate was Thomas Witherell Palmer, who served a single term, from 1883 until 1889; he then became successively minister to Spain and president of the Government Board of the Columbian Exposition at Chicago. Two men who had rendered long and conspicuous service in the House of Representatives were called to the Senate, — Omar D. Conger, who served in the last-named body from 1877 to 1883; and Julius C. Burrows, elected to the Senate on the death of Francis B. Stockbridge, in 1897, and still in service, his colleague being Russell A. Alger, who succeeded James McMillan. During the first administration of President Cleveland, George Van Ness Lothrop, for many years the leader of the Michigan bar, served as minister to Russia; and Don M. Dickinson was the postmaster-general.

Judge Cooley has summarized the succession in the gubernatorial office: —

The successor of Governor Crapo was Henry P. Baldwin, a native of Rhode Island, who for many years had been extensively engaged in business in Detroit as merchant, manufacturer, and banker, and won an enviable reputation for ability, integrity, and liberality. He

[1] Senate Report No. 160; 57th Congress.

held office for two terms, retiring at the beginning of 1873. Succeeding him for two terms was John J. Bagley, a native of New York. In him the State had for executive one of those strong and vigorous characters who, by their native sense, business tact and ability, and promptitude in the performance of duty, do honor to the commonwealth with which they unite their fortunes. Many such have made their homes in Michigan, but none more worthy of honorable mention than John J. Bagley. Charles M. Croswell held office from 1877 to 1881; David H. Jerome, from 1881 to 1883; Josiah W. Begole from 1883 to 1885; and the latter gave place to Russell A. Alger [1885–1887]. Each of these gentlemen as a private citizen was known and respected for the energy, prudence, and success with which he managed his own business interests, and the people expected from each an administration of public affairs which should be prudent, conscientious, and watchful, and in no instance were the expectations disappointed. Governors Croswell and Begole were natives of New York; Governor Alger, of Ohio. To Governor Jerome belongs the proud distinction of being the first governor of Michigan who was born within its limits; the true representative of those who were reared among its stumps and taught in its district schools.[1]

After serving a single term, Governor Alger was succeeded by Cyrus G. Luce, a representative of the agricultural interests, a shrewd and vigorous speaker on the stump, and a man intimately acquainted with the State and the management of

[1] *Semi-Centennial Addresses*, 1886, p. 95.

its institutions. During his administration a banking law, modeled on the national statute, was submitted to the people and adopted. Under the provisions of this law more than one-half of the commercial banking capital of the State finds investment. Since the formation of the Republican party in 1854 but two of the fifteen governors of Michigan have been elected by the opposition; Governor Begole, who has been mentioned, and Governor Winans, who succeeded Governor Luce, a result in each case due to a desire on the part of the Republicans to administer a rebuke to their own party. After a single term, Governor Winans was succeeded by John T. Rich, a farmer candidate, who had served for a time in the National House of Representatives, and who, during four years, gave to the State an intelligent, forceful, and entirely practical administration. He, in turn, was succeeded by Hazen S. Pingree, who also served for two terms (1897–1901), and was succeeded by Aaron T. Bliss.

While the people have strenuously refused to make any general revision of the Constitution, they have yielded to changed conditions by adopting a number of amendments. The number of justices of the Supreme Court was increased to five in 1887 and to eight in 1903, and the salaries were raised to $7000 per annum, with the requirement that the justices shall reside in Lansing. More than one circuit judge has been allowed to certain of the more populous counties; and these counties, together with all counties in the upper peninsula, are permitted to pay circuit judges such salaries as the respective boards of supervisors may determine.[1] In 1894 the salary of the governor was increased to $4000; those of the other elective state officers remain at the former low figures, although four times amendments making general increases have been submitted to the people. Thus has come about the anomaly of the secretary of state, the land commissioner, and the attorney-general receiving a salary of but $800, while their deputies receive $2000; and the treasurer and the superintendent of public instruction receiving only half the salary of their deputies. The practical result has been generally to make these state offices political stepping stones, and in some cases to lead to a division of salaries within the offices. Other amendments provide that foreign-born electors must have been citizens of the United States for two years and a half before they can vote; and that the legislature may provide for the establishment of libraries in each township or city, and all fines for the breach of penal laws must either go to the support of such libraries or else be used for school purposes. Under this latter provision local libraries have been developed throughout the State, and these have been supplemented by an excellent system of "traveling" libraries lodged in factories, schools, and other

[1] Cf. p. 302, 303.

accessible places, the books being exchanged from time to time. In 1902 an amendment was adopted providing for indeterminate sentences, as a betterment of the penal system. The provision of the Constitution prohibiting the State from being a party to, or interested in, any work of internal improvement was successfully invoked to prevent the city of Detroit from purchasing and operating the street railways of that city in 1900, during a temporary demand for the municipal ownership of quasi-public works;[1] but by express provision the city of Grand Rapids may issue bonds for the improvement of the navigation of Grand River.

In 1900 the agitation for increased taxation of steam railroads found expression in an amendment giving to the legislature power to provide for the assessment of property of corporations at its true cash value by a state board of assessors, in place of a specific tax on gross earnings. The legislature is required to provide a uniform rule of taxation for property assessed by such board, and the rate shall be the average rate levied upon other property upon which *ad valorem* taxes are assessed for state and municipal purposes. Also the legislature is required to provide for an equalization of all taxable property by a state board at least once in five years. These amendments were supplemented by legisla-

[1] Cf. p. 293. See also *Quarterly Journal of Economics*, June and October, 1900: articles on "Municipal Ownership of Street Railways in Detroit."

tion providing for the repeal of the special charters held by certain railway corporations, and fixing a means whereby those railways might recover damages (if any) from the State by reason of such repeal. These changes have been far-reaching in their effects, and the measure of advantages gained must await the decisions of the courts as to the many questions now in litigation. The first result has been to add to the rolls over two hundred million dollars worth of property, an increase of about one eighth in taxable property of the State.

The outbreak of the Spanish war, in April, 1898, found Michigan ready to respond to the call to arms. With great promptness five regiments were put into the field; and two of them were among the first to disembark on Cuban soil. If the part assigned to the Michigan soldiers against Fort Aguadores by the commanding general, William R. Shafter (himself a native of Michigan), was such as to create a doubt in the general mind as to the value of those services, at least the regiments carried out the letter of their instructions by holding the enemy in check while more important operations were being conducted at Santiago. At sea, the cruise of the Michigan naval brigade on the Yosemite brought the volunteers from the State into the position of maintaining alone for several days the blockade of San Juan; of driving ashore a Spanish transport, and repulsing the Spanish naval vessel Isabel II and two gunboats. Although laurels were few for the infantry, there was full measure of suffering from the hardships of a tropical campaign. The Secretary of War, during the war portion of the McKinley administration, was Russell A. Alger, the occasion of whose retirement from the Cabinet was the subject of much controversy throughout the country.

The great diversity of natural resources possessed by the State is constantly giving rise to new enterprises. The recent discovery of coal in the Saginaw valley has resulted in an annual production of a million tons of low grade bituminous coal; extensive beds of marl have led to the construction of manufactories of cement; the abundant hard woods have enabled Grand Rapids to become the first city in the country in the production of furniture, the annual market being attended by buyers from every section of the Union; the soil in various localities being well adapted to the production of the sugar-beet, great sugar factories have been constructed, and the best located among them have passed into the control of the Sugar Trust; the salt deposits along the Detroit River have led to the investment of many millions of dollars in plants for the production of soda-ash, bleaching powder, and kindred products; while the celery of Kalamazoo and the peach crop of western Michigan find ready market, with Chicago as the chief point of distribution. Meantime shipbuilding and the manufacture of freight cars are among the leading industries of the State.

The census of 1900 shows Michigan ninth among the States in population, in amount of capital employed in manufactures, and in the production of flour; second in lumber, copper, and iron ore; sixth in the manufacture of agricultural implements and chemicals, and seventh in railway cars; eighth in the production of cheese and of wood-pulp and paper; tenth in manufactures generally; and thirteenth in agriculture.

The extreme beauty of Michigan's sixteen hundred miles of coast line, of the five thousand inland lakes and the numerous islands; the salubrious air of the Great Lakes, and the many streams well stocked with gamy trout, have made the State the resort of thousands of summer pleasure-seekers and sportsmen; while in winter the northern woods still tempt the deer-shooter. The "fairy island" of Mackinaw, with its numerous hotels and villas, adds to marvelous beauty an historic interest running back to remotest times. Old Fort Mackinaw, built by the British Colonel Sinclair in the times of Haldimand, together with the American Fur Company post, recall the last days of the English occupation, the frontier struggles of the War of 1812, and the early days of American enterprise. In 1894, the government, desiring to concentrate the army posts, threatened to sell its wide possessions on Mackinaw Island;

but through the interposition of Senator McMillan, Fort Mackinaw, with its park-like dependencies and its famous natural beauties, was transferred to the State, and is preserved as a park for visitors from all over the land. From Traverse Bay southward even to Berrien County, the shore of Lake Michigan is lined with populous summer cities, as are also the shores of Lake Huron from Saginaw Bay to Port Huron and thence to Lake Erie. Among the marshes of St. Clair Flats a western Venice has built itself, so that for miles along the winding ship-channel a succession of cottages and club-houses, rising from the waters, offers rest to the people of the near-by city of Detroit. At Mount Clemens, where in Revolutionary days fugitives from the Moravian missions of the Ohio country found protection under the British commandant DePeyster, sulphur springs, famed throughout the world, draw thousands to the "Bath City;" and healing waters at other points are only less well known. Lines of fast steamers furnished luxuriously, connect the upper and lower lake cities, offering the summer traveler an uninterrupted journey of from seven to ten days.

In June, 1886, the completion of a half century of statehood was celebrated by the people of Michigan, who assembled at Lansing as at a family gathering to exchange·felicitations over fifty well spent years. The lavish gifts of nature, the progress in education and philanthropy, the changes that the pioneers wrought — such were the themes of the orators. Many of the speakers had seen all and had been part of many of the events they chronicled. Most happy was the summing up by Judge Cooley : —

> What more can be said in praise of the State, than that it has more than kept pace with the astounding growth of the country, and more than kept good the wonderful promise of its earlier years ? Justly and with emphasis of proud satisfaction may its citizens exclaim, as they welcome the stranger to our hospitable board to-day : " Si quaeris peninsulam amoenam, circumspice." Its beauty, its riches, its attractions are everywhere. But not in its wealth, in its beauty, in its numbers does the State chiefly pride itself, so much as in its religious and charitable institutions and its complete system of public education ; and what the people have done and are doing through these and by these, must sufficiently attest: first and foremost the aim of the State has always been to prepare its youth to act well their part in the great drama of life and in its incidental trials and rivalries. If that aim is accomplished, the State may well be content, for material success will abundantly follow.

In 1887 the University of Michigan received the congratulations of sister institutions of learning on the fiftieth anniversary of its foundation. During the past thirty-three years, the fortunes of the University have been entrusted to James Burrill Angell, a native of Rhode Island, a man of sound and elegant scholarship, of infinite tact, and of wide knowledge of men and life. Twice he has been called into the service of the nation to carry on delicate negotiations with the Chinese and the Turkish empires; and the State has ever taken a peculiar pride in the honors bestowed upon a citizen who has won at home so much admiration and respect. On the occasion of the anniversary celebration the delegate speakers representing other colleges made manifest the fact that while the University, through its officers and professors, had ever been an integral part of the great republic of letters, at the same time the institution had been signally successful in maintaining the position, as Professor Bryce has expressed it, " of metropolitan university for the Northwestern States." Akin to the State University is the Normal College, with its centre at Ypsilanti and its branches at Mt. Pleasant, Marquette, and Kalamazoo; the Agricultural College, well equipped and well endowed; and the College of Mines, located in the heart of the Copper country at Houghton. Besides these institutions, the Hollanders have Hope College at Holland; the Presbyterians support a college at Alma, the Baptists one at Kalamazoo, the Free Baptists one at Hillsdale, the Methodists one at Albion, the Congregationalists one at Olivet and another at Benzonia, the Seventh-Day Adventists one at Battle Creek, and the Roman Catholics one at Detroit, each institution being named for the city in which it is located.

A third notable anniversary took place in Detroit in June, 1901, when in a series of pageants the two hundredth anniversary of the landing of Cadillac was celebrated in the streets and on the river. Then the descendants of the old French families came forward, and in a brilliant pantomime revived the sights and scenes of two centuries ago, when, outwardly at least, life presented a gayer aspect than it wears to-day.

On July 6, 1904, the anniversary of the foundation of the Republican party was celebrated under the oaks in the city of Jackson, where the first state convention that adopted the name "Republican" had been held fifty years before. During the half-century every electoral vote of Michigan has been given to the nominees of that party, save in 1892, when the election was held under the so-called Miner Law, passed by a Democratic legislature, whereby electors were chosen by congressional districts instead of by the State at large. The popular vote showed a plurality of over twenty thousand for Harrison; but five out of the fourteen electors returned were Democrats. The law was repealed by the succeeding legislature.

In September, 1904, the war-cry of the War of 1812, "Remember the River Raisin," found renewed expression in the unveiling of a monument erected by the State to the memory of the Kentucky soldiers who perished in that massacre.[1]

[1] Cf. pp. 182–184.

With the opening of the Erie Canal in 1825, a stream of immigration from New England and New York began to flow to Michigan; and since that day the laws and institutions of the State have been patterned largely after those of the parent States. No foreign element, however predominant in a particular section, has had more than a local influence. The descendants of these early settlers congratulate themselves that their lines have fallen in pleasant places. The records of French explorers, the relations of the early missionaries, the stubborn resistance offered by the British to Pontiac, wiliest of savage foes, all give a background of historic romance; the discovery and development of the natural resources afford tales of adventure and achievement, while the great beauty of the inland seas and their picturesque shores have a charm not without decided influence upon the lives of the people. If Michigan has produced no Presidents, and no statesmen of the first rank, at least no national crisis has found the State wanting either in decision or in energy. No people have more sincerely adopted or more fully exemplified in their lives the golden words of the immortal Ordinance of 1787: "Religion, morality, and knowledge being necessary to good government and the happiness of mankind, schools and the means of education shall forever be encouraged."

INDEX

INDEX.

ABBOT, Governor, 91.
Academies, 317.
Adams, John Quincy, 219, 355.
Adrian, 239.
Aigrement, 29, 32.
Alger, Russell A., 390, 391, 396.
American Fur Company, 192, 397.
Amherst, General, 40, 41, 75.
Angell, James Burrill, 399, 400.
Ann Arbor, 239, 317.
Astor, John Jacob, 191.

Bagley, John J., 391.
Baldwin, Henry P., 390, 391.
Barry, John S., 294, 298.
Bates, Judge, 150.
Beauharnais, 35, 36.
Begole, Josiah W., 391, 392.
Bellestre, 43.
Bingham, Kinsley S., 305.
Bird, Captain, 102.
Black Hawk War, 212.
Blair, Austin, 305, 339.
Bliss, Aaron T., 392.
Boundary controversy, 214 *et seq.*
Bradstreet, General, 63, 68.
Brandy, trade in, 31–33, 51, 52.
Brant, Joseph, 106–109, 113, 116, 117.
British posts, detention of, 107, 114, 115, 118.
Brock, General, 174, 175, 177.
Buchanan, President, 339.
Burrows, Julius C., 390.
Burt, William A., 376.

Cadillac, La Motte, 14, 17–34, 401.
Cahokia, 96.
Calumet and Hecla mine, 375.
Campbell, Major, 60.
Canada, colonization of, 5; government of, 8–10, 26; surrender to the British, 40–44; despotic government of, 46, 66–78.
Canals and locks, first a sluiceway, 380; Congress delays construction, 381; constructive problems, 381, 382; canal property valuable, 382; Weitzel lock, 382; Poe lock, 382; supplementary water ways, 383, 384; power canals, 385.
Carleton, Sir Guy, 75, 76, 85, 110, 112, 114.
Cartier, Jaques, 2.
Cass, Lewis, Colonel, 167, 172, 175; made military governor, 187; appointed civil governor, 189; treaties with Indians, 194; visits the upper Lakes, 195, 196; his bravery, 196; his democratic tendencies, 201, 205, 206; organizes counties, 201; becomes secretary of war, 203; his habits, 204; favors general education, 310, 314; obtains grant to University, 312; Nicholson letter of, 334; favors compromise of 1850, 335; speaks for the Union, 342; examines Ontonagon copper rock, 373, 374; statue erected, 387.
Catholepistemiad, 310.
Census of 1900, 397.
Champlain, Samuel de, 3.
Chandler, Elizabeth Margaret, 243.
Chandler, Zachariah, 335, 340, 387, 388.
Charlevoix, 35.
Charter contracts, 300.
Chicago, abandoned in 1812, 181.
Cholera in 1832–34, 212.
Cincinnati, 111.
Civil war, 1861–1865, 330–343.
Clarke, George Rogers, 93–104.
Clay, Henry, 165, 166.
Colbert, 109.
Coles, Edward, 138, 139.
Colonization, European, 1; French, 5.
Company of the Colony of Canada, 26.
Company of the Hundred Associates, 6, 7.
Conger, Omar D., 390.
Congress of Nations, 16.
Constitution of the State of 1835, 225; of 1850, 299–304; amendments of, 304, 392–395.
Constitutions, American, peculiar excellence of, 345; must necessarily change, 347.

INDEX.

Conventions, state, 223, 249; "frost-bitten," 224.
Copper mines, 16, 20, 78, 364; prehistoric workings, 373; first ore shipment, 374; Ontonagon region, 374; Calumet and Hecla, 375; present development, 376; Lake Superior mines, 380.
Corporate charters, 300.
Coureurs de bois, 21, 81, 232.
Craig, Governor-General, 166.
Crapo, Henry H., 292, 390.
Crary, Isaac E., 220, 320, 321.
Crittenden, John J., 337.
Croghan, George, 63.
Croswell, Charles M., 391.
Currency, early, 254 *et seq.*; cut, 257; national, 357–361; wild-cat, 267–278.

Dablon, 11, 12.
Dalzell, Captain, 61.
Dane, Nathan, 167.
Dearborn, Fort, 181.
Dearborn, General, 174.
Defiance, Fort, 182.
Dejean, Judge, 74, 75, 98–100.
De la Barre, 22.
Delegate in Congress, William Woodbridge, 199; Solomon Sibley, 199; Gabriel Richard, 199; Austin E. Wing, 200.
Denonville, 22.
De Peyster, Captain, 91, 101, 102.
Detroit, importance of, 14, 15; founding of, 16–39; siege of, by Pontiac, 40–65; military government of, 66–78; illegal grants at, 68–70; importance of, in the Revolution, 85–103; surrender to the United States, 118; incorporation of, 141; destruction of, by fire, 152; Woodward, plan of, 154; surrender of, by Hull, 175; Colonel Proctor, governor of, 180; evacuated by Proctor, 187; condition in 1837, 237; capital removed from, 296; citizens build peninsula railroad, 384.
Detroit Bank, 155, 257, 258.
Detroit Young Men's Society, 239.
Dickinson, Don M., 390.
Dollier, 16.
Dongan, Governor, 22.
Dubuisson, 34.
Du Lhut, 15.
Du Monts, 3.
Dunmore, Governor, 88.

Education, state, review of, 306–329; support of, 372; university, colleges, and normal schools, 399, 400.
Erie and Kalamazoo Railroad, 279.
Erie Canal, 203.

Explorations, early, 1, 12, 16.

Federal relations in 1837, review of, 226; after the Civil War, 244–371.
Felch, Alpheus, 296.
Findlay, Colonel, 167.
Fort Stanwix treaty, 108, 111.
Forts, Dearborn, 181; Defiance, 182; Le Bœuf, 56, 60; Meigs, 186; Miami, 43, 56, 60, 115–117; Niagara, 56, 60, 62, 63; Ouatanon, 43, 56, 60; Pitt, 56, 60; Pontchartrain, 19, 29; Sandusky, 56, 60; Stephenson, 186; St. Joseph on St. Clair River, 15; St. Joseph on Lake Michigan, 56, 60; Venango, 56, 60.
Fox, Charles James, 84.
Free schools, 303–329.
French farms, 190, 233.
Frenchtown massacre, 182–184.
Frontenac, Count, 9, 10.
Fur trade, American, 4, 22, 23, 29, 191.

Gallinée, 16, 17.
Gallissonière, 37.
General Banking Law, 261, 262, 267, 275.
Gilpin, Henry D., 212.
Girty, Simon, George, and James, 92.
Gladwin, Major, 57.
Grand Council at Huron Village, 109.
Greenly, William L., 296.
Greenville, Treaty of, 117.
Griffin, Judge, 150.

Haldimand, Sir Frederick, 107, 397.
Hamilton, Alexander, 347–349, 351.
Hamilton, Governor, 75, 85, 90.
Harmar, General, 112.
Harrison, William H., governor, 135; general, 182, 186.
Holland Colony, 297.
Horner, John S., 221.
Houghton, Dr. Douglass, surveys copper region, 374; his party finds iron, 376.
Hulbert, Edwin, 375.
Hull, William, 148–163.
Hundred Associates, 6, 7.
Hurons, 4.

Illinois, attempt to legalize slavery in, 137–139.
Immigration to Michigan, 197, 202, 203, 296, 402.
Indian affairs, bad management of, 47–54.
Indian massacres in Northwest Territory, 111, 112.
Indian trade, rivalry for, 4, 22, 23, 29; pathway of, to Quebec, 16.

INDEX.

Indian treaties, how obtained, 159, 169.
Indiana, attempts to legalize slavery in, 133–139.
Indians, conversion of, 20, 21, 23, 38, 142–144; use of, in the Revolution, 86–94.
Industrial development, 372–380, 385–387, 396, 397.
Industries, household, 234.
Internal improvements, 279–293, 296, 384, 385.
Iron mines, 364, 367; discovered, 376, 377; development, 377–379; Lake Superior mines, 380.
Iroquois, 4, 10, 36, 106, 108, 109.

Jackson, President, 207, 218–220, 222.
Jay's Treaty, 118, 136.
Jefferson, Thomas, 125, 126, 130, 147; constitutional views of, 347–349, 351, 371.
Jerome, David H., 391.
Jesuits, 4, 5, 10, 25, 27, 28.
Johnson, Sir John, 110, 112.
Johnson, Sir William, 43, 53, 62–64, 88.
Joliet, 12, 13, 373.
Joques, 10.
Jonquiere, 37.
Judicial officers, election of, 300.

Kaskaskia, capture of, 95, 96.
Kentucky settlements, attacks on, 92–94.
King, Rufus, 127.

La Foret, 135.
Lamothe, 99, 100.
La Motte Cadillac, 14, 17–34, 39, 401.
Land claims, early, about Detroit, 145.
Land speculations, 255.
Langlade, Charles de, 91.
Lansing, capital removed to, 296.
La Roche, 3.
La Salle, 15–17.
Lawyers, early, 248.
Le Baye, 56, 63.
Le Bœuf, Fort, 56, 60.
Legal-tender acts, 360.
Liberty, English, 45, 46.
License laws, 300, 301, 304.
Lincoln, President, 336, 356.
Liquor traffic, 144. See *Trade, Indian*.
Livingston, Robert, 24.
Loan, state, for internal improvement, 283.
Logan, Chief, 88.
Lothrop, George Van Ness, 390.
Lucas, Governor, 218.
Luce, Cyrus G., 391, 392.

Lumber, protection for, 365, 366; annual production, 386, 387.
Lyon, Lucius, 220.

Mackinaw, 102, 118, 143, 170.
Malden, evacuated by Proctor, 187.
Marest, 14, 29.
Marietta, 111.
Marquette, Jaques, 4, 10–13; founds St. Ignatius, 12; death of, 13.
Marshall, village, 239.
Marshall, Chief Justice, 358.
Mason, John T., appointed territorial secretary, 207.
Mason, Stevens T., territorial secretary, 208; acting governor, 208, 220; not of age when appointed, 208–210; elected governor of State, 219; protests against act of admission, 224, 225; on banking, 264–266, 269, 272, 276; on internal improvements, 281–285.
Massacre of Frenchtown, 183, 184.
Massacre, Raisin River, monument to Kentucky soldiers in, 401.
McArthur, Duncan, 167, 175, 312.
McClelland, Robert, 304.
McDougall, Lieutenant, 60.
McMillan, James, manufacturer and philanthropist, 388, 389; notable service in Congress, 389, 390; secures Fort Mackinaw reservation for park, 398.
Meigs, Fort, 186.
Miami, Fort, 43, 56, 60, 115–117.
Michigan Territory, organized, 140; ignorance concerning, 192, 193.
Michigan University, 310–329.
Michilimackinac, 11, 14, 18, 27, 30, 38, 78; mission at, 12, 13, 15, 28; surrender to the British, 43, 44; capture by the Indians, 60, 61; becomes Mackinaw, 102.
Militia in Spanish War, 395, 396.
Miller, Colonel, 174.
"Miner" law, 401.
Money, early, 254–278, 357–361.
Monopoly in banking, 261, 269, 275.
Monquagon, fight at, 174.
Monroe, 239.
Montcalm, 28.
Monteith, John, 200, 309, 315.
Montreal, 3, 40.
Moravian town, fight at, 187.
Mormon colony, 297.
Morris Canal and Banking Company, 286.
Mundy, Edward, 219.
Murray, General, 75.

National banks, 357, 358.
Negro riot, 213.

INDEX.

Newspapers, early, 202.
Niagara, Fort, 56, 60, 62, 63.
Northwest Territory, conquest of, 79–104; reluctant surrender of, 105, 119; land controversy concerning, 105, 120–125; government for, 111, 125.
Norvel, John, 220.
Nouvel, 12.

Office-holders, federal, 370.
Offices as spoils, 207.
Ohio, boundary controversy with, 214 *et seq.*; currency from, 259, 260.
Ordinance of 1787, 125, 127–138, 211.
Ouatanon, Fort, 43, 56–60.

Palmer, Thomas W., 390.
Parsons, Andrew, 305.
Patriot war, 253.
Pawnee slaves, 131.
Peace conference of 1860, 337, 341.
People of the State in 1837, 232 *et seq.*
Perry's victory, 186.
Pierce, John D., 318, 321.
Pingree, Hazen S., 392.
Pitt, Fort, 56, 60.
Pontchartrain, 18, 27, 28, 30.
Pontchartrain, Fort, 19, 29.
Pontiac, chief, 40–66.
Pontiac, village, 239.
Population of Territory, 203, 213.
Population of State, 397.
Porter, George B., 210, 212.
Presque Isle, Fort, 56–60.
Prevost, Sir George, 166, 174.
Printing-press, the first, 202.
Proctor, Colonel, 180–187.
Public lands in market, 195.

Quakers, 247, 248.
Quebec founded, 3; captured, 40, 45.
Quebec Act, 83, 85; boundaries of, 103.

Radicalism in 1849, 298.
Radisson, Pierre Esprit, 375.
Railroads, early, 249; sale of state, 289–291; voting aid to, 292, 293; peninsula extension, 384; increased taxation, 394, 395.
Randolph, John, 134, 162–166.
Ransom, Epaphroditus, 296.
Raymbault, 10.
Reconstruction of States, 362.
Relief measures, 270, 274, 275.
Religion, early, 245, 248.
Repentigny, Chevalier de, 38.
Republican party, dominant power, 392; fiftieth anniversary of foundation, 401.
Resorts, health and pleasure, 397, 398.
Rich, John T., 392.

Richard, Father Gabriel, 141, 199, 200, 309; delegate in Congress, 199; notes of, for St. Anne, 259.
River Raisin massacre, 182–184, 401.
Rivers and harbors, 368.
Roads, territorial, 197, 198.
Roberval, 2.
Rocheblave, 91.
Rogers, Major Robert, 41, 78.
Ruin of Indian trade, 144.

Safety fund for banks, 261.
St. Anne's Church, 199, 259.
St. Clair, General, 110–113; governor, 130, 151, 152.
St. Ignatius mission, 12.
St. Joseph, Fort, on St. Clair River, 15; on Lake Michigan, 56, 60.
Salaries, state, 302.
Salt manufacture, 365, 366, 396.
Sandusky, Fort, 56, 60.
Sastaretsi, Chief, 33, 34.
Sault St. Marie, 10, 15, 38, 63, 144.
Schools, public, 307, 329; endowment for, 321.
Schuyler, General, 89.
Secession, 336.
Semi-Centennial of statehood, 398, 399.
Shafter, General William R., 395.
Sibley, Solomon, 199.
Simcoe, Governor, 114, 117.
Six Nations, 4, 10, 36, 106, 108, 109.
Slavery, 129, 130, 131, 332–343, 356.
Spanish war, militia in, 395, 396.
Speculative mania, 255, 265, 267, 274, 289.
Sports, early, 250–252.
Standard Oil Co., 378, 379.
State and Union in 1837, 226–231; after the Civil War, 344–371.
State Agricultural College, 327, 400.
State credit, not to be loaned, 302.
State currency, taxed out of existence, 359.
State debt, for internal improvements, 283–302; sinking fund for, 301; limitation upon, 301.
State economy, 303.
State government, right to, under ordinance of 1787, 211, 213, 220; petition for, 213; established, 219, 220, 232; recognized by Congress, 224.
State Normal School, 327, 400.
State products in 1880, 364; in 1900, 397.
State railroads, sale of, 289–291, 296.
State School for Dependent Children, 327.
State script, 287, 288.
Steamboat, first, 202.
Stephenson, Fort, 186.
Steuben, Baron, 107.

INDEX. 409

Stockbridge, Francis B., 390.
Strang, John J., 297, 298.
Suspension of specie payments, 263–267.

Talon, Intendant, 373.
Tappan, Henry P., 341.
Taxation, federal, 363.
Tecumseh, chief, 160–162; his reproach of Proctor, 186; his death, 187.
Tecumseh, town, 239, 247.
Temperance laws, 300, 304.
Territorial government, vote on changing, 198; changes made, 200, 201.
Thompson, O. C., 317.
Thurlow, Lord, 84.
Toledo war, 218.
Tontagini, chief, 313.
Tonty, 19.
Trade, Indian, rivalry for, 4; monopolies in, 4–8, 21, 26; intermeddling with, 73.
Traders, Indian, 21, 50–53, 71, 87.
Turnbull, Captain, 74.

Union and State in 1837, 226–231; since the Civil War, 344–371.

University of Michigan, 310–339; income, 372; semi-centennial, 399, 400.

Van Horne's defeat, 173.
Van Raalte, Albertus C., 297.
Vaudreuil, 29, 40, 44.
Venango, Fort, 56, 60.
Vincennes, 96–98.
Voltaire, 45.
Voyageurs, 45, 81.

War of 1812, 163.
Washington, George, 37, 115.
Water highways, 368, 369 (*see also* canals and locks).
Wayne, General, 115–119.
Wild-cat banking, 267–278.
Winans, Edwin B., 392.
Winchester, General, 181–183.
Wing, Austin E., 200.
Wisner, Moses, 305, 339.
Woodbridge, William, territorial secretary, 190; delegate in Congress, 199; acting governor, 205; removed as judge, 210; governor of State, 274.
Woodward, Judge, 136, 149, 180, 258.
Wool in Michigan, 364, 367.